CUSTOMER-BASED
COLLECTION
DEVELOPMENT

CUSTOMER-BASED
COLLECTION
DEVELOPMENT

An Overview

EDITED BY

KARL BRIDGES

An imprint of the American Library Association

CHICAGO   2014

Karl Bridges has been a professional academic reference librarian for more than twenty years. He is the acting dean at Eli M. Oboler Library at Idaho State University. He holds master's degrees in history from Miami University and the University of Illinois, from which he also has an MLS. He has extensive professional writing experience, including scholarly articles in journals such as *American Libraries* and *The Journal of Library Philosophy and Practice*. He has also written three books (two as sole author, one as editor) and a book chapter on various library subjects including Web 2.0, library interviewing, and the future of libraries. He is also a book reviewer for publications including the *Journal of Electronic Resources Librarianship* and *Catholic Library World*.

© 2014 by the American Library Association

Printed in the United States of America

18 17 16 15 14   5 4 3 2 1

Extensive effort has gone into ensuring the reliability of the information in this book; however, the publisher makes no warranty, express or implied, with respect to the material contained herein.

ISBN: 978-0-8389-1192-1 (paper).

Library of Congress Cataloging-in-Publication Data
Customer-based collection development : an overview / edited by Karl Bridges.
    pages   cm
    Includes bibliographical references and index.
    ISBN 978-0-8389-1192-1 (pbk. : alk. paper) 1. Patron-driven acquisitions (Libraries) 2. Academic libraries—Acquisitions—United States—Case studies. 3. Libraries—Special collections—Electronic books. I. Bridges, Karl, 1964- editor.
    Z689.C87 2014
    025.2'1—dc23   2014023029

Cover design by Kimberly Thornton. Images © Shutterstock, Inc.

Text composition by Dianne M. Rooney in the Chaparral, Gotham, and Bell Gothic typefaces.

♾ This paper meets the requirements of ANSI/NISO Z39.48-1992 (Permanence of Paper).

Contents

CRISTINA CAMINITA

1

E-Books and Patron-Driven Acquisitions in Academic Libraries

PATRON-DRIVEN ACQUISITIONS (PDA) IS THE HOT-TOPIC COL-lection development model in academic libraries. Libraries are enthusiastically adopting the model, and librarians are just as enthusiastically reporting the successes and challenges of implementing the model at their institutions. Google Scholar lists over 2,000 results made available online since 2009 for the search "college libraries patron driven acquisitions." EBSCO's *Library Information Science & Technology Abstracts with Full Text* database also lists over 400 articles published since 2009 found using the search terms "college libraries patron driven acquisitions." Even though the user request model, such as acquiring items at the suggestion of faculty and students, is currently used to purchase print materials and has been used in the past to develop collections, the PDA model for e-book purchasing is driving further paradigmatic changes in academic library collection development.

The benefit of patron-driven collection development of e-books for librarians is that it shifts the buying emphasis from the just-in-case model, where items are purchased in the hope that patrons will find them and use them, to the just-in-time model, where patrons search for and access requested items directly. The benefit to patrons of adopting such a model is the ease of access to information. Patrons find records of possible e-book purchases integrated within the library catalog itself. The patron can use the library catalog as they would use Amazon & Barnes & Noble to search for e-books. Patrons can then access the e-books immediately, with no mediating ordering process required. However, e-books carry their own restrictions that can affect patrons' access. Like the Digital Rights Management (DRM) issues that restrict Amazon or Barnes & Noble e-book purchases to specific e-reader devices, DRM e-books purchased through library vendors can usually only be accessed through proprietary websites. These websites may not be accessible on mobile devices. They may also not include accommodations such as font size control or text-to-speech functions for the visually impaired. Preservation of e-book collections can also be a concern if budget issues require cancelling an e-book subscription.

The interlibrary loan of e-book collections is also an issue, since DRM usually restricts or prohibits duplication or loans of items. While implementing PDA of e-books, librarians should become familiar with the challenges e-books present to traditional services provided by academic libraries, and the various software and log-ons users will need to read downloaded e-books on their computers and mobile devices, as well as being aware of the preservation issues facing institutions that purchase large collections of e-books.

THE CHANGING COLLECTION DEVELOPMENT FOCUS OF THE ACADEMIC LIBRARY

The academic library has been experiencing a process of change in focus for the past four decades, and this change in focus has not only followed inevitable changes in academic curricula and research interests on campuses, but has also followed the changes in technology that have transformed the ways that users access information. At the mid-twentieth century, academic libraries were charged with creating substantial research collections to meet the needs of their users. Since the 1990s, academic libraries have increasingly focused on services and instruction to their users in the face of ever-decreasing acquisition budgets as well as the decreasing amount of space on shelves available for the housing of collections. PDA and its particular application to e-book collection building is another response to the various pressures on the academic libraries to make appropriate and justifiable purchases: books and materials that will be used by faculty, staff, and students. This is no longer a question of acquiring a substantial print collection that supports an institution's curricula; it is a question of providing users access to information in the most accessible and least costly format available. The focus on development of e-book collections also addresses the need to repurpose areas of the physical library building for information commons that include computer labs, media centers, and makerspaces.[1] A brief history of the changing landscape of the academic libraries will show how patron-driven acquisition of e-books fits into the development of the academic library as a campus institution.

After World War II, universities grew substantially due to the increased enrollment of students under the GI Bill. With the expansion of curricula and the student body, academic librarians invested in building their collections along a "postwar ideal . . . to build a research library to meet the needs of existing and future patrons."[2] This just-in-case collection development model placed the responsibility of identifying materials for acquisitions on subject specialists. These librarians would purchase materials with the funds allotted to them in the hope that users would identify them through the library catalog and then check them out. Subject specialists would keep their faculty informed about current acquisitions in their subject areas to encourage use of the collection, and reference librarians would assist faculty and students in locating items while using the library's catalog.

Over time, this model of collection development became increasingly untenable as academic libraries began to sustain budget cuts that decreased their purchasing power. Libraries analyzed the use of their collections to make better use of their diminishing purchasing funds. Researchers made an interesting discovery: most items purchased along the just-in-case model had never circulated. The seminal University of Pittsburgh study of use of library materials showed that a "very small portion (perhaps 10%) of the library collection of book titles accounts for the major portion (80% or more) of the circulation and in-house use."[3]

With fewer funds to purchase materials, libraries could no longer justify the expense of books purchased that were never circulated. Coupled with the lack of use of most print collections was the decreasing amount of space to house print collections, even after libraries weeded collections to remove old, damaged, and superseded items, and moved sections of their retained collections to off-site storage facilities. Even with vendor approval plans in place to streamline selection of materials for purchase, academic libraries were spending far more on print materials than were actually circulated or browsed, and oftentimes budget cuts required the suspension of automatic purchasing of items covered by the approval plan.

JUST-IN-TIME COLLECTION DEVELOPMENT: FROM USER REQUESTS TO PDA OF E-BOOKS

Considering user input on acquiring materials is not a new concept in academic libraries. Academic libraries have relied on lists generated from interlibrary borrowing requests for years, and subject specialists responsible for purchasing of materials in their liaison areas have received requests for titles from their faculty and students. The requests in the past have been for print or other physical materials: books, specific government documents, DVDs, CDs, and so on. Users identified a needed information source by searching for a specific title in a library's catalog. If users could not find or access particular items through their library, they then either contacted their library subject liaison to request items for purchase, or contacted their interlibrary loan office to borrow items from another institution. Libraries have also used interlibrary loan (ILL) request records as title lists for print acquisitions. When placing requests through automated ILL systems, users would designate whether titles were recommended for purchase. Subject librarians would review the list of recommended items and then would make their purchases. But this process of purchasing items requested through ILL not only addressed users' need for information after the fact, it also required the library to fund acquiring of the items twice, once by filling the ILL request, and again by purchasing the items.[4]

Libraries then began experimenting with directly purchasing items requested through ILL. Items requested through ILL that met specific criteria would automatically be purchased for inclusion in a library's collection. Criteria for automatic purchase of ILL requests included coverage of designated subject areas, currency, appropriate target audience, and price.[5] Subject specialists assessed and evaluated the direct purchase of ILL requests and found that the items purchased during their experiments were circulated more often than items purchased either by established approval plans or through traditional collection development models.[6] And yet even with this better demand-driven acquisition model in place, users were still required to mediate their access to information sources through ILL.

As users have become more used to the immediate information search and access model provided by Google and other Internet search engines, they have also become less patient with accessing information in print format in academic libraries. Accessing information in print requires users to visit the physical library. Accessing information in print also requires users to become familiar with the organization of physical materials within the library. Many undergraduates who approach the reference desk for research assistance have never located a book on a library shelf using a call number, and busy graduate students and faculty find the lack of older journal articles and books in electronic format an annoyance. If the need for the information in a print source is great enough, users will plan to visit the library, go to the stacks, and find their books. But most users will resist following through with print items. The inconvenience of lacking immediate access to electronic information sources is greater than making the effort to fulfill the information need with a print source. Even with the implementation of book and document delivery plans, with books from the library's collection and journal articles from print journals photocopied and delivered to faculty, staff, and graduate students on university and college campuses, users would prefer the ease of finding and accessing information online.[7]

The adoption of e-book PDA is a response to changes in collection use, the information needs of users, and the needs of libraries to adapt to budget and space concerns. When implementing an e-book PDA model, libraries set up an allocated budget for their e-book program and work with their vendors or with specific e-book vendors, such as ebrary or EBL, to load e-book PDA records into their catalogs.[8] Users can discover these e-book PDA records as they search the catalog or discovery service. If a user decides to click through to view a PDA e-book, the act of clicking through either triggers the purchase of the e-book outright or triggers a short-term loan of the e-book, where the cost of the short-term loan is a percentage of the full cost of the book based on use.[9] The entire process of purchasing the e-book takes place behind the scenes, with users unaware that their search and browsing behaviors have contributed to the development of their library's collections. The process is designed to be seamless and to require no mediation: no subject librarians or ILL staff members need to be contacted to ensure purchase of an e-book that a user wants to access. The just-in-time collection development model is epitomized by this approach to e-book purchasing: the books are only loaned or purchased at the user's point of need. Requiring more physical space to house purchased e-books is not an issue.

The PDA e-book model and purchasing process, "where a user request triggers a purchase, by definition yield a 100 percent circulation rate."[10] Each book purchased through e-book PDA is used, unlike print items purchased in just-in-case models, which resulted in the low use of expensive print collections. However, even though e-book PDA does address the collection development and collection use concerns outlined in this chapter, this collection development is not foolproof, and the added issues surrounding the purchase of e-books must be considered before a decision is made to implement e-book PDA extensively in an academic library.

BIBLIOGRAPHIC AND ELECTRONIC ACCESS ISSUES: THE CASE OF THE DISAPPEARING RECORDS

Budgeting issues may arise with an e-book PDA implementation. A library may find that users quickly download e-books within their PDA records pool and thus spend their allotted PDA budget faster than anticipated. For example, during the e-book PDA pilot at the author's library, the PDA budget was very quickly spent by users clicking through PDA records in the catalog and triggering loans and purchases. Once users exhausted the PDA e-book with their purchases, the catalog records of the PDA titles were suppressed in the catalog to prevent users from discovering them. Soon after the records were suppressed, a very confused faculty member approached the reference desk to ask why he could no longer access a title he had browsed a few days before. The reference librarian assisting the faculty member searched for the title in the catalog in vain; since the title had been suppressed, it was not listed in search results. It was as if the e-book record had vanished. The collection development team soon cleared up the confusion among the reference librarians and the faculty member was informed that the title was no longer available for browsing. The very same issue arose at the Ohio State University Libraries during their 2009 ebrary pilot.[11] After depleting the e-book PDA budget, they suppressed their PDA e-book records.

How does a library explain disappearing records to users? Of course, if a library has funds for further collection development after e-book PDA funds have been depleted, then the materials would be purchased to complete the faculty member's requests. But if such a funding is not available, how does one explain to a confused researcher a collection development process that was designed to be invisible and seamless? Even in traditional models of collection development for print items, users are unaware of the approval plans in place, the purchasing decisions made by subject librarians, and the entire budget allocation process for subject areas. The books appear on the shelves, and users either find them through browsing the physical titles or searching for them through the catalog. Loading e-book PDA records into the catalog confuses this process because the users have become the selectors without having knowledge of the processes of selection or the policies of collection development. Users cannot tell if a particular e-book is owned by the library or not by the information included in the record alone. When users deplete the e-book PDA budget, these records are pulled from the catalog, unlike the records of checked-out books or missing books, which usually state when items are checked out or missing in the simple item information. As William H. Walters notes in his review of patron-driven acquisition and the mission of academic libraries, the practice of shadowing PDA e-book records "is likely to reduce patrons' confidence in the library catalog, especially among students and faculty working on long-term projects."[12]

DIGITAL RIGHTS MANAGEMENT: LICENSING VS. PURCHASING

There is a contradiction in the term *e-book purchasing*. When libraries or individuals purchase e-books, they usually are not purchasing them in the traditional sense, where an exchange of money for a print book occurs. The purchase of most e-books is actually the purchase of licenses for the use of e-books under the rules established by publishers and vendors. The digital technologies that most publishers use to protect their e-books from duplication, mass dispersal, and use on devices or platforms not permissible under contract are called Digital Rights Management (DRM).[13] DRM is included within an e-book's digital file, and it controls how many times an e-book can be checked out or downloaded by an individual; an e-book's circulation time (which may or may not align with a library's circulation policy for print items); onto which devices e-books may be downloaded; if pages from an e-book can be printed; if users can copy and paste information from an e-book into another document, and so on. DRM was designed to protect the rights of creators. However, the inclusion of DRM in e-book files limits the very use of the e-book, and thus requires libraries to modify their traditional lending and accessibility practices. Three major e-book DRM issues will be briefly addressed: accessing e-books on a variety of devices and platforms, the interlibrary loan of e-books, and the preservation of e-books.

WHAT'S YOUR PLATFORM?

Before discussing the various e-book platform issues users may encounter, a warning must be offered to readers: e-books and digital publishing are technologies that are progressing at such a rapid rate that any attempt to summarize platform- or vendor-specific software or websites will be out-of-date as soon, and oftentimes before, it reaches publication. However, as long as DRM remains the standard for preventing duplication of e-books or use of e-books across proprietary platforms, the information presented in this section should provide a general outline of strategies implemented by publishers and vendors to protect their digital books from unauthorized duplication and the scenarios that may arise when users attempt to download checked-out items to their computers or mobile devices.

For standard e-book checkout, vendors may require users to download and install third-party software applications, like Adobe Digital Editions, to read checked-out titles.[14] Adobe Digital Editions also requires users to sign up for an Adobe Digital Editions ID to log in to the application once it is installed. However, requiring third-party software applications to read checked-out titles may present logistical problems for on-campus users such as faculty, staff, and graduate students assigned workstations in offices. As standard practice to secure their computer and wireless networks, most academic institutions do not allow users to make administrative changes such as installing new software on their workstations. Users who require software installation must request service from their IT office. On the other hand, users are free to install third-party software on their own computers, but they may take issue with the entire idea of needing to download a separate piece of software to check out a title. Users may also be hesitant to register at e-book vendor websites or third-party software vendor sites, and may also find having to remember yet another user name and password bothersome.

E-book applications for mobile devices such as the iPhone and iPad, Android phones and tablets, and the Amazon Kindle Fire are available.[15] Two vendors of e-books for academic libraries, ebrary and EBSCO, both require users to register for an Adobe Digital Editions ID.[16] Librarians must be aware of these requirements, and must make an effort to remain up-to-date on the rapidly changing technology requirements, to assist users wishing to view e-book titles on their mobile devices. Even though these applications are free, they do require the patience and willingness of the user to download, install, and log in to them to access an e-book. Considering that one of the e-book PDA model's benefits is to provide access to information quickly and at the user's point of need, the required mediation of third-party software creates obstacles to access. In a *New Library World* article describing possible effective business models for licensing of e-books in academic libraries, Schroeder and Wright briefly mention the issue of DRM and cross-platform compatibility of e-books: "Until users can download books to the device of their choice, they do not have free access to the libraries' purchased collections."[17] To expand upon Schroeder and Wright's point, until library users can download books to the device of their choice without having to register at various third-party sites and download applications, they still do not have free access to e-books purchased through any type of collection development model, PDA or otherwise.

E-BOOKS AND INTERLIBRARY LOAN

As academic libraries have changed focus from collecting print materials to providing access to information, lending and borrowing among libraries through interlibrary loan services have become an integral part of supporting the research needs of users. Critical to the entire enterprise of interlibrary loan has been the protected right of first sale of print items. The right of first sale allows libraries to circulate print books freely, not only to their defined user groups but also to users who request items through interlibrary loan. Once a library purchases a print book, it may dispose of the book according to the use and disposal rules of its institution. Unlike their print counterparts, the way libraries lend e-books beyond their stipulated user community is not protected by the right of first sale because e-books are licensed and not purchased or owned by libraries. Publishers have been reluctant to allow the loaning of e-books through interlibrary loan, fearing that the practice of lending and borrowing e-books outside a library's user group will result in lost sales revenue. Libraries have responded by purchasing and short-loaning more e-book titles, but this approach limits not only what libraries can offer other institutions through ILL agreements, but what materials libraries can borrow from other institutions. Wicht describes alternatives to the traditional model of ILL when e-book ILL requests cannot be filled: short-term purchase (short-term loans), purchase on demand (PDA), print on demand, and consortium-level purchasing.[18] However, these alternatives are merely workarounds to the larger issue: e-book DRM's restriction of access.

PRESERVING E-BOOKS

Digital objects, like e-books, are frequently in danger of becoming obsolete or unusable due to changes in technology. In the e-book world, a number of formats have already become extinct, including Microsoft's .lit format, which was released in 2000 and discontinued in 2011.[19] Just as computers no longer come with floppy drives and .wps (Microsoft Works) files are no longer supported by current Microsoft Office packages, e-book formats and reader devices will modify and evolve, and these changes will require a library's purchased e-book collection to be migrated into a more current format, or to be accessed through emulation software that mimics the original software or hardware required to access the e-book.[20] Libraries will need to work closely with vendors to ensure that the e-books they have purchased will survive the inevitable changes in technology that will occur. Implementation of e-book preservation is lagging behind the established preservation efforts for electronic journals.[21] Portico, a digital preservation and electronic archiving service, is preserving e-books and provides a list of titles currently within its archive.[22] Kirchhoff notes that e-book DRM can complicate preservation efforts because "the purpose of DRM (carefully limit access and replication) is at odds with the purpose of preservation (preserve access for the long term)."[23] The very act of preservation of e-books itself is multifaceted, and not only must consider the possibility of format obsolescence, but also must ensure the library's access to vendor copies of e-books while maintaining consistent metadata at the item and collection levels to preserve discovery of e-books.[24]

CONCLUSION

E-book PDA in academic libraries can provide solutions to issues encountered as collection development evolves to meet the needs of users and the demands of institutional budgets. PDA addresses a user's need for information at the point of demand, and e-books selected through a PDA program provide instant access to information. Increasing e-book purchases through PDA also obviates the space concerns many academic libraries have experienced. E-book PDA also guarantees that items purchased are used, another benefit of this collection development model that avoids the purchase of items that sit unused and uncirculated on library shelves. However, e-book PDA requires a reconceptualization of the library as a provider of access to information rather than a collector of information sources. Providing information access to users as needed by supplying them with e-books demands that the library give up traditional models of service to comply with licensing agreements protected by e-book DRM. E-book DRM limits not only services like interlibrary loan but also limits the manner in which users can download and access e-books on their computers and mobile devices. DRM also complicates preservation efforts. Even though e-book PDA seems to solve many library collection development issues just-in-time, it may cause more costly access and preservation issues in the future.

NOTES

1. Erin Fisher, "Makerspaces Move into Academic Libraries," *ACRL Tech Connect* (2012), http://acrl.ala.org/techconnect/?p=2340.
2. Dracine Hodges, Cyndi Preston, and Marsha J. Hamilton, "Patron-Initiated Collection Development: Progress of a Paradigm Shift," *Collection Management* 35, no. 3–4 (2010): 209.
3. Allen Kent and University of Pittsburgh, *Use of Library Materials: The University of Pittsburgh Study* (New York: M. Dekker, 1979), 6.
4. Judith M. Nixon, Robert S. Freeman, and Suzanne M. Ward, "Patron-Driven Acquisitions: An Introduction and Literature Review," *Collection Management* 35, no. 3–4 (2010): 119–24.
5. Ibid.
6. Kristine J. Anderson, Robert S. Freeman, Jean-Pierre V. M. Hérubel, Lawrence J. Mykytiuk, Judith M. Nixon, and Suzanne M. Ward, "Buy, Don't Borrow," *Collection Management* 27, no. 3–4 (2002): 1–11.
7. Roger Strouse, "The Changing Face of Content Users and the Impact on Information Providers," *Online* 28, no. 5 (2004): 27–31.
8. Norm Medeiros, "Shaping a Collection One Electronic Book at a Time: Patron Driven Acquisitions in Academic Libraries," *OCLC Systems and Services* 27, no. 3 (2011): 160–62.
9. Heather L. Wicht, "The Evolution of E-Books and Interlibrary Loan in Academic Libraries," *Collaborative Librarianship* 3, no. 4 (2011): 205–11.
10. Jonathan Nabe, Andrea Imre, and Sanjeet Mann, "Let the Patron Drive: Purchase on Demand of E-Books," *Serials Librarian* 60, no. 1–4 (2011): 193.

11. Hodges, Preston, and Hamilton, "Patron-Initiated Collection Development," 208–21.
12. William II. Walters, "Patron Driven Acquisition and the Educational Mission of the Academic Library," *Library Resources and Technical Services* 56, no. 3 (2012): 207.
13. Amy Kirchhoff, "E-Book Preservation: Business and Content Management," in *No Shelf Required 2: Use and Management of Electronic Books,* ed. Sue Polanka (Chicago: American Library Association, 2012), 71–91.
14. Adobe, "Adobe Digital Editions," www.adobe.com/products/digital-editions .html.
15. Romana Martin, "The Road Ahead: Ebooks, Etextbooks and Publishers' Electronic Resources" (paper presented at Ascilite Annual Conference, Wellington New Zealand, 2012).
16. ebrary, "New to Downloading Entire Documents as E-Books? Get Started as Follows," http://support.ebrary.com/kb/new-to-ade; EBSCO, "Ebsco Support: How Do I Check-Out and Download an Ebsco Ebook?" http://support.ebsco .com/knowledge_base/detail.php?id5361.
17. Rebecca Schroeder and Tom Wright, "Electronic Books: A Call for Effective Business Models," *New Library World* 112, no. 5/6 (2010): 220.
18. Wicht, "The Evolution of E-Books," 205–11.
19. Steven Musil, "Microsoft Cancels Its Reader E-Book App," CNET.
20. Kirchhoff, "E-Book Preservation."
21. Schroeder and Wright, "Electronic Books."
22. Portico, "Content in the Archive—Portico," 2013, www.portico.org/digital -preservation/the-archive-content-access/content-in-the-archive/e-books.
23. Kirchhoff, "E-Book Preservation," 81.
24. William Walters, "E-Books in Academic Libraries: Challenges for Acquisition and Collection Management," *portal: Libraries and the Academy* 13, no. 2 (2013): 187–211.

REFERENCES

Adobe Digital Editions. "Adobe Digital Editions." 2013. www.adobe.com/products/ digital-editions.html.
Anderson, Kristine J., Robert S. Freeman, Jean-Pierre V. M. Hérubel, Lawrence J. Mykytiuk, Judith M. Nixon, and Suzanne M. Ward. "Buy, Don't Borrow." *Collection Management* 27, nos. 3–4 (2002): 1–11. doi: 10.1300/J105v27n03_01.
ebrary. "New to Downloading Entire Documents as E-Books? Get Started as Follows." 2013. http://support.ebrary.com/kb/new-to-ade.
EBSCO. "EBSCO Support: How Do I Check-Out and Download an EBSCO eBook?" 2013. http://support.ebsco.com/knowledge_base/detail.php?id=5361.

Fisher, Erin. "Makerspaces Move into Academic Libraries." *ACRL Tech Connect*, November 28, 2012, http://acrl.ala.org/techconnect/?p=2340.

Hodges, Dracine, Cyndi Preston, and Marsha J. Hamilton. "Patron-Initiated Collection Development: Progress of a Paradigm Shift." *Collection Management* 35, nos. 3–4 (2010): 208–21.

Kent, Allen, and University of Pittsburgh. *Use of Library Materials: The University of Pittsburgh Study.* New York: M. Dekker, 1979.

Kirchhoff, Amy. "E-Book Preservation: Business and Content Challenges." In *No Shelf Required 2: Use and Management of Electronic Books*, edited by Sue Polanka, 71–91. Chicago: American Library Association, 2012.

Martin, Romana. "The Road Ahead: eBooks, eTextbooks and Publishers' Electronic Resources." Paper presented at ascilite Annual Conference, Wellington, New Zealand, November 25–28, 2012. www.ascilite2012.0rg/images/custom/martin,_romana_-_the_road.pdf.

Medeiros, Norm. "Shaping a Collection One Electronic Book at a Time: Patron-Driven Acquisitions in Academic Libraries." *OCLC Systems & Services* 27, no. 3 (2011): 160–62. doi: 10.1108/10650751111164524.

Musil, Steven. "Microsoft Cancels Its Reader E-Book App." *CNET*, August 15, 2011, http://news.cnet.com/8301-10805_3-20092770-75/microsoft-cancels-its -reader-e-book-app.

Nabe, Jonathan, Andrea Imre, and Sanjeet Mann. "Let the Patron Drive: Purchase on Demand of E-Books." *Serials Librarian* 60, nos. 1–4 (2011): 193–97. doi: 10.1080/0361526X.2011.556033.

Nixon, Judith M., Robert S. Freeman, and Suzanne M. Ward. "Patron-Driven Acquisitions: An Introduction and Literature Review." *Collection Management* 35, nos. 3–4 (2010): 119–24. doi: 10.1080/01462679.2010.486957.

Portico. "Content in the Archive—Portico." 2013. www.portico.org/digital -preservation/the-archive-content-access/content-in-the-archive/e-books.

Schroeder, Rebecca, and Tom Wright. "Electronic Books: A Call for Effective Business Models." *New Library World* 112, nos. 5/6 (2011): 215–21. doi: 10.1108/03074801111136257.

Strouse, Roger. "The Changing Face of Content Users and the Impact on Information Providers." *Online* (Weston, Conn.) 28, no. 5 (2004): 27–31.

Walters, William H. "E-Books in Academic Libraries: Challenges for Acquisition and Collection Management." *portal: Libraries and the Academy* 13, no. 2 (2013): 187–211.

———. "Patron Driven Acquisition and the Educational Mission of the Academic Library." *Library Resources and Technical Services* 56, no. 3 (2012): 207.

Wicht, Heather L. "The Evolution of E-Books and Interlibrary Loan in Academic Libraries." *Collaborative Librarianship* 3, no. 4 (2011): 205–211.

SARAH HARTMAN-CAVERLY,
AMY MCCOLL, NORM MEDEIROS,
AND MIKE PERSICK

2

A Hard DDA's Night

Managing a Consortial Demand-Driven Acquisitions Program for E-Books

THE TRI-COLLEGE LIBRARY CONSORTIUM OF BRYN MAWR, Haverford, and Swarthmore Colleges (Tri-Colleges) was established in 1986 in order to implement a joint online catalog. This system, known as Tripod, facilitates resource discovery and sharing of physical collections across the three institutions. Over the years, the libraries have expanded services to include licensing of databases, development of subject guides, and a collaborative approach to library technologies and systems. Since 2004, the Tri-Colleges have practiced a program of cooperative collection development designed to expand the range of materials available to students and faculty by reducing unnecessary duplication. The centerpiece of this program, a shared approval plan, allows bibliographers to communicate and make decisions among themselves about the books being offered each week. Our foray into demand-driven acquisition (DDA) of electronic books is a natural extension of this cooperative collection building.

This chapter describes the establishment and assessment of a consortial yearlong DDA pilot program with Ebook Library, more commonly known as EBL. It details our approach to planning the pilot, managing profiling and purchase triggers, the effect DDA has had on our shared print approval plan, and the challenge of managing separate print and electronic book processes. We highlight noteworthy usage findings and qualitative user feedback, and we explore the important relationship between electronic and print book use. We discuss implications for loading and bibliographic treatment of MARC records, particularly in light of our discovery layer, which we implemented at the midway point of our DDA pilot. We conclude with areas for further study and considerations for consortial DDA programs.

PREVIOUS RESEARCH

Although there is a rich and growing literature around DDA of e-books in libraries,[1] little has been written to date regarding consortial aspects of DDA. The most significant project in this regard has been undertaken by the Orbis Cascade Alliance of thirty-seven academic libraries in the Pacific Northwest. Hinken and McElroy[2] detail the alliance's requirements for implementing a shared patron-driven e-book project. Their criteria include individual e-book selection, universal access, consortium-level licensing, MARC records, seamless authentication, and integration with YBP Library Services' GOBI system. Stern[3] discusses the need for tailored pricing structures and usage metrics as additional consortia-related DDA criteria. He makes the added point that e-books can serve to supplement dwindling numbers of print books in a consortial setting, a suggestion pertinent to the Tri-Colleges, which seek to reduce unnecessary duplication of print copies among their libraries.

THE PLANNING PROCESS

The Tri-Colleges thoroughly reviewed the offerings of three leading e-book aggregators to determine which to use for the pilot. While each vendor had pros and cons, EBL was selected due to its flexible model, specifically its short-term loan (STL) option.[4] STLs allow a library to pay a percentage of list price for a rental of the book after a trigger condition[5] is met rather than necessitating an outright purchase; use of the book prior to meeting a trigger condition is free. EBL's model also allows libraries to set the number of STLs that triggers a purchase. While the cumulative rental expenditures do not count toward purchase of the book, utilizing EBL's STL model saves money while also providing the greatest access to content. In addition, EBL allowed us to share a single account and access to the same content[6]—an important consideration given our shared catalog.

Once the contract with EBL was signed, budgetary and staffing decisions regarding management of the pilot were made. Each of the three schools contributed an equal amount of money into a central account at EBL, with a librarian at Bryn Mawr managing the invoicing on behalf of the Tri-Colleges. It was decided that we wouldn't be concerned with which school's user triggered an STL or a purchase; all would pay equally since each school would have access to the same content and set of purchased titles. In terms of setting up the pilot, the acquisitions coordinators at Haverford and Swarthmore were selected to manage profiling and associated tasks in LibCentral, EBL's management system. A librarian at Swarthmore was selected to manage the batch import of EBL records into Tripod. Lastly we agreed that the majority of the statistics compiling would be done at Haverford, although each library would generate reports to serve their local interests.

COLLECTION DEVELOPMENT

EBL Profiling

In order to leverage EBL's STL model, paying only a fraction of list price for any given use, and to satisfy potential demand not well-served by our print collection, we decided on a broad profile for both subject and nonsubject parameters. The decisions made were as follows:

EBL Profile Element	TriCollege Decision
Publishers	Mainly U.S. university press, trade, and society publishers; based largely on our print approval plan
Subject areas	No exclusions
LC class numbers	No exclusions
Publication date ranges	2006–present
Title keywords to exclude	No exclusions
LCSH keywords	Exclude: juvenile; textbooks
Purchase price limit	$400
Languages of material	No exclusions
Titles, if any, we wanted to suppress from our EBL profile	All ebrary Academic Complete titles

Triggers and Purchase Models

Once the profile was established, administrative staff overseeing the project made decisions on triggers and notifications. This functionality can be edited by administrators in LibCentral. We decided to trigger auto-purchases after the fifth short-term loan for a given title.

Titles whose use reaches the auto-purchase threshold are acquired via EBL's "nonlinear lending" model when available. This model allows an unlimited number of simultaneous users to access the book for an aggregated total of 325 loan days per year. For instance, if two users borrowed the same book for the same seven-day period, the combined use of fourteen days would assess against the yearly allowable 325 days. We set our default loan length to one day, but patrons can choose from a drop-down menu to borrow books for one, seven, or fourteen days, with the rental price increasing relative to the loan period. Some publishers on EBL's platform choose not to allow this nonlinear lending model for certain titles and instead utilize a "textbook" model, which restricts the number of simultaneous users to three.

In cases where a bibliographer has reason to believe a book will receive heavy use, the title is purchased up front in order to eliminate rental expenses. These purchase requests are sent to the acquisitions coordinators on each campus and then to appropriate Tri-College staff members who have the authorization to make purchases directly in LibCentral. As with auto-purchases, these mediated purchases are paid with our pooled funds, with access to the titles available across the three campuses.

Print Approval and DDA

As noted above, the Tri-Colleges work together to prevent unnecessary duplication of print books. We are now expanding this practice to prevent duplication of print and electronic editions of the same title when such duplication is deemed unnecessary. New titles that match the Tri-Colleges' DDA profile are, in many cases, the same titles that match our print approval plan, managed through YBP. Our DDA profile is considerably broader than our print approval plan, and there is nothing that would match the print plan that would be blocked from the DDA profile. Our desire is to coordinate the acquisition of print and electronic versions so that we only buy a book in print if we know it won't be available electronically, or if we consciously decide that we would prefer print even if the e-book version is available. We don't want to block duplication automatically, but we want to manage that duplication.

DATA MANAGEMENT AND SYSTEM INTEROPERABILITY

Coordination of DDA with YBP/GOBI

In order to coordinate print approval purchasing with DDA, approval slip titles are checked for current DDA availability, a relatively simple but manual process. YBP's online selection and ordering tool, GOBI, provides the ability to search for a title in a customer's ILS; clicking on a record in GOBI performs a search in one's local catalog. Acquisitions staff in the Tri-Colleges click in each GOBI record to launch these searches and then act on the results. A more automated process of checking is desirable, as is the explicit display of DDA profile matches in GOBI.

Because YBP could not show us DDA availability in GOBI at the time of our decision to contract with EBL, we didn't initially see a compelling reason to run our DDA program through YBP. As of this writing, however, YBP has developed a mechanism for displaying DDA availability on a print approval slip. According to initial reports on this feature, YBP can predict a DDA profile match as soon as the print slip becomes available, regardless of the date of availability of the e-book. In other words, GOBI can indicate on a print slip whether a corresponding e-book version is available or is likely to be published in the predictable future. Knowledge of near-term availability of e-books would allow bibliographers to make informed decisions regarding print purchase.

Managing DDA MARC Records

Patron discovery of DDA titles relies on the presence of a MARC record for each title in the local catalog. Libraries are often able to customize the MARC record service as part of an e-book DDA program. File format, size, and delivery; MARC record format (MARC8 or UTF-8); and delivery frequency can all be tailored to the technical requirements and preferences of the library. The library can also choose whether to receive their complete DDA catalog with each update or only files for titles added and deleted during the update period.

The Tri-Colleges elected to receive weekly MARC8 files via FTP. Due to the size of the initial DDA collection of approximately 43,000 titles, we opted to receive only update files for titles added to and deleted from the collection during the week. Librarians responsible for catalog maintenance receive an e-mail notification when the update files are available. In addition to the MARC update files, lists of added and deleted titles are also provided in .csv format. These lists are distributed to bibliographers to keep them apprised of changes to the DDA collection. The Tri-Colleges modify add files according to local metadata standards prior to their being batch-loaded into the catalog. Add files are previewed in MarcEdit to ensure that the expected number of records is present in the file and to validate that the file is structurally sound. The file is processed using a script to make conditional changes to records and fields within the file. The output file is reviewed and validated before being uploaded into the ILS for batch processing.

The MARC/Perl module of Perl is used to execute custom scripts which manipulate MARC metadata in both the add and delete files. In addition to manipulating MARC data to facilitate e-book discovery in the catalog and discovery layer, the Perl script creates a unique collection and title identifier for each record in the add files as a match point for queries, batch updating, and overlaying. Delete files are processed with a similar script that adds a note to each record that can be queried along with the collection/title identifier to compile the records into a file for deletion.

Records for DDA e-books that are purchased in perpetuity are cataloged from the vendor-supplied or OCLC record. Most important, the encoding level of the record is updated in order to prevent the accidental overlay of the record. In addition, a local note field is added with the text "EBL nonlinear purchase" or "EBL textbook purchase" to identify these books as purchases separate from records for nonowned titles.

Metadata accuracy and quality are concerns. EBL's records exhibit incorrect MARC coding and lack of authority control. All subject headings are coded as 650 fields, making it impossible to disambiguate between topical, geographic, and other subject headings for the purpose of display, index searching, or faceting in discovery services. Furthermore, all subject headings lack subfield tags, a problem that initially negated a subject browse and navigation tool in our discovery layer. We have also found nonauthorized name forms, typos, problems with special characters, and extraneous spacer characters in the records. These kinds of problems can be time-consuming to resolve because they require astute attention to detail over a large set of records. Initially we corrected these errors manually; we now use our authority control vendor to correct problems with subject headings in the course of normal monthly record maintenance. We have since learned that YBP's bibliographic records are higher quality than EBL's, which has motivated us to investigate shifting our EBL profiling and bibliographic record service to YBP.

IMPACT ON BIBLIOGRAPHERS

At present, Tri-College bibliographers view titles on our joint print approval plan without knowing if the books will also match our DDA profile. In addition to expressing interest in the print book, they register an opinion about how their interest would be affected by the availability of the corresponding e-book. After all these votes are cast, acquisitions staff check to see if records for DDA versions have been loaded in the online catalog. If a bibliographer expresses satisfaction with the e-book version and it turns out that an e-book version is available, then the print book is not purchased.

One complication for this process is that corresponding print and e-book versions are not necessarily made available simultaneously. A decision might be made about a print book based on the lack of a corresponding e-book; unbeknownst to us, that e-book might appear in as little as a week's time.

Attempts to accurately predict e-book availability suffer from lack of reliable dispatch data. Publisher embargo periods vary, and some publishers withhold certain titles from e-book availability entirely or at least from DDA or rental models. Unfortunately, we don't feel we have a good handle on these variations at this point.

Another complication with our system to manage both formats is the potential for a title to disappear from our DDA e-book stream. Unowned DDA books are vulnerable to being pulled from the platform, whether by deliberate publisher revocation or by an accident of fate such as a corrupt e-book file that renders the book unusable. This uncertainty undermines bibliographer confidence in long-term access to unowned titles.

ASSESSMENT

Effect of DDA on Shared Print Approval Plan

We examined how print approval plan spending was likely affected by the DDA pilot. We expected that the existence of a title in our DDA profile would influence the desire for the book in print. We discovered, however, that bibliographers are not entirely convinced that a not-yet-owned DDA copy of a title is a satisfactory substitute for a permanent print copy on the shelf.

Since 2004 we have run our approval plan jointly, avoiding unnecessary duplication for the consortium where appropriate. The plan consists of slip selection for all subjects and automatic book shipments for many of those subjects, shipping to only one of the three colleges. With the advent of the DDA program and with some number of the print approval titles showing up on the DDA profile, bibliographers were asked to consider whether a title's availability on DDA would be a sufficient replacement for a print book.

We tracked print approval spending[7] for all three colleges for the first three-month period of the DDA pilot, October–December 2011, and compared it to the same period in the previous year (October–December 2010). The combined figures are presented in the following tables:

Entire approval plan, including both slip purchases and automatic book shipments:

	Date	All subjects	Social sciences	Humanities
Expenditures	Oct–Dec 2010	$114,742	$54,415	$60,327
	Oct–Dec 2011	$94,186	$39,232	$54,954
Differences	From 2010–2011	–$20,556	–$15,183	–$5,373
Percentage changes	From 2010–2011	–18%	–28%	–9%

Slip purchases only:

	Date	All subjects	Social sciences	Humanities
Expenditures	Oct–Dec 2010	$96,696	$45,348	$51,348
	Oct–Dec 2011	$77,002	$29,700	$47,302
Differences	From 2010–2011	-$19,694	-$15,648	-$4,046
Percentage changes	From 2010–2011	-20%	-35%	-8%

As can be seen, when comparing 2011 to 2010, expenditures for print dropped in both the social sciences and humanities. Overall, the consortium saw an 18 percent drop in approval and a 20 percent drop in spending on slip selections during this period. Reductions in the social sciences were far greater than those in the humanities.

Using ten random weeks throughout 2012, we examined how bibliographers registered their preference for print over electronic when voting for slip titles. "Print" refers to wanting print even if the title appears as an e-book on our DDA plan; "unless DDA" refers to wanting print only if the title does not appear on our DDA plan. These voting statistics are summarized in the table below:

	# votes	"print" votes		"unless DDA" votes	
All subjects	1,777	1,284	72%	493	28%
Social Sciences	929	556	60%	373	40%
Humanities	848	728	86%	120	14%

The difference in the change in expenditure levels between 2011 and 2010 may be attributed to social sciences bibliographers considering e-books a satisfactory replacement for print more often than their humanities counterparts. Votes from social sciences bibliographers indicated that an e-book copy was a satisfactory replacement (i.e., "unless DDA") 40 percent of the time. In contrast, votes from humanities selectors indicated that an electronic copy was satisfactory only 14 percent of the time. Some humanities bibliographers have stated explicitly that a DDA e-book copy is never an acceptable substitute for print.

Noteworthy Usage Findings and Patron Feedback

LibCentral makes available real-time usage and associated cost data that encompass an array of metrics. The system also enables review of individual patron behavior via a unique persistent identifier assigned to users each time they authenticate into EBL's platform. This identifier provides no means of identifying individuals by name or class (e.g., student, faculty, etc.), but it does support the ability to see user patterns that could be meaningful and even actionable.

At the end of the pilot, we aggregated statistics on various areas, such as use across and within the consortium, expenditures, frequency of use (i.e., the number of books used more than once), and the proportion of e-books used relative to records loaded by publisher, imprint year, and subject. We found that we had financed 3,380 rental transactions on behalf of 1,495 unique users at a total cost of $41,105 ($12.16/use; $27.49/user). Particularly impressive in our minds was the relatively large number of unique users, which represented approximately 30 percent of the total number of students and faculty in the Tri-Colleges.

We paid close attention to those book uses that were repeated, analyzing the degree to which repeat uses came from the same user. Our evidence revealed that there is a strong occurrence of the same patron using the same title more than once, an indicator of a more persistent need than the short-term uses we anticipated:

- In the case of titles rented twice, 52 percent of these uses were by the same individual.
- In cases where a book was rented three times, 40 percent of these uses were by the same individual.
- In cases where a book was rented four times, 31 percent of these uses were by the same individual.

Rather than look at the publishers whose books were used most frequently, we compared the percentage of use for the most heavily used publishers against the proportion of records loaded. Users gravitated to university publishers, with such uses being disproportionately high, while the use of books from commercial publishers was disproportionately low relative to those records loaded. We seeded our catalog with books published from 2006 to the present. Users clearly preferred newer imprints. Approximately 50 percent of the books used were published in 2010 or 2011, though these titles made up only 40 percent of the profiled books.

One motivation for our DDA pilot was to provide access to books not typically purchased in print. In our case this meant profiling subject coverage broadly in order to include areas like business, medicine, and technology that were underserved in terms of our print book purchasing as well as ripe for e-book availability given the importance of timeliness to these areas. Our DDA pilot served these areas, but not as frequently as had been expected. The more significant story was that the humanities fields of philosophy, religion, and literature experienced disproportionately strong use. We had anticipated natural science and social science use to be higher than they were, given those fields' relative acceptance of and satisfaction with electronic content.

Bibliographers were authorized to recommend the preemptive purchase of books they believed would get enough use such that an outright purchase would be less expensive than a series of STLs followed by an auto-purchase. Of the 35 books that were preemptively purchased, however, 15 did not receive any use during the pilot year—evidence that speculative purchasing in a DDA environment may be counterproductive.

During focus groups and informal interactions we learned that students were less enamored with e-books than we originally expected. They reported difficulties navigating platforms, frustration in the amount they were allowed to print, and general difficulties in use. These students conceded appreciation for the abilities to search within e-books and to download them for later viewing. The negative impressions, however, outweighed the positive.

This assessment, coupled with our own interest in format preference, led us to consider the correlation between uses of the same book in print and electronic media. Of those titles that triggered an STL, the corresponding print book, when held at one of the three libraries, was found to be in circulation 40 percent of the time. The STL and print loan occurred within seven days of each other. This temporal similarity between the STL and print circulation was not further studied in order to determine which occurred first. Future assessment will incorporate this component.

CONCLUSION

Areas for Further Study

Although initial setup of the DDA profile was straightforward, managing separate print and e-book workflows is not optimal. Because of this challenge, we are currently investigating merging our DDA and print book profiles within GOBI. Not only will this make the technical management more efficient, it will provide bibliographers with much-needed information regarding the relationship of print books with DDA availability. Moreover, integrating our DDA profile into GOBI is a model that could be extended to other e-book providers as they come on board with YBP.

Assessment of our yearlong pilot revealed some areas worth monitoring. The default one-day loan period seems correct. Although there were some cases where a user rented the same book multiple times, often on consecutive days, the number of these occurrences is not sufficient to consider extending the default loan period. Should a preference for very recent books continue, however, we may opt to shorten the publication window of titles profiled. Given the preference for university press imprints, it may also be worth reducing the number of commercial publishers profiled.

As for assessment measures generally, we need to begin looking at the relationship of browsed e-books—not just STLs—to print book use. Studying this larger set of e-book uses will double the sample size while arguably offering more valid observations than looking at STLs alone, since the brevity of non-STL e-book browses may in many cases indicate a patron's preference for print. Likewise, it's imperative for us to find ways of aggregating qualitative feedback from users, considering these comments in relationship to several factors such as age, major, device, and type of use.

Another subject we'd like to investigate is our bibliographers' attitudes about DDA e-books in relation to corresponding print books. Why do bibliographers consider the e-book format acceptable for certain titles and not for others? Do these attitudes, relative to subject area, correspond to patrons' usage patterns and surveyed preferences? In cases where a bibliographer states that she wants a print copy unless there is a DDA version available, what long- or short-term need does she see the DDA title serving? If this preference assumes long-term access to an unowned title, can we count on that access remaining available?

We have had questions about our purchase trigger and, indeed, about the idea of purchasing books at all. Following the pilot year, we decided to trigger an auto-purchase after the eighth short-term loan rather than after the fifth. The thought was that five loans were too likely to result in unnecessary purchases—ones that would never get enough future use to justify the expense. On the other hand, never purchasing titles that were experiencing significant use might lead to nervousness about long-term access and financial outlay. We compromised on eight loans as being indicative of a fair amount of ongoing interest. At this early date, eight loans reflect a relatively concentrated level of interest. Is there a qualitative difference between such concentrated use and use spread out over time? Studying this issue may elucidate the optimal loan-based purchase trigger at which point we may reasonably expect substantial future use.

However, some of our staff have expressed skepticism over the economic value of purchasing titles at all when short-term loans are available. In this present model, purchasing a title essentially assumes that the title will get a certain, definable level of future use in order to justify the purchase expense. In individual cases, future usage will vary, but more generally is a high level of future use typical enough to suggest that we should always purchase after some number of short-term loans? Long-term observation of use of purchased titles would help answer this question. A further consideration with regard to purchases is that purchasing also ensures the title's availability; owned titles can never be deleted from our DDA stream. We are still uncertain as to how likely it is that we will lose access to a given title in the long term. We have not yet made the decision never to purchase, but we suggest that libraries with a DDA program that allows paid short-term loans consider this option.

Considerations for a Consortial DDA Program

We include here for the benefit of other library groups some questions to consider before and while implementing a shared DDA program:

The Planning Process

- Will content be universally discoverable on all campuses? Likewise, will purchased content be universally accessible?
- Will all members of the consortium share costs equally, or will costs be apportioned based on where the use or purchase occurs?
- Given the unpredictability of expenses, how will the consortium budget for its DDA program? What contingencies are in place should the consortium exhaust its annual budget?
- How will administrative tasks be distributed?
- What authentication method will be employed, and will access to certain members of the user community such as alumni and guests be restricted?
- Who will troubleshoot end-user issues?
- Who will write or assemble documentation?

Collection Development

- Is the role of your DDA program central to collection building in that books accessed or acquired through this means could serve in lieu of print book acquisition, or is the program supplemental, serving subject areas and publishers outside of the consortium's mainstream foci?
- Will your DDA program work in conjunction with an existing print or electronic approval plan?
- Will preemptive purchase of books be allowed, or will purchases be restricted to those triggered by patron use?
- In a program that offers short-term rental access, will auto-purchases be triggered at all?
- Will duplicate e-books offered by separate suppliers be allowed in the joint catalog? Likewise, will an e-book be made discoverable if its corresponding print book is available?

- Will e-books be periodically weeded from the catalog, and if so, what criteria will be used?

Data Management and System Interoperability

- How will you assess the quality of the supplier's MARC records? Relatedly, if the records are deemed subpar, how and on what frequency will they be improved?
- On what frequency will new e-books matching the consortium's profile be ingested into the catalog(s), and who will do this work?
- What mechanism will you develop to facilitate removal of records for e-books no longer available through your supplier?
- What role will your print book vendor's system serve with regard to your DDA program?
- Does the DDA program have implications for your discovery system or resource sharing network(s)?

Impact on Bibliographers

- How will you frame the DDA program in order to gain bibliographer buy-in?
- How will the functional components of bibliographer selection incorporate DDA e-books? Will print and DDA e-book processes be integrative for them?

Assessment

- What quantitative metrics will be collected? How will these be disseminated to appropriate staff? Will these metrics be actionable, and if so, in what ways?
- Will you collect qualitative feedback from end-users, and if so, how?
- How will you determine whether your DDA program is successful?

NOTES

1. For an excellent monograph on this topic, see David A. Swords, ed., *Patron-Driven Acquisitions: History and Best Practices* (Berlin: De Gruyter Saur, 2011).
2. Susan Hinken and Emily J. McElroy, "Consortial Purchasing of E-Books: Orbis Cascade Alliance," in *The No Shelf Required Guide to E-Book Purchasing*, ed. Sue Polanka (Chicago: ALA TechSource, 2011), 8–13.
3. David Stern, "Ebooks: From Institutional to Consortial Considerations," *Online* 34, no. 3 (2010): 29–35.

4. At the time of our decision, EBL was the only vendor that allowed STLs and the ability to set customized purchase triggers.
5. EBL's trigger conditions include printing or copying from a book or five minutes browsing the book.
6. EBL worked with its publishers to establish a feasible pricing model for Tri-College access. Coordinators at Haverford and Swarthmore were selected to manage profiling and associated tasks in LibCentral, EBL's management system. A librarian at Swarthmore was selected to manage the batch import of EBL records into Tripod. Last, we agreed that the majority of the statistics compiling would be done at Haverford, although each library would generate reports to serve their local interests.
7. Science and math are not included in our print approval plan, although they are included in the DDA profile.

JUDITH M. NIXON,
SUZANNE M. WARD, AND
ROBERT S. FREEMAN

3

Selectors' Perceptions of E-Book Patron-Driven Acquisitions

MANY LIBRARIES, ESPECIALLY ACADEMIC LIBRARIES, HAVE established programs to purchase, rather than borrow, their patrons' interlibrary loan (ILL) requested books that meet specific criteria. These programs have had many names over the years, but the term "patron-driven acquisitions" (PDA) is now commonly used. The literature contains many case studies of these libraries' successes. Evaluations of these programs indicate that patrons select high-quality, scholarly books that have a high likelihood of being used again by other patrons.[1]

The success of these print-based PDA programs encouraged librarians to expand the concept into the e-book world.[2] E-book PDA plans differ from the traditional print PDA programs in that they are not based on ILL requests and thus do not wait for the patron to request a specific title before the library acquires it. Instead, librarians work with e-book aggregators to load thousands of records into their OPACs for their patrons to discover. These records are based on the library's predetermined selection profile. When patrons make significant use of a title, the e-book is purchased following a few preliminary short-term-loan rentals.

The first articles about e-book PDA reported on trials in which librarians selected individual titles to include in the PDA pool. In these first experiences, fairly insignificant patron activity, such as opening an e-book for a minute to review the table of contents, triggered purchases, thus depleting program budgets within a few weeks. The challenges encountered by these early adopters led to vendor refinements in PDA plans, resulting in the options that are typically available today, such as titles selected and added based on subject profiles and exclusion criteria; some free browsing; a predetermined number of fee-based, short-term-loan options before purchase; and the flexibility to choose the number of short-term loans before triggering a purchase. Patrons almost always have no idea that their e-book use is driving purchases; the PDA e-book records in an OPAC or discovery layer look identical to those for e-books that the library has already purchased. Several studies document these experiences.[3]

Fifteen years ago, when print-based PDA programs first began, many librarians were skeptical about the concept of programmatically building collections based on patron selections.[4] Would patron selections add too many popular or non-scholarly books? Would a few patrons use the service so heavily that their choices would skew the collection in certain subject areas? Would most of the books only be of interest to the initial patron and not to others? The shift to allowing patrons to select books, even if they were unaware of their role as selectors, seemed to challenge the librarian's responsibility as the collection development expert. For decades, academic librarians—often in consultation with faculty—selected material to support their institutions' research and teaching programs, with the goal of developing well-used collections of the highest quality books. Except for Osorio's survey of Illinois academic librarians,[5] no research has examined whether librarians' perceptions are changing about this newer point-of-need and patron-focused method of collection development.

Why is it important to understand librarians' perceptions about PDA? If this new concept of collection building is difficult for collection development librarians to appreciate at first, other than as a small program in the shadow of traditional collection-building activities, then they might be reluctant to start a program or might favor limiting the program's financial support. The authors wanted to investigate attitudes toward e-book PDA to ascertain whether there were any similarities among librarians at universities similar in size to their own. Therefore, the authors limited this study to large academic libraries that have active e-book PDA programs.

ARGUMENTS IN FAVOR OF E-BOOK PDA PROGRAMS

In the present environment it is possible to delay many book acquisitions until the moment when patrons express a need for specific titles. Academic libraries can avoid the cost of buying tens of thousands of books that their patrons may seldom or never use. A fairly large portion of a library's monograph collection could thus be built on expressed patron need rather than on librarians' best guesses about which titles might be used. With e-book PDA, these acquisitions can occur seamlessly and silently without the patrons ever knowing that their use has triggered a purchase.

ARGUMENTS IN FAVOR OF LIBRARIAN SELECTION

Just as patrons do not realize that the opening of an e-book initiates a purchase, subject librarians, too, might never know what has been purchased. They will become less familiar with and more removed from this part of collection development unless they make an ongoing effort to track PDA purchases. Collection librarians are certainly still needed to establish the PDA profile by deciding what subjects, publishers, and types of books are to be made accessible, but once the program is running, they will usually have to trust the faculty and the students to make useful selections. Another challenge for PDA collection development is that there are many works, such as the hundreds of thousands of new titles published outside of North America in languages other than English that are not available through e-book PDA vendors. As Hodges and her colleagues observed, "even the largest e-book aggregators have rights to distribute only a fraction of the titles published each year in the United States. The content available through patron-driven access programs . . . is only a small subset of what is published."[6] Since relying heavily on PDA builds collections based on e-format availability, traditional selection methods are still needed to acquire works not available through e-book PDA plans. This is certainly the case in subject areas where e-book coverage is inadequate, such as the fine arts, the performing arts, world literatures, and area studies. Combining traditional librarian selection with a PDA program would have the advantage, as Levine-Clark pointed out, of "allow[ing] selectors to spend more time on harder-to-find materials. Ultimately this should provide users a better mix of monographs than they have had in the past."[7]

THE RESEARCH QUESTION

The basic research question was to ascertain what percentage of selectors at large academic libraries favor e-book PDA and to learn what factors influence librarians' attitudes toward patron-driven acquisitions. Rather than ask the straightforward question of attitude toward e-book PDA programs, the authors asked two related questions. To support PDA, librarians need to believe that patrons choose useful titles for their research and also that these books will be useful to other patrons. The first question was written to identify librarians' attitudes toward patrons' ability to choose high-quality books. The second was to determine whether librarians believe that patron-selected books had subsequent circulations. The responses to these two questions were compared with other factors such as personal reading of e-books, time in the profession, and area of subject responsibility. Were librarians who personally read e-books more likely to embrace PDA? Would more recently trained librarians be more positive about PDA? Does disciplinary focus play a role in being more open to the e-book PDA concept? Do these factors have statistically significant impacts on the librarians' attitudes? And what budgets should be used to fund an e-book PDA program? Finally, what factors would influence librarians to expand the e-book PDA program?

Methodology

The authors decided that conducting a survey would be the best way to ask a large number of librarians about their perceptions of e-book PDA. They chose to survey librarians with selection responsibilities at research libraries with active e-book PDA programs within their primary consortium, the Committee on Institutional Cooperation (CIC; www.cic.net). Replies to a query sent to the CIC collection development officers revealed that in July 2012 a total of eight member libraries (the authors' own institution plus seven others) had active e-book PDA programs. The survey was limited to these eight universities: Illinois at Urbana-Champaign, Indiana, Iowa, Minnesota, Northwestern, Pennsylvania State, Purdue, and Wisconsin-Madison. The authors contacted the collection development officer at each of these eight libraries to obtain current e-mail addresses of all librarians involved with collection development. The final list consisted of 349 e-mail addresses. The authors developed a survey and submitted it to Purdue University's Institutional Research Board's (IRB) certification process for human research study approval. The survey was distributed and collected using Qualtrics.

On September 21, 2012, the authors sent the survey via e-mail to the 349 CIC librarians with collection development responsibilities. The survey closed on October 26, 2012; reminders were sent a few days before the deadline. The authors received 83 usable responses for a 24 percent response rate.

Survey Questions and Basic Findings

The survey first defined patron-driven acquisitions as a collection development profile with a vendor loading and periodically adding records to the catalog that meet the profile, and rental fees and purchases triggered by patron use of the PDA titles. The survey consisted of three parts. The first part covered some general demographic information about the librarian's professional background. The second part gathered information on their personal use of e-books and involvement in planning their PDA program, while the third part asked about involvement in the libraries' PDA program.

Part one asked:

- What year did you graduate from library school?
- Approximately how many years have you had collection development responsibilities such as selecting, weeding, and evaluating collections?
- Approximately what percentage of work time do you currently devote to collection development?
- What is your major collection development area? (Six choices, plus an option to indicate general responsibilities and/or several or all areas.)
- Indicate your university name, with an option not to identify the university.

Results indicated a broad spread of years in the profession among the surveyed group. Eighty-two respondents answered this question: 20 percent had fewer than 10 years of experience, 23 percent had between 10 and 20 years of experience, 28 percent had between 20 and 30 years of experience, and 23 percent had more than 30 years of experience. Five respondents (6 percent) did not have a library degree. Likewise there was a broad range of years of collection development experience: 39 percent had fewer than 10 years of experience, 30 percent had between 10 and 20 years, and 31 percent had over 20 years of collection development experience. So there was a fairly even spread of both time in the profession and years of collection development responsibilities. Sixty-six percent of the 83 librarians spent between 10 percent and 30 percent of their time on collection responsibilities. Only 26 percent of the respondents were in the science/technology/engineering/medicine (STEM) fields, while 68 percent either were buying in several areas or were in the humanities or the social sciences (figure 3.1). This emphasis on the liberal arts may in fact represent the proportion of librarians with these responsibilities at the universities. The authors did not have a breakdown by subject area from each library. Some librarians from every institution responded, ranging between 5 and 17. The number of librarians varied widely at each school; Purdue and the University of Minnesota had the most respondents with 16 and 17 respondents respectively.

The second part of the survey asked respondents about their personal use of e-books.

- Do you read e-books on a PC, laptop, notebook, tablet, e-reader? If so,
- How many e-books have you read (at least half of the book) in the last 3 months?

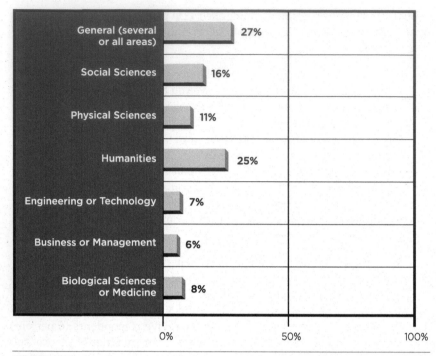

FIGURE 3.1
Major area of collection development.

Seventy-one percent of the librarians in this study personally read e-books; 66 percent of these had read fewer than four books in the last three months. One third of them had read four or more books, and 7 percent read ten or more (figure 3.2). In the comment section at the end of the survey, a number of respondents qualified what they meant by "reading e-books," indicating that they often refer to them, but seldom read them all the way through.

The second part of the survey also asked questions about the librarians' involvement in their local e-book PDA program:

- Are you knowledgeable about e-book PDA processes?
- Were you involved in any aspect of developing your library's e-book PDA program? If so,
- What was your involvement?

Only 34 percent of the respondents were involved in some aspect of the program development. The twenty-eight librarians who were involved in the

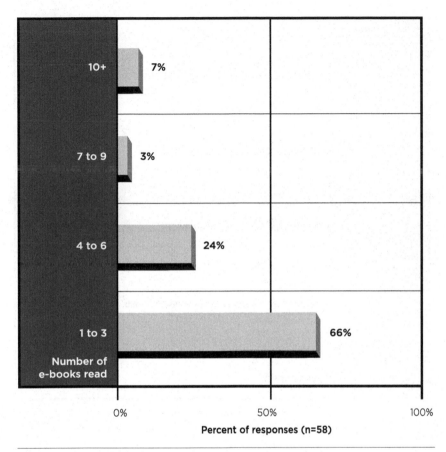

FIGURE 3.2
How many e-books have you read in the last 3 months?

development of the program had a range of involvement. Respondents could select multiple choices; most were on the profile development team; only four made the original proposal (figure 3.3).

The third part of the survey probed the librarians' attitudes about patrons' use of books and about their attitudes toward funding the PDA program.

- I think patrons choose the most useful titles for their research.
- I think the titles that one patron uses will be used by other patrons.
- If I were making decisions on the e-book PDA allocation for my library, I would . . . increase/keep the same/decrease funding.

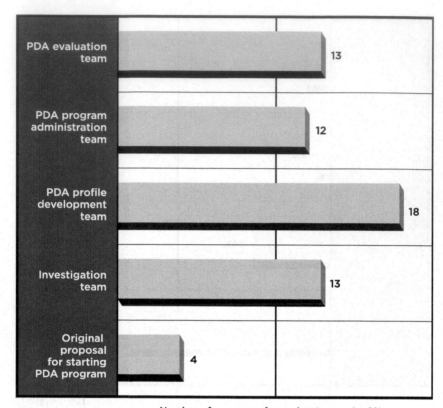

Number of responses for each category (n=28)

FIGURE 3.3
What was your involvement in the development of the e-book PDA program?

Depending on how respondents replied, they were asked one of the next questions.

- To increase funding for my library's e-book plan, I would (if I could) transfer funds from . . . (eight budget choices were given).
- Which of the following arguments would persuade you to INCREASE the PDA e-book budget? (Five choices included increase in annual allocation, overall budget decrease, high usage statistics, gift funds donated for PDA, and patrons asking for more e-books.)
- Of all the e-books purchased on a title-by-title basis (i.e., excluding e-book packages) what percentage should be selected though PDA?

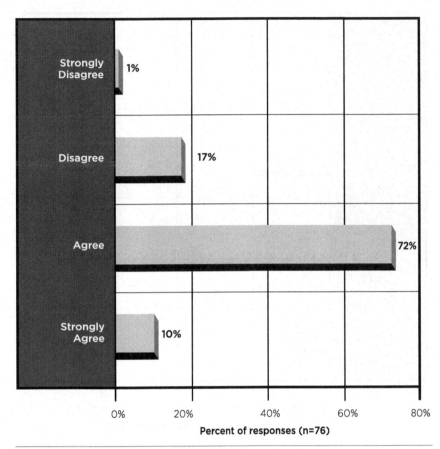

FIGURE 3.4
I think patrons choose the most useful titles for their research.

Not all respondents answered these questions; but of the seventy-six librarians who did, 83 percent agreed or strongly agreed that patrons choose the most useful titles for their research (figure 3.4). Of the seventy-six librarians who responded to the statement "I think the titles that one patron uses will be used by other patrons," 79 percent agreed or strongly agreed (figure 3.5).

Would they increase or decrease funding? Of the seventy-nine librarians who answered this question, 30 percent would increase funding, while 59 percent were content with the allocation; 10 percent would decrease funding. The most persuasive argument to influence those who would decrease funding or keep it at the current level ($n = 54$) was usage statistics for PDA e-books,

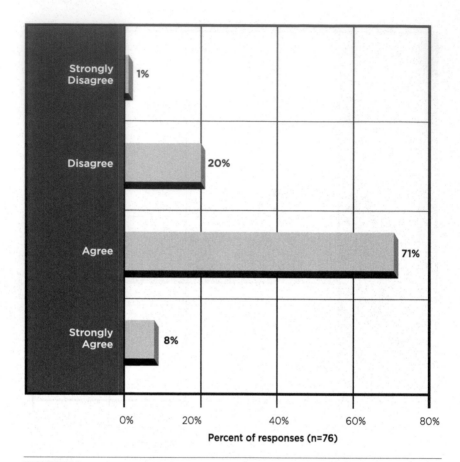

FIGURE 3.5
I think that titles one patron uses will be used by other patrons.

followed by patrons' indications that they would like access to more e-books. If the respondents indicated a preference for increasing funds (n = 54) (figure 3.6), they were also asked which budget lines might be tapped for the increase. Most recommended using the monograph budget as the source of increased funding for the PDA program (figure 3.7).

Librarians overwhelmingly agreed on the value of the PDA program in their library; 90 percent of the respondents agreed that the allocation of funds is sufficient or could be increased. However, there was little agreement on the percentage of the non-package e-books that should come from e-book PDA programs. By "non-package e-books" the authors meant those e-books that are selected on a title-by-title basis, rather than those that come as part of larger

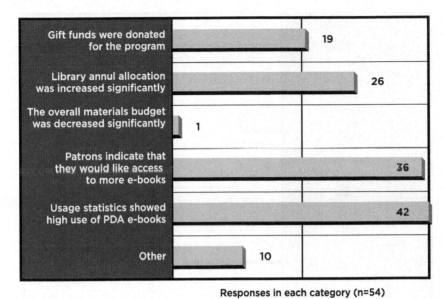

FIGURE 3.6
Which of the following would persuade you to increase
the PDA e-book budget?

publisher or aggregator packages. Forty-three percent of respondents chose 20 percent or less, while 42 percent chose between 21 percent and 49 percent, and 15 percent recommended 50 percent or higher. In retrospect the authors think that this may have been a confusing question. Some respondents may have thought the question was asking what percentage of the entire book budget should be allocated to the e-book PDA program (figure 3.8).

Discussion

The basic research question was to ascertain whether most collection development librarians at large academic libraries favor e-book PDA and what influences these librarians' attitudes toward patron-driven acquisitions. Rather than ask the straightforward question of attitude toward e-book PDA programs, the authors asked two related questions about attitudes toward patrons' book choices: their ability to choose useful titles and the likelihood that patrons' choices would be used later by other patrons. The authors compared the responses to these two questions with other factors such as time in the profession, personal reading of e-books, subject area of collection development responsibility, and involvement in the planning of the e-book PDA

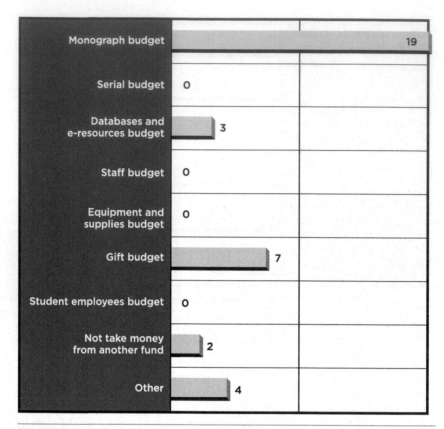

Monograph budget	19
Serial budget	0
Databases and e-resources budget	3
Staff budget	0
Equipment and supplies budget	0
Gift budget	7
Student employees budget	0
Not take money from another fund	2
Other	4

FIGURE 3.7

To increase funding for my library's PDA e-book plan I would (if I could) transfer funds from these categories.

program. These were the four factors that the authors anticipated would be most influential on librarians' attitudes.

How do years of experience in collection development affect responses? To investigate this, the authors merged "strongly agree and agree" and "disagree and strongly disagree" to increase the number of responses for each question. The first question was "Do patrons choose the most useful titles?" A total of seventy-seven respondents answered this question; 82 percent either strongly agreed or agreed, which shows very strong support among collection development librarians for e-book PDA programs. The support level dropped to 74 percent for librarians with more than twenty years of collection development experience. The second question was whether librarians believe that titles one patron used would likely be used by others. Most of the respondents

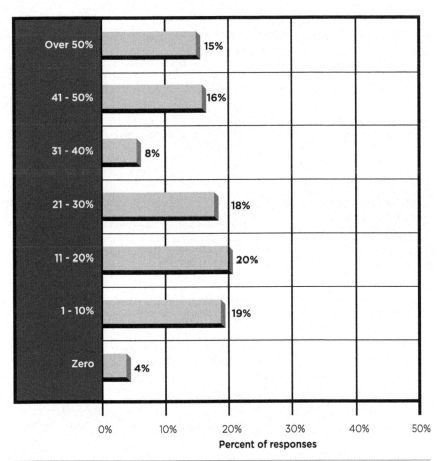

FIGURE 3.8

How many e-books have you read in the last 3 months?

agreed with this: 79 percent strongly agreed or agreed. However, librarians with twenty or more years of collection development experience were less likely to agree; only 68 percent agreed and none strongly agreed (table 3.1).

Personally reading e-books had little effect; 80 percent of the librarians who read e-books agreed or strongly agreed that patrons choose the most useful titles, but 86 percent of those who do not read e-books also agreed or strongly agreed. Personally reading e-books had little effect on whether librarians "thought that titles that one patron uses will be used by other patrons"; 82 percent of those who read e-books strongly agreed or agreed, while only 70 percent of those who do not read e-books agreed. It is important to point out

TABLE 3.1

Librarian by years of collection development responsibility:
Opinions on patrons' choices of PDA titles.

	I think patrons choose the most useful titles for their research.			I think titles that one patron uses will be used by other patrons.		
Years of collection development experience	**Agree, Strongly Agree**	**Disagree, Strongly Disagree**	**Total**	**Agree, Strongly Agree**	**Disagree, Strongly Disagree**	**Total**
Librarians with 20+ years of experience	74% (17)	26% (6)	100% (23)	68% (15)	12% (7)	100% (22)
Librarians with less than 20 years of experience	85% (46)	14% (8)	100% (54)	83% (44)	16% (9)	100% (53)
Total respondents			100% (77)			100% (75)

TABLE 3.2

Librarians who read e-books: Opinions on patrons' choices of PDA titles.

	I think patrons choose the most useful titles for their research.			I think titles that one patron uses will be used by other patrons.		
Do you read e-books?	**Agree, Strongly Agree**	**Disagree, Strongly Disagree**	**Total**	**Agree, Strongly Agree**	**Disagree, Strongly Disagree**	**Total**
Yes	80% (46)	19% (11)	100% (57)	82% (46)	18% (10)	100% (56)
No	86% (18)	14% (3)	100% (21)	70% (14)	30% (6)	100% (20)
Total respondents			100% (78)			100% (76)

that even with merging "strongly agree and agree" and "disagree and strongly disagree" there were fewer than five responses in one category. Because of the small sample size, statistical analysis (e.g., Chi-squared) could not be done; larger sample sizes would increase the frequencies of the numbers, and may allow analysis (table 3.2).

How do the librarians' areas of subject responsibility affect the answers to these two questions? Because of the limited number of responses, the authors merged agree with strongly agree, and disagree with strongly disagree. Then

TABLE 3.3

Librarians by major area of collection responsibility:
Opinions on patrons' choices of PDA titles.

Major area of collection development	I think patrons choose the most useful titles for their research.			I think titles that one patron uses will be used by other patrons.		
	Agree, Strongly Agree	Disagree, Strongly Disagree	Total	Agree, Strongly Agree	Disagree, Strongly Disagree	Total
Biological Sciences or Medicine, Engineering or Technology, Physical Sciences	81% (17)	19% (4)	100% (21)	90% (18)	10% (2)	100% (20)
Business, Social Sciences	78% (14)	22% (4)	100% (18)	78% (14)	22% (4)	100% (18)
Humanities	83% (15)	17% (3)	100% (18)	65% (11)	35% (6)	100% (17)
General (several or all areas)	85% (17)	15% (3)	100% (20)	80% (16)	20% (4)	100% (20)
Total respondents			100% (77)			100% (75)

the subject areas were merged into four broader areas: STEM, Social Sciences, Humanities, and General. When the authors compared the first question, "I think patrons choose useful titles," there were only slight variations, with the social sciences being the lowest in agreement and the humanities and general the highest. This is contrary to what was expected. When the authors compared the second question, "I think that titles that one patron uses will be used by other patrons," with subject responsibilities, 90 percent of the STEM area librarians agreed or strongly agreed. The humanities librarians also agreed, but less enthusiastically, with only 65 percent of them agreeing or strongly agreeing. It is important to point out that with this degree of drilling down, the number of librarians among most groups drops to lower than five.

It is not possible to tell if there is a relationship, using Chi-squared, because in several cases the number of librarians in a category (or cell in the table) is less than five. So there are no conclusions from this survey data on whether librarians in certain subject areas are more likely to support e-book PDA programs. However, large differences between cell percentages indicate that there is a possibility of a relationship. An increase in sample size is necessary to determine any relationship (table 3.3).

Finally, the authors thought that being involved in the planning and development of the PDA program might make a librarian more favorably disposed to the program. Twenty-seven of the 28 librarians who were involved in the development of their e-book PDA program answered the question about whether they felt that patrons choose the most useful titles for their research. Of these 85 percent agreed or strongly agreed, only four disagreed, and no one strongly disagreed. And 80 percent of these librarians agreed that titles used by one patron will be used by other patrons. These statistics paralleled those of the whole group; so being involved in the program development did not noticeably affect opinions toward the e-book PDA program.

Respondents' Comments

The authors invited comments at the end of the survey.

Thirty-seven of the 83 respondents made comments. It would be impossible to assign each comment to a single category or a place on the spectrum of positive and negative attitudes toward e-book PDA. Comments were short or long, narrow or wide-ranging, and enthusiastic or cautious or both at the same time. One comment expressed the ambivalence of many: "I'm really smack dab in the middle. Right now PDA is so new it's hard to tell whether I agree or disagree with the statements." In general, most of the comments addressed either of two issues: the format of e-books or patron-driven selection.

Regarding the format of e-books, several librarians praised the instantaneous accessibility of e-books for distance-education students and other nontraditional students who seldom have time to go to libraries on campus. Only one respondent mentioned the advantage of being able to search e-books for specific terms and phrases. No one commented on how little physical space e-books require. Several respondents commented on the disadvantages of current e-book formats, including "clunky," nonstandard platforms, the difficulty of transferring library e-books to a Kindle, user-unfriendly limitations on printing, and the inability to borrow or lend e-books through ILL due to licensing/ DRM restrictions. A number of librarians saw advantages in both print and electronic formats. For example: "The electronic, everywhere-accessible platform is obviously a great advantage over access to and use of print materials. . . . But I believe it is true that faculty and students still derive significant use of and satisfaction with printed books, . . . The faculty I work with in area studies . . . still work with print and are not likely to abandon the format all together."

Regarding PDA specifically, several comments highlighted these advantages: it meets just-in-time research needs; results in purchases that will probably have more use than librarian selections; involves student and faculty expertise in the selection process; and often fills gaps in the collection. One librarian described PDA as a "safety net" for interdisciplinary areas where it is nearly impossible for librarians to predict user needs. While acknowledging some of these advantages, several librarians expressed caution, and indicated what they feel are problems with PDA. One noted the "unequal distribution" of available and purchased e-books "between subject areas." Another agreed that "it is not clear how many e-books are available in all areas of research." A couple of librarians remarked that patrons are only going to select books they need for immediate assignments. One warned against too many undergraduate purchases, and would prefer to see "PDA selections among graduate level students and faculty only." Several others worried about "not acquiring something for the future before it is no longer available." For example: "I do not want us to forego purchasing a significant number of research titles that we may not be able to retroactively acquire. I work in the humanities and it can take a long time before a book is used." Another wrote: "I think of [e-book PDA] as offering the equivalent of instantaneous ILL. However, in a large research library, I fear that subscribing to the 'just in time' notion will come back to haunt my successors in years to come, in terms of quality of the collections and for sure in costs for ILLing what we didn't acquire—if indeed the material will even be available through ILL." One commenter warned that PDA would contribute to the decline of collection librarians' expert knowledge: "The reason I answered that I wouldn't put more money into PDA is because it is simply another example of the collection and the library being further removed from its stewards and custodians. With PDA, the publishers and providers of e-books learn more about the borrowing community than the librarians know." Finally, one librarian commented that many selectors like PDA, "but it remains to be seen how much they would like it if a percentage of their subject funds were skimmed at the beginning of the FY to partially cover the costs."

CONCLUSIONS

An important finding in this research was that librarians at large institutions with e-book PDA programs are highly supportive of the programs; they feel that patrons can choose appropriate books for their own research and that these books are likely to circulate to other students and researchers. This attitude does not appear to be influenced by the percentage of time spent on collection management activities, personal reading habits of e-books, or by being involved in the planning of the e-book PDA program. Area of subject responsibility, which the authors also investigated, might have some effect, but the research was inconclusive.

Based on the survey's findings, librarians at institutions that do not yet have a PDA program may want to give serious consideration to starting one.[8]

FURTHER RESEARCH

It is interesting to discover that in a mere fifteen years, academic librarians' attitudes toward formal programs for patron-selected books have gone from highly skeptical (early ILL book purchase programs) to highly supportive (e-book PDA plans). However, this present study focused on large research institutions and on librarians with collection development responsibilities. It would be interesting to discover if academic librarians in general embrace the same attitude, or if perceptions about PDA change significantly depending on institution size. The authors have conducted a similar survey of library directors in all sizes and types of academic libraries in their home state of Indiana.

Specific questions that the authors propose for further research are:

- Do librarians with certain subject responsibilities favor e-book PDA programs? Are STEM librarians more supportive or less supportive than humanities or social science librarians, and why?
- Why do some librarians at smaller institutions seem reluctant to start an e-book PDA program?
- What specific obstacles do librarians face in recommending and starting an e-book PDA program?
- This study indicates that statistics showing high patron use of e-books would positively influence librarians who may be reluctant to support PDA as a collection tool. Further statistical studies analyzing e-book use as a result of PDA programs are needed.
- What are the qualitative differences between patron-selected and librarian-selected books?

ACKNOWLEDGMENTS

Susan E. Niskanen, Purdue Libraries research assistant, who assisted with statistical analysis.

Dave Nelson, assistant director of the Center for Instructional Excellence at Purdue University, who advised on survey creation.

NOTES

1. Kristine J. Anderson et al., "Buy, Don't Borrow: Bibliographers' Analysis of Academic Library Collection Development through Interlibrary Loan Requests," *Collection Management* 27, no. 3–4 (2002); Kristine J. Anderson et al., "Liberal Arts Books on Demand: A Decade of Patron-Driven Collection

Development, Part 1," *Collection Management* 35, no. 3–4 (2010); Marianne Stowell Bracke, "Science and Technology Books on Demand: A Decade of Patron-Driven Collection Development, Part 2," *Collection Management* 35, no. 3–4 (2010); Judith M. Nixon and E. Stewart Saunders, "A Study of Circulation Statistics of Books on Demand: A Decade of Patron-Driven Collection Development, Part 3," *Collection Management* 35, no. 3–4 (2010); Jennifer Perdue and James A. Van Fleet, "Borrow or Buy? Cost-Effective Delivery of Monographs," *Journal of Interlibrary Loan, Document Delivery & Information Supply* 9, no. 4 (1999); David C. Tyler et al., "Just How Right Are the Customers? An Analysis of the Relative Performance of Patron-Initiated Interlibrary Loan Monograph Purchases," *Collection Management* 35, no. 3–4 (2010); David C. Tyler et al., "Patron-Driven Acquisition and Circulation at an Academic Library: Interaction Effects and Circulation Performance of Print Books Acquired via Librarians' Orders, Approval Plans, and Patrons' Interlibrary Loan Requests," *Collection Management* 38, no. 1 (2013).

2. William Breitbach and Joy E. Lambert, "Patron-Driven Ebook Acquisition," *Computers in Libraries* 31, no. 6 (2011); Karen S. Fischer et al., "Give 'Em What They Want: A One-Year Study of Unmediated Patron-Driven Acquisition of E-Books," *College & Research Libraries* 73, no. 5 (2012); Dracine Hodges, Cyndi Preston, and Marsha J. Hamilton, "Patron-Initiated Collection Development: Progress of a Paradigm Shift," *Collection Management* 35, no. 3–4 (2010); Dracine Hodges, Cyndi Preston, and Marsha J. Hamilton, "Resolving the Challenge of E-Books," *Collection Management* 35, no. 3–4 (2010); Michael Levine-Clark, "Developing a Multiformat Demand-Driven Acquisition Model," *Collection Management* 35, no. 3–4 (2010); Jason S. Price and John D. McDonald, "Beguiled by Bananas: A Retrospective Study of the Usage and Breadth of Patron vs. Librarian Acquired Ebook Collections" (paper presented at the 29th Annual Charleston Conference, November 4–7, 2009), *Library Staff Publications and Research, Paper 9* (2009).

3. Breitbach and Lambert, "Patron-Driven Ebook Acquisition"; Melissa De Fino and Mei Ling Lo, "New Roads for Patron-Driven E-Books: Collection Development and Technical Services Implications of a Patron-Driven Acquisitions Pilot at Rutgers," *Journal of Electronic Resources Librarianship* 23, no. 4 (2011).

4. Candice Dahl, "Primed for Patron-Driven Acquisition: A Look at the Big Picture," *Journal of Electronic Resources Librarianship* 24, no. 2 (2012).

5. Nestor L. Osorio, "A User's Participatory Selecting Model: Librarians' Point of Views" (paper presented at the Illinois Library Association Annual Meeting, Rosemont, IL, October 19, 2011), http://eprints.rclis.org/16507/1/PDA -paper.pdf.

6. Hodges, Preston, and Hamilton, "Patron-Initiated Collection Development: Progress of a Paradigm Shift," 219.

7. Levine-Clark, "Developing a Multiformat Demand-Driven Acquisition Model," 206–7.
8. Suzanne M. Ward, *Guide to Implementing and Managing Patron-Driven Acquisitions* (Chicago: Association for Library Collections & Technical Services, American Library Association, 2012).

REFERENCES

Anderson, Kristine J., Robert S. Freeman, Jean-Pierre V. M. Herubel, Lawrence J. Mykytiuk, Judith M. Nixon, and Suzanne M. Ward. "Buy, Don't Borrow: Bibliographers' Analysis of Academic Library Collection Development through Interlibrary Loan Requests." *Collection Management* 27, no. 3–4 (2002): 1–11.

———. "Liberal Arts Books on Demand: A Decade of Patron-Driven Collection Development, Part 1." *Collection Management* 35, no. 3–4 (2010): 125–41. doi:10.1080/01462679.2010.486959.

Breitbach, William, and Joy E. Lambert. "Patron-Driven Ebook Acquisition." *Computers in Libraries* 31, no. 6 (2011): 16–20.

Dahl, Candice. "Primed for Patron-Driven Acquisition: A Look at the Big Picture." *Journal of Electronic Resources Librarianship* 24, no. 2 (2012): 119–26. doi:10.1080/1941126X.2012.684557.

De Fino, Melissa, and Mei Ling Lo. "New Roads for Patron-Driven E-Books: Collection Development and Technical Services Implications of a Patron-Driven Acquisitions Pilot at Rutgers." *Journal of Electronic Resources Librarianship* 23, no. 4 (2011): 327–38. doi:10.1080/1941126X.2011.627043.

Fischer, Karen S., Michael Wright, Kathleen Clatanoff, Hope Barton, and Edward Shreeves. "Give 'Em What They Want: A One-Year Study of Unmediated Patron-Driven Acquisition of E-Books." *College & Research Libraries* 73, no. 5 (2012): 469–92.

Hodges, Dracine, Cyndi Preston, and Marsha J. Hamilton. "Patron-Initiated Collection Development: Progress of a Paradigm Shift." *Collection Management* 35, no. 3–4 (2010): 208–21. doi:10.1080/01462679.2010.486968.

———. "Resolving the Challenge of E-Books." *Collection Management* 35, no. 3–4 (2010): 196–200. doi:10.1080/01462679.2010.486964.

Levine-Clark, Michael. "Developing a Multiformat Demand-Driven Acquisition Model." *Collection Management* 35, no. 3–4 (2010): 201–7. doi:10.1080/01462679.2010.486965.

Nixon, Judith M., and E. Stewart Saunders. "A Study of Circulation Statistics of Books on Demand: A Decade of Patron-Driven Collection Development, Part 3." *Collection Management* 35, no. 3–4 (2010): 151–61. doi:10.1080/01462679.2010.486963.

Osorio, Nestor L. "A User's Participatory Selecting Model: Librarians' Point of Views." Paper presented at the Illinois Library Association Annual Meeting, Rosemont, IL, October 19, 2011. http://eprints.rclis.org/16507/1/PDA-paper.pdf.

Perdue, Jennifer, and James A. Van Fleet. "Borrow or Buy? Cost-Effective Delivery of Monographs." *Journal of Interlibrary Loan, Document Delivery & Information Supply* 9, no. 4 (1999): 19–28. doi:10.1300/J110v09n04_04.

Price, Jason S., and John D. McDonald. "Beguiled by Bananas: A Retrospective Study of the Usage and Breadth of Patron vs. Librarian Acquired Ebook Collections." Paper presented at the 29th Annual Charleston Conference, November 4–7, 2009. *Library Staff Publications and Research, Paper 9* (2009).

Stowell Bracke, Marianne. "Science and Technology Books on Demand: A Decade of Patron-Driven Collection Development, Part 2." *Collection Management* 35, no. 3–4 (2010): 142–50. doi:10.1080/01462679.2010.486742.

Tyler, David C., Christina Falci, Joyce C. Melvin, MaryLou Epp, and Anita M. Kreps. "Patron-Driven Acquisition and Circulation at an Academic Library: Interaction Effects and Circulation Performance of Print Books Acquired via Librarians' Orders, Approval Plans, and Patrons' Interlibrary Loan Requests." *Collection Management* 38, no. 1 (2013): 3–32. doi:10.1080/01462679.2012.730494.

Tyler, David C., Yang Xu, Joyce C. Melvin, Marylou Epp, and Anita M. Kreps. "Just How Right Are the Customers? An Analysis of the Relative Performance of Patron-Initiated Interlibrary Loan Monograph Purchases." *Collection Management* 35, no. 3–4 (2010): 162–79. doi:10.1080/01462679.2010.487030.

Ward, Suzanne M. *Guide to Implementing and Managing Patron-Driven Acquisitions.* Chicago: Association for Library Collections & Technical Services, American Library Association, 2012.

JAMIE L. CONKLIN AND
ERIK SEAN ESTEP

4
Flying in Late

A Pilot PDA on a Microscopic Budget

LOVEJOY LIBRARY OF SOUTHERN ILLINOIS UNIVERSITY IN Edwardsville was late to the party with its patron-driven acquisition (PDA) program; however, party guests often learn a lot by arriving near the end. Lovejoy was also unique because of the low $4,000 budget. The pilot was implemented quickly and was live for just one month before all of the funds were expended. The total length of the pilot was brief as well. The Task Force was formed in October 2011, and we implemented the pilot in the spring semester, analyzed the results in the summer, and presented our final report to the Collection Management Committee in December. But before we get to the lessons learned in our own pilot, it is important to analyze the strengths and weaknesses of our predecessors.

Purdue University implemented the first large-scale PDA program in January 2000 and was called Books on Demand. Bucknell College had tried in 1990 but was hamstrung because of books being out of print or the requirement of prepayment. Only the rise of online bookselling allowed for the implementation of a PDA in a large manner.[1] Purdue used their ILL system to run a Liberal Arts Books on Demand program and the librarians found that requests from users in six liberal arts departments—English, Foreign Language & Literatures, History, Management, Philosophy, and Political Science—continued to be the heaviest users. The librarians also found that 79 to 93 percent of the requests were in scope and would have been purchased anyway by the bibliographers. However, the Purdue librarians did get needed requests for *interdisciplinary* titles. Ranges of 40 percent to 80 percent of the books within subject call numbers were requested by users outside of those disciplines. The Purdue librarians conclude that while the pilot was successful, user requests should not entirely take the place of subject expertise.[2]

More recently, librarians at the Ohio State University Libraries (OSUL) implemented two programs: (1) an interlibrary loan purchase program (ILPOD) and (2) two tests of ebrary's PDA program that were triggered by patron-driven usage. Although the authors make the case that academic libraries are experiencing a paradigm shift to more patron-driven input through PDAs, they also argue that subject librarians still have a large role to play. Their most interesting suggestion for future PDAs is to have the patron-driven use of the e-book be set at a higher level before the library purchases the book; this is a needle that punctures some of the PDA boosterism that is seen in too many articles.[3]

With those important case studies in mind, we carefully designed our own PDA in the fall and winter of 2011/12. At Lovejoy, collection development decisions are made collectively. We have a Collection Management Committee (CMC) that meets twice a month and is chaired by the acquisitions librarian and electronic resources librarian. All subject selectors are invited to participate, as well as other professionals involved in the collection development process. We come to decisions and then submit them to our dean for final approval. It was at these CMC meetings that the parameters of our pilot PDA were hashed out.

PARAMETERS AND TIME LINE

Previous literature has shown that selecting appropriate parameters for a PDA project helps ensure its success.[4] Therefore, in February 2012, the Task Force decided to set several limits (see table 4.1). The items added to our pilot would include only e-books provided by EBL and published since 2008. The humanities librarian recommended adding French, German, and Spanish e-books since the university offers these languages as degree programs, and the Task Force agreed with this recommendation. A monetary limit of $175 eliminated expensive textbooks and reference sets.

Our acquisitions librarian acted as liaison between the Task Force and our YBP representative. He set up the $4,000 fund for the project and shared our

TABLE 4.1

PDA pilot project parameters.

Format	E-book
Languages	English, French, German, and Spanish
Publication date	> 2007
Price	< $175
Limit	No monographs already owned
LC Classification	Vendor-selected titles within predetermined profile

parameters. He also provided the Task Force with a vendor profile that librarians created in June 2009, which the Task Force used as a starting point to save time. YBP sent 55,000 slips in fiscal year 2011 that matched this profile, so these records were then cross-referenced with our project parameters. In March 2011, YBP provided 36,000 e-book titles for the project.

In addition, the Task Force chose an unmediated project so that users had control over their catalog experience. We allowed three short-term loans, each set with a one-day loan duration, before triggering a purchase. Each short-term loan totaled 10 to 15 percent of the e-book list price.

During one of our CMC meetings, librarians voiced concern about the ability to review the e-book records before we uploaded them into the catalog. Due to time constraints and the emphasis of this project as a pilot, we urged them to allow the Task Force to handle this process. We received 36 folders, each containing 1,000 items, to review. We divided up the folders and randomly skimmed through them. One member of the Task Force commented, "I have gone through two folders, and my eyes are about to fall out of my head." In the end, there were too many records to analyze thoroughly, and we decided that keeping the entire list would be best for the purpose of a pilot.

By March 18, approximately 33,500 PDA records were uploaded to our catalog. The director of technical services identified approximately 400 records with errors that she then removed from the pilot. Some of these records were duplicates for titles we owned through other e-book packages, while others were titles librarians had ordered but had not yet received.

We had the option to continually add more titles that matched our profile as they became available. We decided to stick with the initial number of records to keep it simple. On March 27, we received our first report, which indicated students had already used a quarter of our budgeted amount (see table 4.2). Within a little more than a month, students spent the $4,000 allocated to our pilot project.

An analysis of the number of short-term loans triggered throughout the project showed that students browsed the e-books more during the beginning

TABLE 4.2

Time line of expenditures.

Date of report	# of short-term loans	Cost of short-term loans	# of purchases	Cost of purchases	Total spent
March 27	121	$1,097.00	1	$ 55.00	$1,152.00
March 30	160	$1,463.60	2	$340.00	$1,803.60
April 9	227	$2,032.99	3	$369.99	$2,402.98
April 17	330	$2,584.60	4	$389.99	$2,974.59
April 23	382	$2,996.79	4	$389.99	$3,386.78
April 25	406	$3,164.75	5	$454.99	$3,619.74
April 27	437	$3,407.62	6	$549.94	$3,957.56

of the week, especially on Tuesdays. Usage decreased over the weekend and even dropped to zero over the Easter holiday weekend. These trends match both our door count and reference transaction patterns.

BENEFICIAL PILOT PROJECT OUTCOMES

Just-in-Time Access

Perhaps the most beneficial outcome of our pilot was that students were able to gain access to e-book content when they needed it. For example, students enrolled in the university's introductory biology course needed resources related to plant pollination for a lab report. Due to the large number of enrolled students, the library's print collection for this topic was depleted. Therefore, students could rely on the e-books from our pilot project, which triggered the purchase of *Pollination and Floral Ecology*. Another title, *Evolution of Plant-Pollinator Relationships*, had three short-term loans but no trigger to purchase.

Students' Needs and Interests

Since subject librarians perform reference, instruction, and collection development for specific academic courses and disciplines, we sometimes focus only on student development in academics. However, much research has shown that students develop in other areas while in college, including social, personal, practical, and occupational aspects.[5] When choosing items for our pilot project, we first took the narrow focus of scholarly books for academic purposes. However, when reviewing the folders of e-books, we noticed some popular titles related to dating, cooking, personal care, and other topics that are typically found in public rather than in academic libraries. Instead of removing the titles, we decided to leave them in to see if students would search for them.

During our pilot, students did browse some e-books considered more popular than scholarly. Therefore, librarians could expand their orders to include items that students can use for self-growth outside of academics. For example, students read several *For Dummies* titles, including one on finance, a second on living vegetarian, and a third on starting a business. However, this was the exception rather than the norm.

Our pilot project indicated that students are focused on job obtainment either during or after their education. Several browsed titles included how-to books on writing cover letters and resumes, as well as selecting jobs and studying for employment-related exams. Some examples include *200 Best Jobs for Renewing America, Step-by-Step Cover Letters, Expert Resumes for Military-to-Civilian Transitions, Police Officer Exam for Dummies,* and *Cover Letter Magic.*

It is difficult to maintain a print collection of these types of books in the library since they tend to go missing. However, the ability to view these in e-book format eliminates this issue. Student interest in this area opens up possibilities for librarians to partner with the campus career center, to hold workshops, and to provide helpful career information to students.

Another area of interest uncovered by our pilot is that of the effect of technology and social media on students' lives. Students browsed titles on Internet addiction, the impact of mobile communications, and the philosophy of technology. They also searched for material that would help them learn some technological tools, including Twitter, Prezi, JavaScript, and many other programming languages. As with the career books, this could lead to opportunities of hosting programs on social media, presentation, and other technological tools, as well as developing collections in these areas.

Data for Collection Development

The majority of titles browsed during our pilot project did align with academic coursework, thus assisting librarians with collection development in specific disciplines. There were several disciplines with more than ten short-term loans (table 4.3). While librarians already knew that students in the health, computer science, and engineering disciplines rely heavily on e-books, others were surprised to see the heavy use in literature, social sciences, and mathematics. Our pilot project demonstrated that students in these disciplines readily use e-books when available.

TABLE 4.3

Short-term loans by LC Classification.

LC Classification	Total loans	% of loans
PN-PT: Literature	66	15%
R, RA, RC, RG, RJ, RM: Medicine	50	11%
HM-HT: Sociology	36	8%
LA-LJ: Education	24	5%
HD: Labor	20	5%
HV: Social Pathology, Social and Public Welfare, Criminology	20	5%
TA-TP: Engineering	20	5%
HF: Commerce	16	4%
JC-JZ: Political Science	15	3%
E, F: History (American)	14	3%
QA 75-76: Computer Science	13	3%
QA: Mathematics	13	3%
QH-QL: Botany and Zoology	12	3%

Comparing print circulations to short-term loan data proves useful for determining whether or not students sought materials in the same disciplines or subject matters in both print and e-book formats. Circulation data shows that many of the same disciplines most used in the pilot project, including literature, history, sociology, and medicine, were also most likely checked out in person (table 4.4). Medical books in e-book format (11 percent of short-term loans) were more popular than print books (5 percent of total print circulation), while American history was the opposite with 3 percent of short-term loans and 10 percent of print circulation. Anthropology was another discipline where print was preferred to e-book format.

Surprisingly, dental students checked out twelve print books but did not view any e-books. Chemistry students followed suit with eight print checkouts and no e-book usage. It is possible that these students rely more heavily on journals rather than books. Although we did not perform an analysis on the number of e-books uploaded into the project by LC Classification, the exercise of comparing print and e-book statistics can still be a starting point for determining student preferences and for beginning a conversation with faculty and students in different disciplines.

Overall, our list of browsed titles provided evidence of what information students needed, whether for class assignments, personal interest, or other purposes.

TABLE 4.4

Total print circulations by LC Classification.

LC Classification	Total circulations	% circulations
PN-PZ: Literature	247	17%
E, F: History (American)	148	10%
DA, DD, DR, DS: History	103	7%
HM-HT: Sociology	73	5%
HV: Social Pathology, Social and Public Welfare, Criminology	67	5%
R, RA, RC, RG, RJ, RM: Medicine	65	5%
B-BD, BJ: Philosophy	54	4%
N-NX: Visual Arts	53	4%
PA-PM: Languages and Literature	51	4%
L-LJ: Education	44	3%
JA-JZ: Political Science	40	3%
BF: Psychology	38	3%

Increased Usage

It is interesting to note that of the 438 short-term loans, 138 (31.5 percent) were for duplicate titles. Several studies have shown that an advantage to PDA titles is that they circulate more frequently than titles ordered by librarians.[6] Although we cannot know for sure whether the same student viewed the same title multiple times, our pilot demonstrates that students in the same classes with the same projects may find the same titles useful. Since our small pilot only resulted in six purchases, we will be unable to determine too much about future circulation data.

Students had the option to download titles or view them online. The e-book format chosen for the pilot created the opportunity for more students to access a specific title compared to our print collection. Since undergraduates may check out print books for four weeks, most circulated titles would have been unavailable to additional students during the month-long pilot.

CHALLENGES AND LESSONS LEARNED

Communication with Librarians

One of our largest challenges arose due to timing. We started our pilot project in March, which is when librarians order the bulk of their monographs for the fiscal year. When we initiated conversations about our pilot project in the previous October, librarians agreed to hold off on purchasing titles that would be part of the pilot. As the looming ordering deadline approached, some found this agreement difficult to keep. Each title uploaded as a PDA record in our catalog was given a message viewable in Gobi, our ordering site. This made it easy for librarians to determine whether or not a title was part of the pilot. Our pilot included Choice titles and other highly valued titles librarians wished to purchase. After much discussion, librarians were allowed to order titles that fell within the range of our project in order to meet the impending deadline.

This challenge would easily be eliminated if a future pilot project was run well in advance of monograph ordering deadlines. That way, librarians could use data from the PDA pilot as a tool for ordering high-interest titles viewed by students.

E-Book Training

The pilot project reiterated the need for future e-book training for students and library staff alike. Introducing more than 33,000 e-book records into our catalog created a huge impact on individual searches. It was nearly impossible to perform a search without pulling up at least one e-book in the first page of results. While at the information desk, library faculty and staff found themselves providing more one-on-one instruction in the use of e-books. It became necessary to make sure that everyone knew how to respond to student questions related to these materials.

The fact that students triggered 437 short-term loans for e-book titles in the short time of our project indicates that they are ready and willing to accept this format. On the other hand, the increase in questions related to e-books shows the necessity of providing training to students. Therefore, our library plans to offer future drop-in classes on how to use e-books and will investigate the possibility of implementing a technology zoo at the desk where students can use iPads and other reading devices to learn how to access, download, and use e-books.

One minor obstacle we had not considered at the start of our project was how to demonstrate e-book usage to students without triggering a short-term loan or purchase. We settled on two options. If a student showed definite interest in a specific title, we asked her to log in using her credentials so that a short-term loan would associate with her account for later viewing. Otherwise, if a student was more interested in the mechanics of downloading or browsing a title rather than the content of a specific title, we would demonstrate how to do so with an e-book we had purchased prior to our pilot.

Short-Term Loan Considerations

Providing the short-term loan option allowed more students to access titles at least once, which in turn gave librarians a broader picture of student needs. If we had set the parameters to trigger a purchase on the second view, we would have purchased sixty-nine titles and gone through our budget much more quickly. A triggered purchase on the third view would have resulted in twenty-two purchases at a total of $1,230.67. Since the average short-term loan price was $7.80, students would have missed the opportunity of obtaining access to eighty-seven short-term loan titles and the pilot would have most likely ended a week earlier. On the other hand, the library would have added an additional sixteen titles to its e-book collection.

Hence, librarians implementing a PDA pilot project should consider what would be the optimal number of short-term loans to trigger a purchase. If the purpose is to gather as much information as possible on students' information needs, then a larger number of short-term loans allows for more title viewings. However, if the library's priority is to build the e-book collection, a smaller number of short-term loans would be advisable.

What Is to Be Done?

The $4,000 spent on our pilot project was well worth the funds for the information it provided about student e-book usage and preferences as well as their information needs. Some subject librarians who feel the project was especially successful in their subject areas would like to pursue small pilot projects limited to their disciplines in the future. The monthlong study gave some indication as to the appropriate amount to set aside for PDA. This would entail figuring out how to set up subject funds and more specific subject profiles.

Subject librarians will use the results of the pilot to start a conversation with faculty liaisons about the use of e-books in their disciplines. Others will simply order more or fewer e-books in the future based on the trends shown by the pilot. In addition, librarians will purchase some of the e-books that received multiple short-term loans and develop collections in areas that proved popular by students.

Unfortunately, Southern Illinois University–Edwardsville, like so many schools in this age of austerity, is facing serious budget cuts at the time of this writing. No commitment has been made from the administration to permanently implement a PDA. However, if we do decide to continue with a PDA we will likely use our pilot project as a way to improve our efforts. For instance, we will recommend starting the program at the beginning of a semester rather than in the middle of it, with work done during the summer to make sure the program is implemented properly. As always, we will once again gather input from our colleagues to make sure they are comfortable with the project. Even if we don't go forward, this pilot proved that even on a very small scale, a PDA can have a positive impact on collection development and can give librarians at all levels of involvement vital information to make more informed selections.

NOTES

1. Judith M. Nixon, Robert S. Freeman, and Suzanne M. Ward, "Patron-Driven Acquisitions: An Introduction and Literature Review," *Collection Management* 35 (2010): 119–24.
2. Kristine J. Anderson, Robert S. Freeman, Jean-Pierre V. M. Herubel, Lawrence J. Mykytiuk, Judith M. Nixon, and Suzanne M. Ward, "Liberal Arts Books on Demand: A Decade of Patron-Driven Collection Development, Part 1," *Collection Management* 35 (2010): 138–39.
3. Dracine Hodges, Cyndi Preston, and Marsha J. Hamilton, "Patron-Initiated Collection Development: Progress of a Paradigm Shift," *Collection Management* 35 (2010): 220.
4. Karen S. Fischer, Michael Wright, Kathleen Clatanoff, Hope Barton, and Edward Shreeves, "Give 'Em What They Want: A One-Year Study of Unmediated Patron-Driven Acquisition of eBooks," *College & Research Libraries* 73 (2012): 469–92, http://crl.acrl.org/content/73/5/469.full.pdf+html; Hodges, Preston, and Hamilton, "Patron-Initiated Collection Development," 208–21.
5. Karma El Hassan, "Identifying Indicators of Student Development in College," *College Student Journal* 42 (2008): 517–30; Nixon, Freeman, and Ward, "Patron-Driven Acquisitions, 119–24.
6. George D. Kuh, "In Their Own Words: What Students Learn outside the Classroom," *American Educational Research Journal* 30 (1993): 277–304; Fischer, Wright, Clatanoff, Barton, and Shreeves, "Give 'Em What They Want," 469–92.

REFERENCES

Anderson, Kristine J., Robert S. Freeman, Jean-Pierre V. M. Herubel, Lawrence J. Mykytiuk, Judith M. Nixon, and Suzanne M. Ward. "Liberal Arts Books on Demand: A Decade of Patron-Driven Collection Development, Part 1." *Collection Management* 35 (2010): 125–41.

Fischer, Karen S., Michael Wright, Kathleen Clatanoff, Hope Barton, and Edward Shreeves. "Give 'Em What They Want: A One-Year Study of Unmediated Patron

Driven Acquisition of eBooks." *College & Research Libraries* 73 (2012): 469–92, http://crl.acrl.org/content/73/5/469.full.pdf+html.

Fountain, Kathleen Carlisle, and Linda Frederiksen. "Just Passing Through: Patron-Initiated Collection Development in Northwest Academic Libraries." *Collection Management* 35 (2010): 185–95.

Hassan, Karma El. "Identifying Indicators of Student Development in College." *College Student Journal* 42 (2008): 517–30.

Hodges, Dracine, Cyndi Preston, and Marsha J. Hamilton. "Patron-Initiated Collection Development: Progress of a Paradigm Shift." *Collection Management* 35 (2010): 208–21.

Kuh, George D. "In Their Own Words: What Students Learn outside the Classroom." *American Educational Research Journal* 30 (1993): 277–304.

Nixon, Judith M., Robert S. Freeman, and Suzanne M. Ward. "Patron-Driven Acquisitions: An Introduction and Literature Review." *Collection Management* 35 (2010): 119–24.

Reynolds, Leslie J., Carmelita Pickett, Wyoma vanDuinkerken, Jane Smith, Jeanne Harrell, and Sandra Tucker. "User-Driven Acquisitions: Allowing Patron Requests to Drive Collection Development in an Academic Library." *Collection Management* 35 (2010): 244–55.

NAOMI IKEDA CHOW
AND RYAN JAMES

5

A Case Study for PDA
on a Shoestring Budget

An Evolving Vision for Collection
Development through Three Pilot Projects

THE UNIVERSITY OF HAWAI'I AT MĀNOA (UHM) IS UNIQUE FOR
its geographic isolation, situated in the Pacific Ocean, nearly 3,000 miles
from the nearest major land mass, including the continental United States.
UHM is the flagship of a 13-campus statewide University of Hawai'i (UH) system, spread out over 4 islands covering nearly 350 miles. UHM has the largest enrollment, physical facilities, and program offerings in the UH system
(table 5.1). The student and faculty populations are quite diverse in ethnicity,
nationality, and socio-economics, representing all 50 states and 108 coun-
tries. Roughly 70 percent of the students are in-state, 20 percent are from out
of state, with the remaining 9 percent international (Mānoa 2012).

The university's funding support is derived mainly from state funds, supplemented by national-level research grants brought in by faculty investiga-
tors. As a mid-level-sized research university, UHM supports a full range of
academic and professional programs covering a wide variety of subject areas.
Research and academic strengths lie in the areas of astronomy, oceanography,
scholarship related to China, Japan, Korea, South and Southeast Asia, and
Hawaiian and Pacific studies.

TABLE 5.1
University of Hawai'i at Mānoa quick facts.

Date founded	1907
Type	Public (land-, sea-, and space-grant)
Enrollment	20,249 • 14,402 undergraduates • 6,027 graduate & professional • 1,012 unclassified
Faculty	1,229 FTE
Bachelor's degree	92 fields
Master's degree	83 programs
Doctoral level	51 programs
Professional programs	Medicine, law, business
Accreditation	Western Association of Schools and Colleges (WASC)

SOURCES: University of Hawai'i at Mānoa. 2012. "About UH Mānoa." Accessed May 23, 2013. http://manoa.hawaii.edu/about; University of Hawai'i at Mānoa. 2012. "A Brief History of UH Mānoa". Accessed July 5, 2013. http://www.uhm.hawaii.edu/academics.

UHM LIBRARY BACKGROUND

Soon after the founding of the university, the library collections were established in 1908, with a dedicated stand-alone building constructed in 1920 (Morris 2006). The library's collections are middle-ranked in strength for academic breadth and depth in the general subject areas. Reflective of the UHM's academic and research priorities, the Hawaiian, Pacific, and Asia collections are among the library's areas of strengths. Our collection includes roughly 3.4 million volumes with 40,008 serials subscriptions. The majority of our serials in the general collection are in electronic format, with a small, but growing, collection of e-books.

At UHM, interlibrary loan (ILL) services have historically supplemented the physical and electronic collections for our patrons. Like other academic libraries, expanded means for discovery have led to increased demand for a diverse set of research materials by the UHM graduate students and faculty that cannot be fully addressed by materials within the collections. With the rapid increase to patron direct access to electronic databases in conjunction with the implementation of the embedded link to our electronic ILL request submission system, ILLiad, the number of UHM ILL requests increased by 112 percent from 2003 to 2009. Although the rate has dropped slightly due to the introduction of several local services and the increase in provision of electronic journal and book content, UHM remains a net borrower, processing over 27,000 requests on behalf of UHM patrons annually, providing 5,522 loans and 15,686 articles in FY2011–12. The continued high rate of interlibrary loan use is also fueled by the library's diminished collections budget and cuts in serials over the years.

ECONOMICS

The UHM Library's annual collections budget falls in the lower third ranking of the Association of Research Libraries (ARL), so our overall ability to acquire materials has always lagged compared to other ARL institutions (Kyrillidou, Morris, and Roebuck 2010–2011). Our efforts have been further reduced recently due to the university's austerity measures enacted in response to the recent downturn of the U.S. and global economies from 2008 to the present (2013). In FY2009–10, the library incurred a 10+ percent budget reduction and hiring freeze, along with the rest of the university. The majority of the cuts were felt in the library's materials budget. Our FY2009–10 materials budget was $7.2 million and has been held at this level through FY2011–12. In comparison, our previous budget for FY2008–09 was $8.1 million.

The depressed economy has had a detrimental effect on the overall collection efforts of the library. These cuts are on top of continual serial cancellation projects to address the spikes in serials costs that all academic libraries have been facing. The monograph-gathering (approval) plan has been placed on hiatus, and some serials as well as electronic databases have been cut. With the economic downturn, we have been unable to purchase as many firm order books as in previous years. For the past four years, we have not been systematically or broadly collecting monographs for our general collections in the social sciences, humanities, and sciences/technology as well as our specialized collections.

To sum up our institutional environment, we are physically quite far away from other major academic research institutions, have specialized academic strengths that draw upon our unique geographic and geological attributes, and although not the poorest in our peer group, we are not the strongest overall. The end result for our library collections is that they are very strong in specialized areas, not as strong in more general collection areas, and we are a heavy net borrower for interlibrary loan books on behalf of our UHM patrons for a variety of reasons.

SETTING THE STAGE FOR PDA AND POD

In 2009, the library world was again heating up with enthusiasm for patron-driven-acquisitions (PDA) endeavors including purchase-on-demand

(POD) (Nixon, Freeman, and Ward 2010). Within our main consortium group, the Greater Western Library Association (GWLA), individual libraries including Brigham Young University, Oregon State University, Southern Illinois State University, University of Arizona, University of Arkansas, University of Nebraska (GWLA member at the time), and the University of Texas at Austin were beginning forays in the areas selecting to purchase book titles generated by ILL requests (POD) and electronic book title record loading (PDA) (Gibson and Kirkwood 2009; Hussong-Christian and Goergen-Doll 2010; Reynolds et al. 2010; Tyler et al. 2010; Dillon 2011; Nabe, Imre, and Mann 2011; Schroeder 2012). UHM's later adoption of PDA/POD allowed us to benefit from the experiences of other libraries, including our consortia partners, in implementing our local projects. Nationally, several institutions including Grand Valley State University, the University of Denver, and the University of Arizona at Tucson were pursuing fairly large scale PDA/POD projects in terms of monies allocated and scope of potential titles targeted (Way 2011a; Levine-Clark 2010; Jones 2011).

Our Collection Development (CD) librarian at the time, Kristen Anderson, as well as other library selectors were quite interested in starting PDA/POD efforts at the UHM Library. One of the potential benefits of PDA/POD programs for our library was the speed of delivery of the materials that were known to be in demand by local patrons. By tapping into the quick access of electronic books (e-books) and purchasing from speedy services for print-books (p-books) such as Amazon or Barnes & Noble or directly from publishers, we wanted to decrease the time it takes to obtain a book to add to our collections compared to the traditional library book vendor ordering. Being very geographically distant from the book vendors such as Blackwell North America (BNA) or Yankee Book Peddler (YBP), the vendors would batch-send p-books to economize on shipping costs. Regular acquisition book shipments are, therefore, slower than for our mainland continental library counterparts.

The library needed to consider several parameters when setting up its PDA/POD programs: limitations in budget, staffing, and shelf space. The library budget was limited, therefore, the monetary allocations would be modest, under $20,000 per effort. As our staffing had been, up until recently, quite short in areas traditionally key to collection development and management such as selection, acquisitions, and cataloging, the mechanisms for our POD/PDA programs would need to be sustainable with minimal staffing interventions. Last, common for many libraries are the space limitations of the book stacks (Lugg 2011, 8). Our library stacks are at full capacity, having an overflow shelving situation for the past several years, with volumes residing on the floor in certain call number ranges (Wermager 2008). Due to careful weeding of duplicate copies and items available in electronic format such as JSTOR titles and reference materials, we are currently able to shelve materials, but at a zero-growth scenario. P-book titles selected for purchase would ideally be high in academic value and impact in order to justify much-coveted shelf space. E-book format would also be an attractive alternative to consider.

Through careful planning, we have experimented with three small programs using different methods to implement patron-driven acquisitions that emphasize quick turnaround times and potential high value. This chapter aims to show that even a modest institution with a small budget allocation and minimal staffing can implement thoughtful choices that have a positive, timely impact on the information needs of its patrons.

Three Small-Scale PDA Projects

The PDA and POD programs serve as starting points for the UHM Library, with hopes that their initial, small, but groundbreaking steps for our library would segue into potentially larger applications within the library. The pilots offer small-scale explorations into what does and does not work for the library staff and our patrons, including how to best structure workflows in order to have a fast turnaround time to meet patron needs. Ultimately, the pilots have shown us how departments can work together in new communication streams to quickly address patron needs while adding items of value to the local collections.

The two out of the three projects discussed in this chapter have been spearheaded under the guidance and vision of our then Collection Development librarian, Kristen Anderson. She worked with the UHM Library's Collection Development and Management Committee (CDMC) to shape parameter-driven pilots for e-book patron-driven acquisitions (PDA) via record loading into the library's Voyager OPAC, and the interlibrary loan (ILL) purchase-on-demand (POD) program. The third POD program has evolved from the informal practice of purchasing items using the ILL unit credit card or other purchase methods outside of our normal library acquisitions process for items that are difficult to find through traditional ILL networks due to the newness or unusual nature of the topic. Currently, two out of the three programs have been adopted as methods to place titles into the library's selection stream.

MyiLibrary E-Book Record Loading into the Online Catalog

The MyiLibrary project was our library's initial experiment with record loading of e-book titles to explore how it might work for our environment: How difficult were the technical requirements to get records loaded in the online catalog? How quickly would we run through the allocated money? Would a title selected by PDA provide a good indicator of future use? When setting up our small program, we benefitted from anecdotal reports from other academic institutions whose earlier forays into PDA with e-book record loading fore-warned that loading a large number of records might allow for rapid depletion of allocated funds. Discussions and planning for the pilot began in mid-2009, and it was implemented in early 2010 with a $15,000 deposit account allocation.

We pursued our pilot through a PDA opportunity negotiated through (GWLA) consortia with MyiLibrary through the vendor, Coutts. The article by Nabe, Imre, and Mann (2011) provides a good overview of the general struc-ture of the GWLA MyiLibrary program. It reports on the process Southern Illi-nois University Carbondale (SIUC) used and reviews the experience that uses a parameter-driven model to select and load a pool of approximately 9,000 e-book title records. The SIUC program, which began in 2008, was broader and larger than the program eventually implemented at UHM.

The collection development librarian worked with the UHM Library's Collection Development and Management Committee to establish the param-eters for a modest subset of records to be extracted from the MyiLibrary col-lection for e-book PDA via record loading into the library's Voyager catalog. The CDMC is comprised of librarians who represent selection area disciplines and departments that dovetail with collections: Asia; Business, Humanities and Social Sciences; Government Documents; Hawaiian/Pacific; Science/Tech-nology; Sinclair Library (covering audiovisual materials, music, and course reserves); Access Services, including interlibrary loan/document delivery; Acquisitions; Serials; and Preservation.

The goal was to extract a smaller but still viable pool of titles to load. The selectors wanted to create a profile that would be manageable in size yet include titles that would cover a variety of disciplines from publishers deemed to offer high-quality content, appropriateness of scholarly level, potential for continued future use, and items considered appropriate for our collections. We also wanted to negotiate a trigger point for purchases that balanced the potential for quick patron "browsing" with longer patron "use" that was fair and reasonable. The collection development and e-resources librarians wanted an ongoing notification mechanism regarding what titles were being purchased and how quickly the deposit was being spent. Total amount expended would be controlled by the deposit amount—once it was spent, the pilot would end.

The profile parameters established to create the set of MyiLibrary records to be loaded into our Voyager OPAC are found on table 5.2.

The implementation of the record-loading project took a concerted effort by the collection development librarian, Anderson, working in consultation with the library selectors via the Collection Development Management Com-mittee for subject areas, publishers, price parameters, and with the e-resources librarian, Lori Ann Saeki, to set up the mechanism for purchase and access, and the initial work with the Library Systems Office, with Carol Kellet, systems

TABLE 5.2

Record-loading profile and PDA selection parameters.

Publisher	University presses plus some additional agriculture-related presses
Level	Academic/Research
Format	Electronic book (e-book)
Subject Areas	Approval/Gathering Plan profiles established for book vendor (BNA)
Intial Record Load	1,586 records (eventually pared to 914 records)
Time Frame	Most current 3 years (began March 2010)
Price Ceiling	$200 per title
PDA Decision	Made by patron
Browsing	Unlimited browsing of table of contents
Purchase	3-click viewing of text results in purchase
Deposit Account	$15,000
Invoicing	Monthly, automatic
Notifications	E-mail about purchases sent to e-resources and collection development librarians; list of titles purchased forwarded to selectors via e-mail

librarian, to receive and upload the records into the catalog. The initial load included 2,450 records. Records for 864 titles that duplicated items already in our collection were removed. This left 1,586 potential PDA titles. An additional 672 were removed in April 2011 when price increases went above the $200 parameter. Currently, we have 914 records in our catalog, of which 90 have been purchased via the PDA program. The 90 titles account for 6 percent of the original eligible titles (post de-duplication) or 10 percent of the adjusted final pool. This is a bit lower than other universities' forays into e-book record loading (8 to 12 percent) (Swords 2011, 182; De Fino and Lo 2011, 335), but this may be due to the more limited nature of the record load in terms of both sheer volume and type of works as compared to other institutions' loads since it excludes commercial academic publishers.

The pilot shows (table 5.3) that the parameter-focused title load is worthwhile for our library. If we apply the average cost of $107 per title, calculated from the results of our pilot's purchased MyiLibrary e-books thus far, to estimate the potential cost of the 914 titles, we have loaded approximately $98,000 worth of titles into our catalog. Instead of having to expend the entire $98,000 at a single time, it is doled out over time, as needed, available

TABLE 5.3

MyiLibrary® PDA pilot results (April 2010–June 2012).

Number of titles purchased	90 (623 hits)
Average number of titles purchased per month[a]	3.3 (range 1 – 10 purchases)
Amount expended	$9,671.81
Average price per title	$107.47
Average cost per hit[b]	$15.53
Average # hits per title[c]	7 (range = 3 – 107)
Number of titles viewed >3 times	53 (58.9% of titles)
Number of titles viewed 7 or more times	24 (26.7% of titles)

a. Purchases began in April 2010 with purchases in every month through June 2012
b. Definition: 1 hit = 1 access to the text of the book
c. 3rd hit triggers purchase

to the patron instantly at the click of the mouse. In comparison, it would take several weeks at a minimum for a print book to come in from the book vendor's normal processing rate, at least 12–24 hours for an e-book order via the book vendor, and a minimum of 5–7 days in total processing time for the title to arrive by interlibrary loan. Implementation and title record loads are relatively inexpensive as there is no charge from the vendor's side, and minimal costs on the library side aside from the system librarian's programming time to add the records to our online catalog. The average of $15.33 per view, especially considering our geographic distance, is comparable to and at times lower than what we calculated in FY2012 that it would cost to borrow and process the paper print book via interlibrary loan (overall average of $21–$13 for reciprocal consortia; $29 for OCLC ILL Fee Management [IFM] charging libraries).

Titles selected for purchase were used on average 7 times, ranging from 3 to 107 uses per title. Quite a wide variety of subjects were purchased, including science, technology, law, and medicine. This may reflect the nature of university press subject breadth in general. The most highly used titles fell in the areas of social sciences and humanities as reflected by the list of the top fifteen titles ranked by views (table 5.4). The highest-use book title with 107 uses falls into the area of Hawaiian and Asian studies, topics within our academic fortes. Specific data regarding the pattern of purchasing and use of titles by subject that also compares the three methods of PDA/POD at UHM will be explored at the end of this chapter.

TABLE 5.4

Top 15 titles by usage for MyiLibrary®.

Title	Hits ($n = 623$)	% of total charges	LC call no.	(Collection*)
Ethnicity and Inequality in Hawai'i: Asian American History and Culture	107	17.2%	DU624.6	(Hawaiian)
Language Classification: History and Method	27	4.3%	P143	(General)
Free for All: Fixing School Food in America	18	2.9%	LB3479.U6	(General)
Brain Landscape: The Coexistence of Neuroscience and Architecture	18	2.9%	RC343	(General)
Cognitive Grammar: An Introduction	17	2.7%	P165	(General)
Cambridge Handbook of Linguistic Code-switching, The: Cambridge Handbooks in Language	16	2.6%	P115.3	(General)
Everything but the Coffee: Learning about America from Starbucks	14	2.2%	TX415	(General)
Dark Green Religion: Nature Spirituality and the Planetary Future	13	2.1%	BL65.N35	(General)
Survivance: Narratives of Native Presence	12	1.9%	E98.S67	(General)
Corporate Power in Global Agrifood Governance	11	1.8%	HD9000.5	(General)
Art of the Gut, The: Manhood, Power, and Ethics in Japanese Politics	11	1.8%	HQ1090	(Asia)
Conversation Analysis and Psychotherapy	11	1.8%	RC506	(General)
Comanche Empire, The	10	1.6%	E99.C85	(General)
Overcoming Alcohol Use Problems: A Cognitive-Behavioral Treatment Program Workbook	10	1.6%	HV5276	(General)
Japan Since 1980 (The World Since 1980)	9	1.4%	HC462.95	(Asia)

* UHM collection that would be assigned for a print book

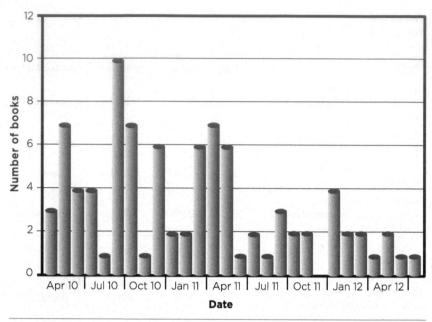

FIGURE 5.1

MyiLibrary® purchases 2010–2012.

The e-format provides the twin savings of physical library shelf space and staff time to handle the physical item. Though the rate of adding three or four titles a month might not seem like much, for our library's zero-growth situation, every inch saved is worthwhile. If an average book takes one inch of shelf space, the current 914 titles in the catalog would equate 76 linear feet. The ease of adding and subtracting to our collection is another great advantage of e-book PDA record loading. The effort to add the 2,450 volumes and then subtract 1,536 volumes from the physical print collections would have taken many staff hours, whereas the systems librarian is able to add or delete records within hours or days rather than weeks and months. These were also 914 fewer cataloging records that the catalogers and cataloging staff needed to process.

Even though the pilot had only one initial load that is now over two years old, there is continued use and new purchases throughout the two-year period, although the highest rate of purchasing occurred during the first year of the pilot (figure 5.1). It is recommended to rerun the analysis every two or three years with results by publication date to see if the trend for purchases and usage continues or drops off after a certain time period to provide data to formulate a weeding policy for e-book record loading. At the moment, we do not have a retention policy about the length of time to keep non-purchased records in the catalog. The concept of "weeding" the library's electronic book collection has not yet been thought out and perhaps should be incorporated into the collection development policy as it is for print materials as implemented at Rutgers University (De Fino and Lo 2011). If the steady use and purchase rates continue, it may be worthwhile to keep all of the records for the university press e-book titles in the OPAC indefinitely. If additional funds could be found to replenish the deposit account, it is recommended to add an update of titles through the current year screened under the initial selection parameters. We could also target a few narrow subject areas and/or publishers to broaden titles beyond the university presses to see if the same type of trends for use and purchase occur.

ILL Request-Generated POD Program

The UHM Library administration recognized that UHM is historically a heavy interlibrary loan borrower of "returnables" (i.e., book loans) and supported the concept of a purchase-on-demand (POD) program based upon ILL requests submitted by UHM faculty and students. The POD program would provide an alternative avenue for supporting patron needs with a quick turnaround time. The aim was to capture books for the local collection that would have a high probability for reuse by future patrons. There were already well-established precedents for use of ILL patron requests as a means of patron-driven collection development, including the Books on Demand program instituted at Purdue University in 2000 (Nixon and Saunders 2010), and the program based on a decision matrix to purchase or borrow instituted at the University of Minnesota Law Library in 2007 (Zopfi-Jordan 2008), as well as programs established within our GWLA consortia. During the summer of 2009, the UHM collection development librarian, Anderson, approached the interlibrary loan unit librarian, Naomi Chow, about formally implementing a purchase-on-demand (POD) program based upon ILL requests submitted by UHM patrons. The UHM Library had recently established and hired a new managerial position in the ILL unit in May 2009 in part to administer the POD program. The CD librarian's vision was to capture titles to add to the local collection that might not otherwise be selected, or selected as quickly.

A POD program based on UHM patron ILL requests was logical to investigate in terms of cost-benefit factors including (1) high rate of returnables requested via ILL (opportunity to capture essential or core items that the library was not purchasing); (2) high cost of shipping ILL returnables (mainly books) due to both our high volume of loans and the geographic distance; (3) increased length of shipping times that affects the timeliness of receipt (some lenders will choose to send library/media rate, which can average 3–4 weeks till receipt, although we are fortunate to belong to a consortium with a high benchmark for quick turnaround time reducing the majority of our loans to be received and processed within 5–7 days); (4) understandable reluctance for some potential lenders to lend due to the great geographic distance; (5) "sending" shipping costs for items we borrow (we offer to pay for expedited shipping via courier such as FedEx or UPS to encourage libraries that might not otherwise be able to cover the shipping costs to lend items to us and to reduce shipping time); and (6) difficulty in borrowing newer materials that are often not available from the normal library networks due to policy or unavailability.

Benefits envisioned for the patron would include a comparable or faster speed of delivery compared to traditional ILL borrowing practices, and increased length of loans using locally defined loan periods: UHM offers loans of 28 days for undergraduates, 13 weeks for graduate students, 26 weeks for faculty, all with possibility of renewals. Contrastingly, ILL loan periods generally span 1–3 months, with some giving as short as 3 weeks and some (though very few) libraries generously offering 6-month loans, without any guarantee of renewal. The benefits for the library would be that highly valued titles are added to the collection, and the potential reduction in repeated ILL requests for the same title with their associated ILL fees and shipping costs. It might be more cost-effective for UHM to purchase than borrow, as the 2011 analysis of the University of Nebraska Library ILL purchase on demand program shows (Tyler et al. 2011).

The creation and establishment of the ILL POD program have been heavily collaborative, cutting across and connecting departments throughout the library for both work processing and closer, direct communication. Under the initial guidance from the CD librarian, the ILL librarian coordinated the creation of the ILL POD policies and procedures with input, review, and approval of the CD librarian and the library's Collection Development Management Council. This included working with staff from acquisitions, cataloging, interlibrary loan, and circulation/access services to establish the procedural framework for the program. The program itself has been implemented and managed by the ILL unit manager, Ryan James, who has provided insightful feedback and incorporated changes since the program's successful implementation over three years ago.

The ILL POD program applies the parameters set up by selectors established for the print monograph vendor's profile plans. Table 5.5 summarizes the ILL Print-Book (P-Book) POD program's parameters, including a price ceiling, a publication date time frame, and availability from commercial book vendors (e.g., Amazon and Barnes & Noble, chosen for their quick fulfillment turnaround as well as priority/rush shipping) and, when needed, individual consultation with the subject selectors when a title falls into an area that might not be so clear-cut. The ILL manager sends weekly e-mail notifications with a

TABLE 5.5

ILL POD print book selection parameters.

Selection pool	ILL loan book requests submitted by UHM patrons
Publishers	Approval/Gathering Book Vendor Plan profiles (BNA, YBP)
Level	Academic/Research classification as described by: • Library book vendors (BNA, YBP) • Publishers • Book reviews • Commercial sellers (e.g., Amazon, Barnes & Noble)
Format	Paper book (p-book)
Subject areas	Approval/Gathering Book Vendor Plan profiles (BNA, YBP)
Special areas of interest	Hawaiian, Pacific, and Asia subject areas
Time Frame	Latest 3 years (began October 2009)
Price ceiling	$150.00
Availability	Amazon or Barnes & Noble
POD decision	ILL manager
Allocation of funding	$5,000 initial allocation (total 1st year allocation = $10,000)
Invoicing	University p-card (credit card)
Notifications	Weekly list of titles e-mailed to the CDMC subject representatives for dissemination
Exclusions	• Popular works • Undergraduate level textbooks • Items held/available within the greater UH library system • Previous editions held at UHM

list of titles ordered to the library's CDMC subject area representatives. The ILL manager also compiled and shared two POD titles circulation usage studies with the CDMC during the first two years of the project.

The timing of the ILL P-Book POD program implementation in late 2009 is also significant since the library's approval plan has been temporarily shut down due to budget cuts from fall 2009 and was not restarted until May 2013. The ILL POD program provides the library with an alternative method to pick up on newly published titles to supplement the firm order selection process by the library's subject selectors. In our ILL unit, we find that patrons are quick to discover and submit requests for newly or soon-to-be-released books due to the plethora of information dispersal (e.g., direct e-mail from publishers to faculty and students, web search engines locating pre-print information from publishers' websites, etc.).

TABLE 5.6
ILL POD print book pilot results (as of August 2012).

Number of titles purchased	263 (with 888 charges)
Average number of titles purchased per month[a]	13 (range 2 – 43 purchases)
Amount expended	$16,442.27
Average price per title	$63.48
Average cost per charge[b]	$18.92
Average # checkouts/charges per title[c]	3.4 (range = 1 – 13)
Number of titles in original circulation as of 8/2012	33 (not yet returned from first POD patron)
Mode number of charges	2
Number of titles viewed >2 times	146 (55.5% of titles)
Number of titles viewed 7 or more times	11 (4.2% of titles)
Average number of holds per title	2.6 (ranging from 0 – 25 holds on 259 titles) #

a. Purchases began in October 2009 with purchases in 17 out of 20 months through May 2011
b. Definition: 1 charge = 1 use of book (does not take into account length of checkout period)
c. Calculated February 2013

The program began with a modest initial allocation of $5,000. The total allocation for the initial year was expanded to $10,000, of which $9,000 was expended. A brief summary of the analysis of the program from its inception in October 2009 through August 2012 (May 2011 was the date the last p-book was purchased via POD) is presented in table 5.6. Similar to the MyiLibrary results, the average cost per use per ILL P-Book POD title of $18.92 is lower than the estimated cost of an ILL loan book (overall average of $21–$13 for reciprocal consortia; $29 for OCLC IFM charging libraries), with the added benefit of potential further local use. The 2011 analysis of the University of Nebraska Library ILL five-year-old purchase-on-demand program shows similar cost-effective per use results (Tyler et al. 2011). Cost factors not taken into consideration for this study include the cost of rush shipping from Amazon or Barnes & Noble, nor staff costs for acquisitions and cataloging processing.

The ILL P-Book POD titles had, on average, 3.4 checkouts per title. Our rate is similar to the findings of 4.1 circulation uses in the analysis of ten years' worth of data for the Purdue ILL-based Books on Demand program at Purdue University (Nixon and Saunders 2010). In return shipping costs alone at an estimated $11 (average of USPS priority and courier $6–$16), four uses of an ILL title would be $44. This does not include any potential ILL fees for the loan

TABLE 5.7

Top 15 titles by usage for ILL POD print.

Title	Charges (*n* = 869)	% of total charges	LC call no.	Collection
History of White People	13	1.50%	E184.A1 P29 2010	General
SAGE Handbook of Organizational Research Methods	13	1.50%	HD30.4 .S252 2009	General
Communication Power	13	1.50%	HM1206 .C376 2009	General
Qualitative Research: A Guide to Design and Implementation	13	1.50%	LB1028 .M396 2009	General
Writing Your Journal Article in 12 Weeks: A Guide to Academic Publishing Success	13	1.50%	Z471 .B45 2009	General
Handbook of Language Teaching	12	1.40%	P51 .H3265 2009	General
Multilevel and Longitudinal Modeling with IBM	11	1.30%	HA32 .H39 2010	General
Reading in a Second Language: Moving from Theory to Practice	11	1.30%	P53.75 .G73 2009	General
Analyzing Qualitative Data: Systematic Approaches	9	1.00%	H62 .B438 2010	General
Discovering Statistics Using SPSS: (And Sex and Drugs and Rock 'n' Roll)	9	1.00%	HA32 .F54 2009	General
Eating Animals	9	1.00%	TX392 .F58 2009	General
Gender and Labour in Korea and Japan: Sexing Class	8	0.90%	HD6060.65.K6 G43 2009	Asia
Feminism and Visual Culture Reader	8	0.90%	N72.F45 F46 2010	General
Language Learning and Study Abroad: A Critical Reading of Research	8	0.90%	P118.2 .K53 2009	General
Big Short: Inside the Doomsday Machine	7	0.80%	HC106.83 .L5 2010b	General

itself. If factored at $16 per loan, the loan fees could add up to $64. So shipping plus loan fees for a book borrowed via ILL four times could potentially add up to $108, more than the average cost of $63.48 to purchase a POD title.

All ILL P-Book POD titles were given brief cataloging-on-the-fly records that were entered in the online public catalog to enable items to be checked out following the standard library procedures (Appendix 5A: "ILL P-Book POD Workflow/Procedures"). There are thirty-three titles that are still in circulation as of August 2012 that have not yet received full cataloging since their initial purchase over one year ago, seventeen of which were originally purchased in 2010. The originally requesting patron is able to borrow and renew the book loans using locally defined UHM loan policies. Such lengthy use could not be easily provided with the short-term nature of ILL loan books. Another statistic that reflects the high value of the ILL P-Book POD titles is that UH patrons have requested 673 holds via the library's ILS online catalog, equating an average of 2.6 holds per title with a range from 0 to 25 holds as of February 2013. Only 11 (4 percent) titles have not had an additional hold placed on them. Similar to the MyiLibrary pilot results, the subject areas found in the list of the top fifteen most heavily used titles were in the humanities and social sciences (table 5.7). (Specific data regarding the pattern of purchasing and use of titles by subject that also compares the three methods of PDA/POD at UHM will be explored at the end of this chapter.)

Changeover to Electronic Book ILL POD

In April 2011, the ILL manager suggested that the library switch to electronic book (e-book) ordering for POD titles. Upon approval from the CDMC, he coordinated changes in the processing for ordering and receipt including cataloging and access with staff in acquisitions, cataloging, and the e-resources librarian. The ILL unit manager's reasoning for a change in format included several factors: (1) potential speedup of turnaround time for delivery for the patron, and less time spent on physical item processing on behalf of the staff; (2) e-format could address the concern about our library's at-capacity-for-shelving space issue; (3) printed paper book straps placed on the p-books to identify them as POD titles would occasionally come off, and in essence, the books would become "lost" somewhere in the library, still in need of full cataloging and labeling for shelving.

The revised program has evolved into an e-book firm order process with the benefits of (1) speed of access for patrons (within 24–48 hours of order placement); (2) ease of ordering/payment (via book vendor with invoicing rather than using a library credit card); and (3) ease of cataloging (no need to wait until physical item returned to library). Otherwise, the same selection parameters applied except that the e-book title needs to be available from our

TABLE 5.8

ILL POD electronic book selection parameters.

Selection pool	ILL loan book requests submitted by UHM patrons
Publishers	Approval/Gathering Book Vendor Plan profiles (YBP)
Level	Academic/Research classification as described by: • Library book vendors (BNA, YBP) • Publishers • Book reviews • Commercial sellers (e.g., Amazon, Barnes & Noble)
Format	Electronic book
Subject areas	Approval/Gathering Book Vendor Plan profiles (YBP)
Special areas of interest	Hawaiian, Pacific, and Asia subject areas
Time Frame	Latest 3 years (began April 2011)
Price ceiling	$150.00
Availability	YBP Gobi
Platform preference	EBL, then ebrary
POD decision	ILL manager
Allocation of funding	$3,000 initial allocation with total of $8,000 made available (April 2011–August 2012)
Invoicing	YBP invoicing via acquisitions
Notifications	Weekly list of titles e-mailed to the CDMC subject representatives for dissemination
Exclusions	• Popular works • Undergraduate level textbooks • Items held/available within the greater UH library system • Previous editions held at UHM

book vendor's, Yankee Book Peddler, GOBI ordering system. As noted in table 5.8, our library's preferred e-book platform is Ebook Library (EBL), followed by ebrary.

The average POD purchase cost of an electronic book ($88) is higher than for print books ($63) (table 5.9). Although the funding does not go as far as with ILL P-Book POD, the advantages outlined above about the speed of delivery and "anytime/anywhere" remote access as well as not taking up shelf space may outweigh the increase in cost. There was an initial concern about whether patrons would reject e-format, but this seems to have been unfounded. We have received very few complaints and very rarely were asked to order the paper item.

TABLE 5.9

ILL POD electronic book pilot results (as of August 2012).

Number of titles purchased	90 (over 10 months)	
Average number of titles purchased per month[a]	9 (range 3 – 16 purchases)	
Amount expended	$7,939.69	
Average price per title	$88.22	
E-book platforms	EBL (51 titles)	ebrary (25 titles)
Total number of hits	169	3432
Average cost per charge[b]	$26.62	$0.64
Average # hits per title	3.3 (range = 1 – 18)	137.3 (range = 1 – 980)
Average # hits per month all titles combined	7	143

a. Purchases began in April 2011 thru May 2012 with purchasing allowed 10 out of 13 months; average is 7 titles per month if prorated over entire 13-month period

b. Definition: 1 EBL hit = 1 login of book (does not take into account length of use, number of section views); 1 ebrary hit = 1 view of 1 section (e.g., chapter) of a book (does not take into account length of time used), thus one person could account for several hits on a single title if multiple chapters are viewed

The reduced average number of titles purchased per month (13 titles for p-books versus 9 titles for e-books) may also be due to two other changes: (1) the second and third years' ILL POD funds have been more slowly disbursed compared to the initial program year of 2009–2010 due to budgetary constraints; and (2) the purchase method changeover from university acquisitions unit credit card (p-card) to standard invoicing via the library's book vendor reduces the number of months when titles may be ordered due to the fiscal accounting cycle of the university, with periods of nonavailability of funds during the start and end of the fiscal year (8–9 months for invoicing versus 11 months for credit/p-card billing).

A challenge for comparison of usage and cost analysis for ILL E-Book POD is that the two primary platforms, EBL and ebrary, count usage using two different algorithms. EBL counts initial log-in access to the book, while ebrary counts hits on sections of the book (i.e., one patron can account for many hits by reviewing many pages/chapters within a book). With this in mind, the cost per use differs greatly between EBL ($26) and ebrary ($0.64) titles (table 5.9). The average cost per use for EBL titles is still within the range of average prices for ILL loans ($13–$29) though a bit higher than for p-book titles. For a comparable cost and less staff time, whether in the ILL unit to borrow/return

TABLE 5.10

Top 15 titles by usage for ILL POD EBL e-book.

Title	Hits ($n=169$)	% of total hits	LC call no.	(Collection*)
Multilevel Analysis: Techniques and Applications	18	10.6%	HA29	(General)
Coming to Terms with the Nation: Ethnic Classification in Modern China	10	5.9%	DS730	(Asia)
Coming to Terms with the Nation: Ethnic Classification in Modern China	10	5.9%	LC243.B55	(General)
The Cambridge Handbook of Creativity	8	4.7%	BF408	(General)
Handbook of Self-Regulation of Learning and Performance	8	4.7%	LC32	(General)
Japan's Wartime Medical Atrocities: Comparative Inquiries in Science, History, and Ethics	8	4.7%	D804.J3	(Asia)
Spaces between Us: Queer Settler Colonialism and Indigenous Decolonization	7	4.1%	E98.S48	(General)
Transnationalism and the Asian American Heroine: Essays on Literature, Film, Myth and Media	7	4.1%	PS153.A84	(General)
Cognitive-Behavioral Strategies in Crisis Intervention	6	3.6%	RC480.6	(General)
The Social Psychology of English as a Global Language	6	3.6%	PE1074.75	(General)
Language Life in Japan: Transformations and Prospects	4	2.4%	P57.J3	(Asia)
Alternative Approaches to Second Language Acquisition	4	2.4%	P118.2	(General)
Anonymity in Early Modern England: What's in a Name?	4	2.4%	PR121.A56 2011	(General)
Occupying Power: Sex Workers and Servicemen in Postwar Japan	4	2.4%	HQ247.A5	(Asia)
Collaborative Nationalism: The Politics of Friendship on China's Mongolian Frontier	3	1.8%	DS19	(Asia)

* UHM collection that would be assigned for a print book

TABLE 5.11

Top 15 titles by usage for ILL POD ebrary e-book.

Title	# of hits (*n* = 3432)	% of total hits	LC call no.	(Collection*)
Adopted Territory: Transnational Korean Adoptees and the Politics of Belonging	980	28.6%	HV875.5	(Asia)
Shakespeare and the Just War Tradition	626	18.2%	PR3069.W37	(General)
Aesthetic Constructions of Korean Nationalism: Spectacle, Politics and History	519	15.1%	DS916.35	(Asia)
Health Informatics: Designing User Studies in Informatics	216	6.3%	QA76.9.H85	(General)
Juvenile Justice: Advancing Research, Policy, and Practice	192	5.6%	HV9051	(General)
Crustacean Issues: Phylogeography and Population Genetics in Crustacea	188	5.5%	QL435	(General)
Libertine's Friend: Homosexuality and Masculinity in Late Imperial China	159	4.6%	HQ76.3.C6	(General)
Sensuous Surfaces: The Decorative Object in Early Modern China	145	4.2%	NK1068	(Asia)
Truman Administration and Bolivia: Making the World Safe for Liberal Constitutional Oligarchy	70	2.0%	E183.8.B6	(General)
Songs and Stories of the Ghouls	53	1.5%	PS3564.O79	(General)
Treasures of the Earth: Need, Greed, and a Sustainable Future	48	1.4%	HC79.C6	(General)
Earthscan Water Text Series: Right to Water: Politics, Governance and Social Struggles	38	1.1%	K3260	(General)
Apoha: Buddhist Nominalsim and Human Cognition	30	0.9%	BC25	(General)
Multivariate Applications: Longitudinal Data Analysis: A Practical Guide for Researchers in Aging, Health, and Social Sciences	28	0.9%	H62	(General)
Keeping the Nation's House: Domestic Management and the Making of Modern China	26	0.8%	TX101	(Asia)

* UHM collection that would be assigned for a print book

a p-book or in the acquisitions and cataloging unit to process a p-book for the library's collection, the patron receives the item much more quickly with a broader access point that is not restricted to library hours, nor does it require the patron to come to the library to pick up the item. Note: It may be that since the e-book titles have been available to UHM patrons for a shorter time period of up to 10 months than the ILL POD p-books of 18 months up to 3 years, the number of uses may increase, and therefore associated cost per use may become lower, if comparable lengths of time were analyzed.

A review of the top fifteen titles by usage for EBL (table 5.10) and ebrary (table 5.11) weigh heavily for titles in the humanities and social sciences. Several high-use titles on EBL and ebrary lists fall into research areas that are closely aligned with the University of Hawai'i at Mānoa's strength in Asian studies. (Specific data regarding the pattern of purchasing and use of titles by subject that also compares the three methods of PDA/POD at UHM will be explored at the end of this chapter.)

ILL-Purchased Print Books

As stated previously, the third POD program has grown through the informal program of purchasing items using the ILL unit credit card for items that are difficult to find through traditional ILL networks either due to newness or the unusual nature of the topic. The ILL unit has traditionally had access to a university purchase card (p-card), similar in nature to a credit card. It was originally established to allow more streamlined purchasing of materials via commercial document delivery and sources for dissertations/theses as well as entire issues of journals when purchasing directly from the publisher is deemed less expensive than the combined ILL fees plus copyright royalty fees per article. The unit also has access to book vendors such as Alibris via the OCLC Resource Sharing network and its ILL Fee Management (IFM) payment process.

The ILL unit staff discussed the possibility of purchasing print monographs when it was either not feasible to pursue via the normal interlibrary loan routes (either via OCLC or ALA-approved interlibrary loan forms) and there was a possibility to purchase the item requested, whether via a book vendor, online bookstore, or directly from the publisher for a reasonable cost. Often the publisher is a small press or not a mainstream resource (e.g., museum press, independent press, overseas publication, even self-published items). If the item were approximately the cost of an average ILL loan fee plus shipping (under $50), it was viewed as a viable option to purchase. The items were treated as loans to the patrons, and then routed to selectors to decide whether to retain them for the library's collections. Occasionally, the ILL librarian would consult with the subject selectors if the item were more expensive and, in essence, received a preapproval for addition to the library's collections.

A concern emerged from this inconsistent treatment as there were some titles that were purchased without selector consultations that were in the end considered not appropriate for our university's research collection. Although some libraries opt to give the items for patrons to keep similar to nonreturnables (articles), due to the limited budget of our library, purchasing solely for the use for a single patron to keep as her or his own was deemed not a wise use for limited funds. Additionally, the practice of treating a monograph as a nonreturnable falls outside of the conventions of state law regarding monograph purchases made with state monies. After discussion with the CDMC about ILL purchases, it was decided to apply parameters and consistent processing to ILL purchases for monographic materials beginning in fall 2011 (table 5.12). The program now also picks up some hard-to-find/new titles that might be available only in p-book format that would not be picked up under the parameters of the ILL POD e-book program. If an item is not appropriate for addition to the collection, the patron is sent an explanation regarding the cancellation of the ILL request as it is not available via loan, the patron is referred to the subject selector for further consultation about possible alternative resources, and the patron is referred to the website where the patron could purchase the item for individual use.

A positive outcome of the revised process has been a closer working relationship between the ILL librarian and subject selectors, especially with regard to newly published material or hard-to-find items. The benefits of a more formalized ILL-selector collaborative program at the University of Oregon at Eugene has been discussed by Bean and Rigby (2011). Often the selectors provide insight into the patron's information needs as they are already working with the patron and are familiar with the person's research. The selectors are sometimes able to find alternative resources available on hand or via ILL loan, while other times they confirm that the purchase would be worthwhile both for the patron and as an addition to the library's collection. There have been times when items are unavailable to borrow from library sources or purchase via the Internet, however, the selector has better access to acquiring the materials and the patron is able to wait for the more lengthy acquisitions process, such as for materials acquired from another country in Asia or the Pacific. The open communication process has allowed the patron's information request to flow full circle with the referral from the ILL unit to the subject selector with the ultimate aim to aid the patron as best as we can within the library as an overall entity.

One benefit is that the p-card process or order on Alibris via OCLC precludes the schedule constraints of the university's accounting cycle. Purchasing can continue for longer periods even when the university accounts

TABLE 5.12

ILL p-card print book selection parameters.

Selection pool	ILL loan book requests submitted by UHM patrons
Publishers	Open (no restrictions)
Level	Academic/Research classification as described by: • Publishers • Book reviews • Commercial sellers (e.g., Amazon, Barnes & Noble)
Format	Print book
Subject areas	Fit into UHM collections
Special areas of interest	Hawaiian, Pacific, and Asia subject areas
Time Frame	Open (no restrictions)
Price ceiling	$150.00
Availability	Commercial book vendor, publisher's website, online bookstore, Alibris via OCLC
POD decision	ILL librarian in consultation with subject selectors
Allocation of funding	No current allocation (case-by-case basis); funding from ILL budget
Invoicing	University p-card (credit card), OCLC IFM
Notifications	Individual consultations with subject selectors previous to purchase
Exclusions	• Popular works • Undergraduate level textbooks • Items held/available within the greater UH library system • Previous editions held at UHM

cannot be accessed for ordering via the normal acquisitions process. Several titles have been ordered when the selectors' funds were unavailable during the closing and reopening of the fiscal year between April to September. This appears to be a common challenge among academic institutions, for example as reported by De Fino and Lo (2011, 331) at Rutgers University. It may be worthwhile for the library to consider providing access to purchase cards to the selectors, whether as individuals or as a department, for their own "purchase on demand" requests for items that need to be requested quickly, and when normal acquisitions processes are unavailable due to the university's accounting cycle, for example, when the selectors receive requests from individual faculty and graduate students for purchase requests.

It should be noted that the size of the pool of ILL purchased materials is quite small, thus the data analysis and conclusions must be taken accordingly

TABLE 5.13

ILL p-card/Alibris book results (as of August 2012).

Number of titles purchased	27 (with 42 charges)
Average number of titles purchased per month[a]	1.08 (range 0 – 3 purchases)
Amount expended	$2,125.70
Average price per title	$78.73
Average cost per charge[b]	$50.61
Average # checkouts/charges per title	1.6 (range = 1 – 3)
Number of titles in circulation as of 8/2012	5
Mode number of charges	1
Number of titles borrowed >2 times	9 (33% of titles)

a. Purchases began in April 2010 with purchases in every month through June 2012
b. Definition: 1 charge = 1 use of book (does not take into account length of checkout period)

TABLE 5.14

Top 9 titles by usage for ILL p-card print book.

Title	Charges (*n* = 42)	% of total charges	LC call no.	Collection
Applied Conversational Analysis: Intervention and Change in Institutional Talk	3	7.10%	P95.45 .A65 2011	General
California's Ancient Past: From the Pacific to the Range of Light	3	7.10%	E78.C15 A793 2010	General
Disability and New Media	3	7.10%	HV1569.5 .E45 2011	General
Musical Cognition: A Science of Listening	3	7.10%	ML3830 .H4813 2011	Music
Painted King: Art, Activism, and Authenticity in Hawai'i	3	7.10%	NB230.H3 W53 2012	Hawaiian
Post-American World: Release 2.0	3	7.10%	CB161 .Z34 2011	General
Hiroshima: Ground Zero 1945	2	4.80%	D767.25.H6 B37 2011	General Folio
Rethinking Cultural Resource Management in Southeast Asia: Preservation, Development, and Neglect	2	4.80%	DS523 .R48 2011	Asia
Service Design and Delivery	2	4.80%	HD9980.5 .S46 2011	General

(table 5.13). The materials also represent items that are hard to locate and are thus unusual or very specific topics. The lower rate of circulation use of 1.6 checkouts per title is in some ways to be expected due to their unusual nature. It would be worthwhile to analyze use data for the titles after an additional ten-year time period has elapsed to see if further, longer-term use has evolved, either from local patrons or via ILL requests from other institutions. It would also be interesting to find out how valuable the item was to the originally requesting patron's academic or scholarly work. Average cost per use at $51 is high as compared to the average ILL loan costs; however, the item is not available from traditional ILL resources. The titles are also heavily based in the humanities and social sciences, and also relate to the research that is closely aligned with the University of Hawai'i at Mānoa's unique strengths in Hawaiian/ Pacific/Asia studies (table 5.14). (Specific data regarding the pattern of purchasing and use of titles by subject that also compares the three methods of PDA/POD at UHM will be explored at the end of this chapter.)

Comparative Analysis of Three PDA/POD Programs

The purchases for each PDA/POD program were analyzed by LC Classification as assigned either by the UHM Library's cataloging staff, or from designations from OCLC WorldCat records (UHM Library does not assign call numbers to electronic books). The purchases were then sorted and tallied using the broadest classification category. The individual program results may be seen in Tables 5.15 to 5.18. The ILL POD program results are broken into two tables, one for p-books, and the other for e-books.

In comparing the purchase patterns among the three distinct programs at UHM, there is an interesting similarity in trends in subject areas (table 5.19). In purchase trends by LC subject area, P (Language and Literature) and H (Social Sciences) classifications rank consistently within the top two or three classes of titles purchased for all three PDA/POD programs. Another category that ranked high for two out of the programs and occurred in the top five for three of the programs was the LC Class D (World History and History of Europe, Asia, Africa, etc.). The LC Class for Q (Science) also showed up in rank 4 or 5 for two of the three PDA/POD programs. Our findings can be contrasted with the Southern Illinois University at Carbondale's findings of social science, engineering, and general science as most viewed areas (Nabe, Imre, and Mann 2011, 195).

In terms of the possible reasons for our particular results, it may be that our academic programs are more heavily skewed in the literature and social sciences so that demand in these areas is reflectively high. Alternatively, it could be that our print and electronic collections are not as strong in these areas for the current literature (as two out of the three programs emphasize the acquisition of recent monographs within the latest three publication

TABLE 5.15

MyiLibrary® LC Class by % purchased.

Call no. range	# of titles (n = 90)	% of total purchases	LC Classification*
P	19	21%	Language and Literature
H	18	20%	Social Sciences
B	10	11%	Philosophy, Psychology, Religion
D	10	11%	World History and History of Europe, Asia, Africa, etc.
R	8	9%	Medicine
E	4	4%	History of the Americas
J	4	4%	Political Science
L	4	4%	Education
Q	3	3%	Science
C	2	2%	Auxiliary Sciences of History (incl. Archaeology)
G	2	2%	Geography, Anthropology, Recreation
M	2	2%	Music and Books on Music
T	2	2%	Technology
K	1	1%	Law
S	1	1%	Agriculture

* SOURCE: Library of Congress. "Library of Congress Classification Outline." 2013. http://www.loc.gov/catdir/cpso/lcco/.

years). As stated previously in the chapter, our gathering/approval plan and ability to order monographs by firm order has greatly diminished since 2009, so the trends may also reflect the holes in our normal collecting, with the PDA/POD programs filling in some of the gaps in the meanwhile. That being said, though, our science/technology collections have been similarly affected by budget cuts, so it may also reflect the general patterns of social science and humanities scholarship and research reliance upon the monographic treatise, whereas science and technology emphasize a faster communication cycle of the journal literature (Anderson et al. 2010, 128).

Another hypothesis is that the science/technology monographs tend to run higher in cost than the humanities and social sciences, therefore skewing them outside of the PDA/POD parameters ($200/$150 price cap), although the Stowell Bracke's analysis of average cost of books in various fields of science and technology for 2007–2008 shows that Purdue's Books on Demand

TABLE 5.16

ILL POD print book LC Class by % purchased.

Call no. range	# of titles ($n = 259$)	% of total purchases	LC Classification*
H	60	23.2%	Social Sciences
P	57	22.0%	Language and Literature
G	20	7.7%	Geography, Anthropology, Recreation
Q	18	6.9%	Science
B	16	6.2%	Philosophy, Psychology, Religion
R	16	6.2%	Medicine
J	15	5.8%	Political Science
D	12	4.6%	World History and History of Europe, Asia, Africa, etc.
N	9	3.5%	Fine Arts
L	8	3.1%	Education
T	7	2.7%	Technology
Z	5	1.9%	Bibliography, Library Science, Information Resources
E	3	1.2%	History of the Americas (America, United States)
K	3	1.2%	Law
U	3	1.2%	Military Science
F	2	0.8%	History of the Americas (US Local History, British America, etc.)
M	2	0.8%	Music and Books on Music
A	1	0.4%	General Works
C	1	0.4%	Auxiliary Sciences of History (Archaeology)
S	1	0.4%	Agriculture

* SOURCE: Library of Congress. "Library of Congress Classification Outline." 2013. http://www.loc.gov/catdir/cpso/lcco/.

price cap of $150 would appear to have been generally more than adequate when it compared the average cost of books, including items selected by the librarians (Stowell Bracke 2010, 149). Monographs purchased by UHM via purchase order and invoices for 2010–2012 averaged $64.21 per title. A review of more general resources for book prices by subject area using the *Library and Book Trade Almanac* and the "Academia" web lists provided by YPB book

TABLE 5.17

ILL POD e-book LC Class by % purchased.

Call no. range	# of titles (*n* = 75)	% of total purchases	LC Classification*
H	16	21%	Social Sciences
P	16	21%	Language and Literature
B	8	11%	Philosophy, Psychology, Religion
D	7	9%	World History and History of Europe, Asia, Africa, etc.
Q	6	8%	Science
G	5	7%	Geography, Anthropology, Recreation
L	5	7%	Education
N	3	4%	Fine Arts
E	2	3%	History of the Americas
C	1	1%	Auxiliary Sciences of History (Archaeology)
J	1	1%	Political Science
K	1	1%	Law
M	1	1%	Music and Books on Music
T	1	1%	Technology
U	1	1%	Military Science
Z	1	1%	Bibliography, Library Science, Information Resources

* SOURCE: Library of Congress. "Library of Congress Classification Outline." 2013. http://www.loc.gov/catdir/cpso/lcco/.

vendor shows that the hard sciences would have a higher percentage of titles above the $150 price ceiling than for humanities and social sciences (Appendixes 5B: "Average Monograph Price by Subject Area [YBP Sampling]" and 5C: "Average Monograph Price by Subject Area"). The percentage and probability of purchasing science and technology POD titles might therefore be lower than for humanities and the social sciences related to the price differentials.

We also analyzed our PDA/POD data by use statistics. It is a bit more difficult to compare usage between programs directly due to the different definitions used for "use." For the p-books, one use is considered one checkout on the library's ILS circulation system, whereas e-books vary in terms of usage depending upon the platform (MyiLibrary, EBL, or ebrary). MyiLibrary and EBL count a single log-in as a usage, whereas ebrary will count the number of times each individual section (similar to a chapter) is utilized. Ebrary usage

TABLE 5.18

ILL p-card print book LC Class by % purchased.

Call no. range	# of titles (*n* = 27)	% of total purchases	LC Classification*
P	4	15%	Language and Literature
D	3	11%	World History and History of Europe, Asia, Africa, etc.
H	3	11%	Social Sciences
M	3	11%	Music and Books on Music
Q	3	11%	Science
C	2	7%	Auxiliary Sciences of History (Archaeology)
S	2	7%	Agriculture
Z	2	7%	Bibliography, Library Science, Information Resources
E	1	4%	History of the Americas
J	1	4%	Political Science
N	1	4%	Fine Arts
R	1	4%	Medicine
T	1	4%	Technology

* SOURCE: Library of Congress. "Library of Congress Classification Outline." 2013. www.loc.gov/catdir/cpso/lcco.

numbers are therefore much higher in total number as compared to EBL and MyiLibrary results. Due to this difference, we have chosen to compare percentage of use as compared to total usage within an individual PDA/POD program to give us an idea of relative use for comparison. On figures 5.2, 5.3, 5.4, and 5.5, the percentage of uses are visually compared with the percentage of purchases as a baseline to see if use and purchase trends coincide. In most cases, they do parallel in percentages. For others, it appears that there may be one specific, individual title that received extraordinarily high usage (refer back to tables 5.4, 5.7, 5.10, 5.11 and 5.14). Tables 5.4 and 5.11 each have one title that received extremely high use; for table 5.4, one title had 17.2 percent of the total use followed by 4.3 percent for the next highest title; for Table 5.11, one title received nearly a third of all the usage for the program titles, with the next highest title receiving 18.2 percent of the usage.

Our findings show that of the PDA/POD titles, the majority of the usage is accounted for by titles in the humanities and social sciences as opposed to the science/technology areas for monographs. Our analysis for results for use by LC class is similar to an in-depth review of ten years of ILL POD at Purdue

TABLE 5.19

LC Class purchase rankings by UHM PDA/POD program.

Purchase rank	MyiLibrary®	ILL P-POD	ILL e-POD	ILL p-card
1	P (21%)	H (23%)	P (21%)	P (15%)
2	H (20%)	P (22%)	H (21%)	D (11%)
3	D (11%)	G (8%)	B (11%)	H (11%)
4	B (11%)	Q (7%)	D (9%)	M (11%)
5	R (9%)	B (6%)	Q (8%)	Q (11%)

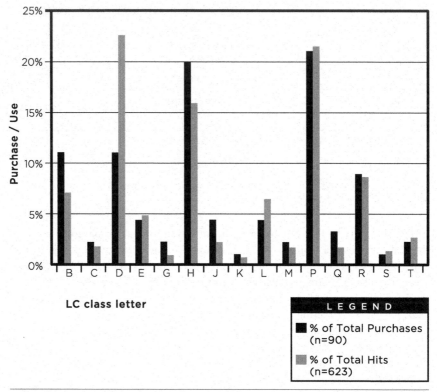

FIGURE 5.2

MyiLibrary® purchase compared with use by LC Class.

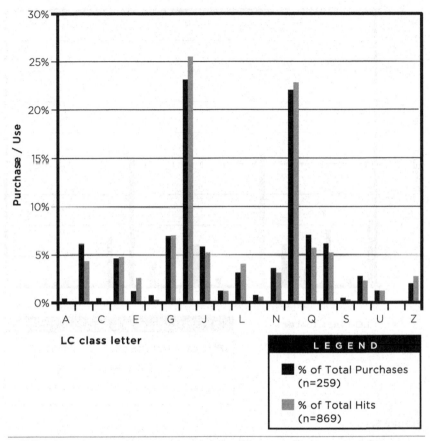

FIGURE 5.3

ILL p-book POD purchase compared with use by LC Class.

University that found usage of 85 percent for humanities/social sciences compared with 15 percent for science/technology (Stowell Bracke 2010, 143).

For the UHM Library, the implications are that any future OPAC record loading for PDA could best be concentrated on the humanities and social science titles as these areas are in demand both in terms of acquisition and high use. In discussions with the current chair of the CDMC at UHM, Ross Christenson, who is a subject specialist in the humanities, he said it may be that monographic PDA would better suit the needs of our undergraduate population since the students traditionally turn to monographs for their academic/research level studies, and turnaround time is of the essence to this population (e.g., it's Thursday and the paper is due next Monday). A quick analysis of the institutional status of the requester (table 5.20) shows that undergraduates

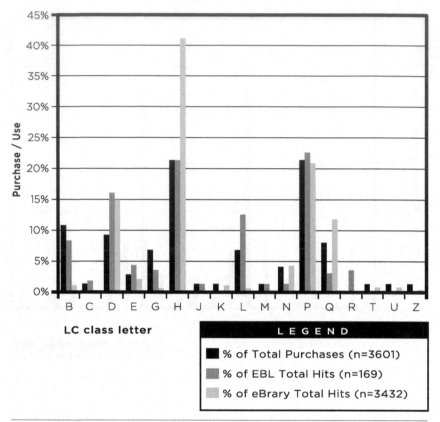

FIGURE 5.4

ILL e-book POD purchase compared with use by LC Class.

TABLE 5.20

UHM institutional status of PDA/POD initial requester.

PDA Program	Faculty	Graduate level	Undergraduate	Other
MyiLibrary® PDA[a]	51.2%	22.9%	23.5%	2.3%
ILL P-POD[b]	51.6%	38.4%	7.3%	n/a
ILL E-POD[b]	44.6%	46.7%	6.5%	2.2%
ILL p-card[b]	50.0%	32.5%	12.5%	5.0%

a. Based on patron status of first use of title.
b. Status of patron placing ILL request.

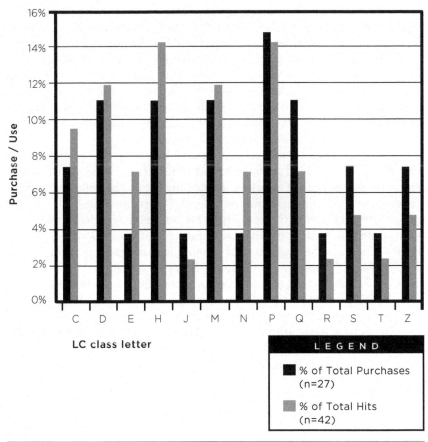

FIGURE 5.5
ILL p-book p-card purchase compared with use by LC Class.

log into the MyiLibrary e-books as the first user at a higher rate as compared to being the initiator of a request that is selected for ILL POD or p-card selections. It would be logical that the undergraduates look for resources that are readily available, and therefore use the OPAC to find books in the local collection or that are instantly accessible. PDA e-books in the OPAC would provide a good method of supporting undergraduate needs, especially if our ability to purchase books more widely and broadly via our firm order and approval plan processes continue to be curtailed.

The interlibrary loan service at UHM, on the other hand, is more heavily utilized by our graduate student and faculty patrons. By extension, the ILL loan titles that meet the POD parameters tend to be requests submitted by graduate students and faculty compared to undergraduates (table 5.20). The faculty and graduate students are aware of and submit the ILLs for items outside of the local holdings, including items that are new or cutting edge. Often times the items may not yet be easily available on ILL loan as many newer items are in use or restricted by ILL institutional policy to allow home institution patrons the first chance at the new materials. ILL POD would continue to serve a good niche for providing service while adding to our library's collection for the higher academic levels of research and scholarship.

The newer ILL POD selections appear to have a broader body of use as shown by their continued use by, assumedly, more than one individual, reflecting the high value of the selection. In shaping future ILL policy, should ILL concentrate upon loan items that are older and therefore unavailable by other means? Should anything that is available for purchase be purchased and added to the collection because the chances of future use by other local patrons are high? Or perhaps the application of the profile parameters as set up for the ILL E-Book POD program, or the individual, case-by-case consultation with selectors as done for those hard-to-find or extremely new items outside of the e-book POD parameters, provides the appropriate overlay as a filter for items that are "high quality" or a "good fit" for the library's collections.

The items selected from the record loading and ILL POD programs are high value as confirmed by selectors' post-review feedback that the items were appropriate for the collections and would be items that they would select and by patrons as reflected by high use. For the future, the library administrators would like to allocate more funds for PDA/POD efforts as they are convinced of the bang for the buck for PDA/POD expenditures by the high reuse rates as supported by analysis of the long-term ILL patron-driven collection development program at Purdue University, which examines a large pool of titles (over 9,000) over a long period of potential use (ten years) (Nixon and Saunders 2010; Stowell Bracke 2010, 146). Library selectors are beginning to consider expanding the PDA program for OPAC record loading, but there is much concern about how this might impact the quality of our collection's well-roundedness for future generations since at the moment the funding for PDA/POD would come at the expense of the more traditional approval/gathering plan and firm order selections.

CONCLUDING REMARKS

PDA/POD can be done on a small scale that is affordable. It does not need to have a large sum of funds allocated to it ultimately, and in a timely manner it benefits the institution's patrons. It does not need to be a complex process that involves many staff, though there is an initial investment of time to set up the procedures. PDA and POD do not need to completely exclude consultation with and the expertise of subject selectors.

As others have suggested, PDA/POD should be viewed as simply another tool to complement, not supplant, the myriad of selection methods currently in use (Dillon 2011; Way and Garrison 2011; Dahl 2012; Hodges Preston, and Hamilton 2010). Nardini (2011) notes that PDA is not a completely new concept; before the existence of gathering/approval plans, academic libraries often relied upon faculty purchase requests and suggestions to select materials for their collections. The difference from the past practice of processing faculty requests is that PDA via catalog record loading, for example, takes advantage of technology to address patron-based suggestions more quickly and efficiently in an unmediated fashion, whereas ILL-based POD taps into another avenue for capturing patron-based requests to supplement requests sent directly to library selectors.

Additionally, the fulcrum has swung full circle to widen the field of selectors to include all potential library patrons, beyond academic faculty and librarians. Studies have shown that patron groups are not only valid selectors when compared with librarians, but can add items that complement librarian efforts in unexpected ways. Anderson et al. (2010) show that graduate student PDA selection was on-track and produced appropriate selections. A study by Shen et al. (2011) also shows that patron selections are comparable in quality though overlapping in selection with librarian-selected titles. Both studies show that the overlap was great, but patrons chose materials that the librarian selectors did not pick up as well such as interdisciplinary (Anderson et al. 2010) and niche subject areas (Shen et al. 2011).

In the current economic climate, most institutions need to make tough choices about where and how to place their dollars for both their collection resources and staffing. We can no longer afford to collect and select as we have for the past 20 or 30 years. Carefully, narrowly defined PDA programs, such as the UHM university press title project, could release time and monetary pressures, allowing selectors to concentrate upon areas that require more intensive review and attention. Monies that would have been spent on immediate and definite purchases could be freed by moving subject areas or publishers to PDA e-book record-loading access, where expenditures are often made at a lower rate as well as spread out over a longer period of time. This could free funds that could then be reallocated to subject area specializations that are considered core to the mission of the local institution, in our case in Hawaiian, Pacific, and Asian studies.

The chair of our library's CDMC has suggested another way to provide quick access while further reducing cost; e-book record loading could be set up to have patron use trigger a short-term lease for e-books for immediate temporary access to titles for a portion of the full purchase price. This would be similar to the e-book record-loading model that Grand Valley State University has used where a title has short-term loans for the first 3–5 uses, with purchase after the threshold has been hit (Way 2011b; Way and Garrison 2011). A modified program could be set up to send the selectors a list of all titles utilized for additional review for full purchase consideration. Selectors would make the final decision as to whether to add the titles to the permanent collection, similar to the way repeated use of ILL print books can be used as a gauge for purchasing a title. A higher threshold for automatic purchase could be integrated so that high-demand titles could automatically be added to the collection without the need for selector review.

Providing PDA for the patron currently in front of us, however, does not mean that we have to give up just-in-case access for future patrons. Ideally, if potential PDA e-book titles, for example, are retained in the catalog indefinitely with potential access guaranteed in perpetuity, it would not be much different than purchasing books on an approval plan. This potential for simultaneous just-in-time and just-in-case e-titles requires that we advocate as a profession for the perpetuity of access to monographs and journals whether in electronic or print format as exemplified by the efforts of organizations such as JSTOR, Project Muse, HathiTrust, Internet Archive, and the WEST Repository, as a few examples, and also by working with publishers and vendors on perpetual access to and archiving of electronic materials such as is being addressed by the NISO Working Group for DDA (Demand-Driven Acquisitions) Best Practices.

Our efforts bring up many new questions and issues for our library to address, but this in turn shows that the library is a living organism, one that is willing to examine its practices and to adapt to changing times. PDA/POD is no longer a "new invention," and it is flexible enough to fit into any type of academic institution (large or small, wealthy or not so). The ever-changing technology helps to change the procedural matters on how to enact PDA/POD, whether via OPAC record loading en masse with a deposit account, or item-by-item purchasing using an established book vendor for e-book purchase and delivery, or the simple institutional p-card for individual items that could not have been so easily accessed ten years ago before the advent of websites where products may be ordered instantly, and delivered within days. It requires an openness to change, an openness to embrace a different way of processing materials. We are fortunate to have staff in acquisitions, cataloging/cataloging support, and systems that are willing to do things differently and help to solve the question of "how" things can be accomplished, in addition to selectors willing to try new ways to get the patrons what they need.

The authors would like to acknowledge and thank the staff members at the UHM Hamilton Library who have provided data and support for our program analyses: Lori Ann Saeki (E-Resources); Carol Kellett (Systems); Frederick Allen (Systems); Jaeyeon Sung (Access Services, Head), Nackil Sung (Acquisitions, Head), and Wing Leung (Desktop Network Support).

REFERENCES

Anderson, Kristine J., Robert S. Freeman, Jean-Pierre V. M. Herubel, Lawrence J. Mykytiuk, Judith M. Nixon, and Suzanne M. Ward. 2010. "Liberal Arts Books on Demand: A Decade of Patron-Driven Collection Development, Part 1." *Collection Management* 35 (3–4): 125–41.

Bean, Margaret H., and Miriam Rigby. 2011. "Interlibrary Loan Reference Collaboration: Filling Hard-to-Find Faculty Requests." *Journal of Interlibrary Loan, Document Delivery and Electronic Reserve* 21 (1–2): 1–7.

Dahl, Candice. 2012. "Primed for Patron-Driven Acquisition: A Look at the Big Picture." *Journal of Electronic Resources Librarianship* 24 (2): 119–26.

De Fino, Melissa, and Mei Ling Lo. 2011. "New Roads for Patron-Driven E-Books: Collection Development and Technical Services Implications for a Patron-Driven Acquisitions Pilot at Rutgers." *Journal of Electronic Resources Librarianship* 23 (4): 327–38.

Dillon, Dennis. 2011. "Texas Demand-Driven Acquisitions: Controlling Costs in a Large-Scale PDA Program." Chap. 10 in *Patron-Driven Acquisitions: History and Best Practices* edited by David A. Swords, 158–67. Berlin: de Gruyter Saur.

Gibson, Tess M., and Patricia E. Kirkwood. 2009. "A Purchase-on-Demand Pilot Project at the University of Arkansas, for the Proceedings of the Materials Research Society Symposiums." *Journal of Interlibrary Loan, Document Delivery and Electronic Reserve* 19 (1): 47–56.

Hodges, Dracine, Cyndi Preston, and Marsha J. Hamilton. 2010. "Patron-Initiated Collection Development: Progress of a Paradigm Shift." *Collection Management* 35 (3–4): 208–21.

Hussong-Christian, Uta, and Kerri Goergen-Doll. 2010. "We're Listening: Using Patron-Feedback to Assess and Enhance Purchase on Demand." *Journal of Interlibrary Loan, Document Delivery and Electronic Reserve* 20 (5): 319–35.

Jones, Douglas. 2011. "On-Demand Information Delivery: Integration of Patron-Driven Acquisition into a Comprehensive Information Delivery System." *Journal of Library Administration* 51 (7–8): 764–76.

Kyrillidou, Martha, Shaneka Morris, and Gary Roebuck. 2010–2011. "ARL Statistics 2010–2011." Association of Research Libraries. http://publications.arl.org/ARL -Statistics-2010-2011.

Levine-Clark, Michael. 2010. "Developing a Multiformat Demand-Driven Acquisition Model." *Collection Management* 35 (3–4): 201–7.

Lugg, Rick. "Collecting for the Moment: Patron-Driven Acquisitions as a Disruptive Technology." 2011. Chap. 1 in *Patron-Driven Acquisitions: History and Best Practices,* edited by David A. Swords, 7–22. Berlin: de Gruyter Saur.

Mānoa, University of Hawai'i at. 2012. "About UH Mānoa." University of Hawai'i at Mānoa. http://manoa.hawaii.edu/about.

Morris, Nancy J. 2006. "History of Libraries, University of Hawai'i, Mānoa." University of Hawai'i at Mānoa Libraries. http://library.manoa.hawaii.edu/about/library_history.html.

Nabe, Jonathan, Andrea Imre, and Sanjeet Mann. 2011. "Let the Patron Drive: Purchase on Demand of E-Books." *Serials Librarian* 60 (1–4): 193–97.

Nardini, Bob. 2011. "Approval Plans and Patron Selection: Two Infrastructures." Chap. 2 in *Patron-Driven Acquisitions: History and Best Practices,* edited by David A. Swords, 23–43. Berlin: de Gruyter Saur.

Nixon, Judith M., Robert S. Freeman, and Suzanne M. Ward. 2010. "Patron-Driven Acquisitions: An Introduction and Literature Review." *Collection Management* 35 (3–4): 119–24.

Nixon, Judith M., and E. Stewart Saunders. 2010. "A Study of Circulation Statistics of Books on Demand: A Decade of Patron-Driven Collection Development, Part 3." *Collection Management* 35 (3–4): 151–61.

Reynolds, Leslie J., Carmelita Pickett, Wyoma Vanduinkerken, Jane Smith, Jeanne Harrell, and Sandra Tucker. 2010. " User-Driven Acquisitions: Allowing Patron Requests to Drive Collection Development in an Academic Library." *Collection Management* 35 (3–4): 244–54.

Schroeder, Rebecca. 2012. "When Patrons Call the Shots: Patron-Driven Acquisition at Brigham Young University." *Collection Building* 31 (1): 11–14.

Shen, Lisa, Erin Dorris Cassidy, Eric Elmore, Glenda Griffin, Tyler Manolovitz, Michelle Martinez, and Linda M. Turney. 2011. "Head First into the Patron-Driven Acquisition Pool: A Comparison of Librarian Selections versus Patron Purchases." *Journal of Electronic Resources Librarianship* 23 (3): 203–18.

Stowell Bracke, Marianne. 2010. "Science and Technology Books on Demand: A Decade of Patron-Driven Collection Development, Part 2." *Collection Management* 35 (3–4): 142–50.

Swords, Davis. 2011. "Elements of a Demand-Driven Model." Chap. 11 in *Patron-Driven Acquisitions: History and Best Practices,* edited by David A. Swords, 168–88. Berlin: de Gruyter Saur.

Tyler, David C., Joyce C. Melvin, Yang Xu, MaryLou Epp, and Anita M. Kreps. 2011. "Effective Selectors? Interlibrary Loan Patrons as Monograph Purchasers: A Comparative Examination of Price and Circulation-Related Performance." *Journal of Interlibrary Loan, Document Delivery & Electronic Reserve* 21 (1–2): 57–90.

Tyler, David C., Yang Xu, Joyce C. Melvin, Marylou Epp, and Anita M. Kreps. 2010. "Just How Right Are the Customers? An Analysis of the Relative Performance of Patron-Initiated Interlibrary Loan Monograph Purchases." *Collection Management* 35 (3–4): 162–79.

Way, Doug. 2011a. "The Implementation of a Patron-Driven Acquisitions Program at Grand Valley State University." Paper presented at American Library Association Annual Conference, New Orleans, LA.

———. 20111b. "Patron-Driven Acquisitions: Transforming Library Collections in the Virtual Environment. Presentations. Paper 23."

Way, Doug, and Julie Garrison. 2011. "Financial Implications of Demand-Driven Acquisitions: A Case Study of the Value of Short-Term Loans." Chap. 9 in *Patron-Driven Acquisitions: History and Best Practices,* edited by David A. Swords, 138–56. Berlin: de Gruyter Saur.

Wermager, Paul. 2008. "Sabbatical Project during July 1, 2008 to December 31, 2008 (Space Inventory of the UH Manoa Library)." Honolulu, HI: University of Hawaiʻi at Mānoa Hamilton Library. http://scholarspace.manoa.hawaii.edu/handle/10125/25872.

Zopfi-Jordan, David. 2008. "Purchasing or Borrowing: Making Interlibrary Loan Decisions That Enhance Patron Satisfaction." *Journal of Interlibrary Loan, Document Delivery and Electronic Reserve* 18 (3): 387–94.

ILL POD print book processing steps.

Review by selection criteria	Narrow possible titles for POD	"No" to POD reverted to and borrowed via ILL
Review of OCLC holdings	Special interest in three areas:	
	"Core" title	Collected by many academic libraries - a title that may be considered basic to an academic collection
	"Pearls" treasures subject areas	Falls into Hawaiian, Pacific, and Asia subject areas
	Newly published/rarely held	Few library holdings in OCLC; hard to borrow via ILL
Review of local OPAC	Subject fits into established collections? Previous editions? Held elsewhere in UH system?	Would this fit into UHM established collections?
Consultation with selectors	As needed: Item appropriate to UHM collections?	Would this be appropriate for UHM collections?
Place order	E-mail notice to acquisitions	
Quick fulfillment and delivery turnaround	Orders placed with Amazon or Barnes & Noble	Purchased with p-card (credit card) via acquisitions department
Patron access first, minimal OPAC records	• Brief order record by acquisitions staff in OPAC and library name stamp • Rush acquisitions processing - item sent directly to ILL (barcode, brief circ record, security tattle tape) • Circulates as is until returned • Then sent to cataloging for full record and labeling	• Other: UHM patrons may place holds upon new record; some books have circulated continuously with full cataloging for two years since inception of program • Plus: patrons can gain access to item readily • Minus: identifying book band may fall off/be discarded - hard to identify POD by sight to then send to cataloging (two books have been "lost")

APPENDIX B

Average monograph price by subject area (YBP sampling).

Subject area	Average price	#titles	# titles > 150	Range
Allied Health[a]	$83.32	199	6%	14.25–325.00
Anthropology[b]	$81.61	278	5%	14.00–1,295.00
Bio Nano Technology[a]	$143.32	126	33%	25.00–445.00
Child Development[b]	$88.95	238	6%	10.00–1,450.00
Computer Studies[a]	$66.38	260	3%	13.00–199.95
Earth Sciences[a]	$129.01	263	28%	11.95–1,595.00
East Asian Studies[b]	$66.09	316	4%	15.00–335.00
Ethnic Studies[b]	$72.30	456	2%	14.95–350.00
Evolution Natural History[a]	$72.37	196	4%	11.95–549.00
Family Studies[b]	$70.69	207	6%	15.00–550.00
Geography[b]	$92.69	192	12%	11.95–940.00
Human Rights[b]	$80.68	350	4%	14.95–625.00
Life Sciences[a]	$87.54	310	10%	11.95–900.00
Literary Essentials[c]	$45.23	444	2%	7.95–495.00
Multicultural Studies[b]	$79.07	239	3%	11.95–380.00
Oceania[b]	$62.71	147	3%	12.95–180.00
Performing Arts[c]	$71.03	582	2%	9.00–2,095.00
Poetry Essentials	$30.82	98	2%	12.95–350.00
Public Policy[b]	$71.57	325	6%	15.00–264.95
Renaissance Studies[c]	$88.28	168	7%	19.95–595.00
Urban Studies[b]	$71.98	371	9%	9.95–1,425.00
Overall Average	**$78.84**		**7%**	
SciTech Average[a]	**$96.99**		**14%**	
Social Sciences[b]	**$76.21**		**5%**	
Humanities[c]	**$58.84**		**3%**	

SOURCES: YPB/Baker and Taylor. "Academia." 2013. www.ybp.com/acad/index.htm. Including subtopics of:

YPB/Baker and Taylor. "Academic Essentials." 2013. www.ybp.com/acad/EssentialsCover.htm.

YPB/Baker and Taylor. "Literary Essentials." 2013. www.ybp.com/acad/literaryessentials.htm.

YPB/Baker and Taylor. "Poetry Essentials." 2013. www.ybp.com/acad/poetryessentials.htm.

YPB/Baker and Taylor. "Area and Ethnic Studies." 2013. www.ybp.com/acad/area.htm.

APPENDIX C

Average monograph price by subject area.

Hardcover average per-volume prices, 2011			
Science/Technology		**Humanities & Social Sciences**	
Computers	$136.22	Architecture	$79.24
Mathematics	$128.77	Art	$75.03
Medical	$163.77	Education	$118.46
Science	$189.92	Foreign Language Study	$119.03
Technology and Engineering	$164.03	History	$83.49
Average	$156.54	Language Arts and Disciplines	$116.38
		Literary Criticism	$89.90
		Music	$87.88
		Philosophy	$98.77
		Political Science	$106.94
		Psychology	$112.89
		Religion	$78.01
		Social Science	$103.02
		Average	$97.62

SOURCE: *Library & Book Trade Almana.* 2012. 57th edition.

KAY DOWNEY

6

Technical Services Aspects of Demand-Driven E-Book Acquisitions

D EMAND-DRIVEN ACQUISITION (DDA), ALSO KNOWN AS PATRON-
driven acquisition (PDA), is a business model whereby print or electronic book purchases are made as a result of library user activity. In January 2012 Kent State University Libraries (KSUL) implemented a DDA purchasing model that uses a combination of the acquisition services provided by YBP, our primary book jobber, and the access services provided by an e-book distributer, ebrary. Upon initiation, KSUL loaded 22,555 DDA-eligible records into their catalog, making the e-books accessible to library users for discovery and access to the e-book source on the publisher or aggregator platform. The library then began purchasing selected e-books based on use or trigger activity. Each week as new ebrary e-books became available KSUL received a new set of discovery records from YBP, which were added to the catalog. Today there are well over 34,000 DDA records in the KSUL catalog, and authorized KSUL users across all ten campuses are triggering purchases for about fifty e-books per week. The following chapter will provide an overview of Kent's DDA program; project development, technical services aspects and the advantages of using book jobber mediation; as well as the implications for program modification and improvement.

E-BOOK ACQUISITIONS

E-books are becoming increasingly important to KSUL for a number of reasons. The first is logistics. Kent State University has ten campuses dispersed across a large geographic region that spans the entire northeastern quadrant of the state of Ohio. Acquiring e-books provides KSUL with the ability to more easily share content across all of the Kent campuses. It also provides cost efficiencies as e-books do not require physical circulation, shelf maintenance, or associated costs of book transit or document delivery. Besides geographic expanse, the increasing number of online and distance learning classes and rising patron expectations for electronic content also contribute to KSUL's need to acquire e-books. Libraries benefit from using a variety of e-book acquisition methods.

One method may prove to be more effective than another depending on factors such as type and size of library, budget, subject matter, or academic level. There are advantages and disadvantages for each method depending on the circumstances of the need, subject matter, and intended use. Each institution must sort through the available options to determine what method or combination of methods works best to build a balanced, utilitarian collection. Over the past decade, KSUL has successfully acquired e-books through a variety of methods, including consortia participation, subscription packages, firm orders, and DDA.

E-book aggregator subscription packages are another low-cost way of providing access to a large quantity of content, but record maintenance and content management may be time-consuming since titles in subscription packages are frequently added and removed by participating publishers. Title-by-title e-book selection can help to build specialized collections necessary to serve local programs or targeted users; however, in contrast to consortia deals, local e-book purchases are more costly and in effect create silos of collections that cannot be shared with other libraries.

CONSORTIA DDA

In the past KSUL acquired the majority of their e-books as a benefit of Ohio-LINK (OL) membership through consortia purchases for e-book packages accessible through the OhioLINK Electronic Book Center (EBC). Although consortia e-book package deals make up a small percentage of KSUL's overall monograph purchases, they do provide the benefit of a shared collection and are an economical way to quickly acquire a large volume of e-books.

More recently, OhioLINK has been preparing to launch a consortia e-book pilot that includes a DDA component. This initiative has been planned in cooperation with YBP and three participating publishers including Ashgate, Rowman & Littlefield, and Cambridge University Press. YBP set up approval profiles for the consortia based on analyses of past print purchases by Ohio-LINK member libraries. Because YBP is a major supplier for the majority of OL libraries it can effectively control the supply of books to individual member libraries, and prevent duplication. For e-books not supplied automatically via the profile a DDA model will be used to facilitate e-book purchases. MARC records for profiled e-books and discovery records for the DDA will be made available by YBP on a weekly basis. These records will be uploaded to the Ohio-LINK central catalog and also placed on the OhioLINK server so that member libraries may download the records into their local catalog if so desired.

Another example of this type of initiative is the DDA program developed by the Orbis Cascade Alliance consortia. Like OhioLINK, they are working in partnership with YBP to manage DDA acquisitions. This approach also utilizes YBP's approval-profiling algorithms to ensure that suitable e-books are eligible for purchase and that duplication is controlled across member libraries (Doyle & Tucker, 2011).

Consortia purchase e-book package deals that are based on the broadest community need so that they can serve the widest possible user base. The homogenous nature of these collections can be a disadvantage, as it may not necessarily provide for the specified local programmatic needs. Although consortia acquisitions are KSUL's preferred method of acquiring e-books, increased user demand and greater flexibility in e-book purchase options for academic libraries have contributed to the decision to also acquire e-books in other ways.

Demand-driven acquisition models for either print or electronic books offer definite advantages for libraries, the most obvious of which is the provision of immediate electronic access to a large quantity of content with the insurance that funds are being expended for content that is actually being used. Because the acquisition is automatic, DDA can save time for selectors and may be a cost-effective alternative to interlibrary loan (ILL). There is evidence to suggest that user-selected resources have the same potential for long-term use as those selected by bibliographers. The DDA model has also been shown to strengthen collections for emerging areas of study and inter-disciplinary categories that often fall outside of the bibliographer's area of responsibility (Anderson et al., 2002; Fischer et al., 2012). DDA works especially well when the library has control over the content eligible for selection and is able to maintain predictable spending patterns.

BOOK JOBBER-MEDIATED DDA

Most recently KSUL has been acquiring e-books using the DDA model. One way of managing DDA is through approval service providers such as YBP. This DDA model uses patron-triggered acquisitions for e-book purchases with the added benefit of the technical components available via traditional print approval services. Book jobbers can provide definite advantages over PDA programs managed directly by an aggregator or publisher.

Today many academic libraries have either experimented with or implemented DDA for e-book acquisitions. Some of the first experimental DDA programs, such as the pilot conducted at Ohio State University, provided access to large sets of e-books with little or no restriction on content. Funds allocated for these projects quickly ran out (Hodges, Preston, and Hamilton, 2010). Since these first DDA programs, librarians began to specify restrictions to narrow the PDA-eligible content in an attempt to control spending. Some began using book jobbers such as Coutts or YBP to assist in the customization DDA plans based on Library of Congress classification and other non-subject parameters. Two examples of DDA that use the book jobber–mediated approach are programs run by the University of Iowa and the University of Kansas Libraries (KU Libraries), which both worked with YBP and used their YBP approval profiles and historical purchase data to craft the parameters and calculate projected expenditures (Fischer et al. 2012; Currie and Graves 2012).

In the summer of 2011, KSUL began the planning for a DDA pilot project supported with $50,000 of central collection funds. The planning phase took six months, during which time librarians, in conjunction with YBP representatives, developed the e-book approval plan and wrote specifications for associated MARC records. Systems librarians developed and tested scripts for record loads, provided holding data to YBP, and loaded a back file of ebrary-hosted e-books to KentLINK, KSUL's online catalog. In January 2012, KSUL loaded 22,555 DDA-eligible MARC records into the catalog. Following this, KSUL added new e-book records to the catalog on a weekly basis as delivered by YBP. The pilot continued for six months during which time KSUL had acquired about 550 new e-books via DDA at an average cost of $95 per e-book. At the conclusion, the program was analyzed with collection managers and selectors who recommended the program continue for the following fiscal year. (See table 6.1.)

The primary benefit of using the book jobber–mediated DDA is their ability to create a customized profile, which preselects the e-books eligible for user-generated purchases. This profile can mirror the existing profile for print book selection based on Library of Congress classification and other

TABLE 6.1

DDA technical process sequence.

Schedule	Prompted by	Workflow / Action
June 2011	Collection manager	Appropriated funding for Pilot ($50,000)
August 2011	YBP/ KSUL acquisitions librarians	Created new DDA approval account
Sept. – Nov. 2011	YBP / KSUL acquisitions catalogers and systems librarians	•Created technical specifications •MARC discovery records •MARC point of invoice records, including 9XX fields for order and invoice data •Developed and tested scripts for record loads
November 2011	YBP	Loaded KSUL >= PD 2009 non-YBP holdings into GOBI
December 2011	TS and systems librarians	Initial Record Load for retrospective file, suppressed from public view
January 2012	KSUL collection manager, acquisitions, catalogers, and systems librarians	•Opened Access, unsuppressed retrospective file •Workflow organization and training •Selector communications
weekly	YBP	Notifies KSUL via e-mail that a new DDA discovery record file is available for pickup
weekly	KSUL cataloger	Using the III's Batch MARC Load Tool discovery records are loaded into KentLINK
weekly	Library user	Triggers an e-book purchase on ebrary platform
weekly	ebrary	Notifies YBP within 24 hours of the trigger purchase
weekly	YBP	Initiates the order with ebrary and creates an invoice for KSUL
weekly	YBP	Notifies KSUL that point of invoice records for purchased e-books are ready for pick up
weekly	ebrary	Trigger reports are e-mailed to KSUL collection manager
weekly	KSUL cataloger	Loads point of invoice records which overlay discovery records matched on the MARC 001 field and generates an order record
weekly	KSUL acquisitions staff	Invoices are processed via electronic invoicing
	KSUL cataloger	Add holdings data to OCLC WorldCat manually and overlay point-of-invoice bibliographic record with OCLC record
monthly	KSUL cataloger	Performs ebrary record deletes from discovery pool
monthly	Collection manager	Deduplication / sends holdings to YBP for non-YBP purchases
periodic	Collection manager	Review and analysis

nonsubject parameters. In this way, the library knows that funds are expended for resources that will truly fit collection development guidelines.

Once the DDA e-book profile is established, MARC records for e-book titles that match the profile are made available to the library and loaded into the library's catalog. YBP provides customized MARC records that automate bibliographic and order record creation, making it possible to incorporate the process into existing acquisitions workflows such as electronic invoicing. Once the records are accessible via the catalog, library users discover and link to the e-book source on the publisher or aggregator platform. The library then purchases select e-books based on use or trigger activity. Purchase triggers commonly consist of 10 page views, 10 consecutive minutes of use within a title, or one page (or portion thereof) copied or printed. Once triggered, the e-book is automatically purchased by the library, new MARC records that include order information are supplied, and the cost is applied against a deposit account.

Other management benefits provided by YBP are their de-duplication services. Because YBP has KSUL's profiling data, it maintains a record of the library's' purchasing history and therefore facilitates automated de-duplication of DDA-eligible records against existing YBP orders. This process minimizes duplication across both print and electronic purchases. However, KSUL purchases print and e-books from suppliers other than YBP. To compensate for this gap YBP provides a holdings load service whereby the library reports ISBNs for non-YBP purchases which allows them to reflect more complete KSUL holdings in GOBI, YBP's online approval management system. By adding non-YBP holdings data to GOBI it allows them to prevent duplication against records for all print and e-book acquisition plans, including DDA. This service is crucial to program success since Kent purchases more than a third of their books from Amazon and a number of publishers and book vendors.

One of the drawbacks to DDA e-books acquisitions is that it can demand a significant amount of preparation time and maintenance, particularly during the initial stages. Integrating e-book acquisitions into the workflow involves systems and technical services librarians who ensure the access records and metadata meet the library specifications. Program coordinators must also invest time in communicating with selectors and provide training across cataloging and acquisitions departments.

Another complicating factor is that publishers will often delay access to an e-book until the print edition has been on the market for a certain period. This delay is referred to as an embargo period. E-books released within six weeks of the print release date are regarded as simultaneous publication. Today about 40 percent of all e-books are dispatched simultaneously with the print equivalent. Another point to consider is that high-demand content, such as textbooks, may not be made available in electronic format at all. This delay introduces additional steps in the selection and acquisition process to avoid duplication of e-book and print books.

There is also a considerable amount of time in record maintenance once DDA is activated. One reason for this is that publishers regularly remove content from the aggregator site, making it necessary to update the discovery pool to accurately reflect eligible e-books. Regular catalog updates and record deletes are part of the DDA workflow.

License negotiation may be another challenging component to e-book acquisitions. Although book jobbers can supply e-books from a number of e-book suppliers, the library must still have a contract on file for each individual aggregator or publisher from which they wish to purchase e-books. Contract negotiations can be complicated processes because license terms vary from one provider to another. In some cases, negotiations may end in an impasse due to restrictive terms.

Two types of records are made available for the DDA program: discovery records provided for e-books that are eligible for purchase, and point of invoice records for e-books that triggered a purchase. Most of these e-book records are derived from records for the print format. Each standard record includes LC classification, site-specific URLs that link to full text, and a unique control number output in the 001 field for match/overlay purposes. They all contain unique data that allows the library to distinguish them from other records in the catalog so that the library can identify and suppress or remove them from the catalog when necessary. Record customization options are available from YBP for a fee.

Standard discovery records are provided on a weekly schedule by YBP. The discovery records adhere to the Program for Cooperative Cataloging (PCC) Provider-Neutral E-Resource MARC Record Guidelines, which are available at www.loc.gov/aba/pcc/scs/documents/PCC-PN-guidelines.html. KSUL edits these records with an in-house Batch MARC Load program that modifies them during the load process in order to meet local record specifications. The MARC fields modified include the 001 primary identification number, addition of a local note in the 506 and the 910, the swap from 856 to the 956 for access data.

YBP also supplies KSUL with new records for triggered e-books on a weekly schedule which when loaded overlay the discovery records matched on the 001 MARC field. These Point of Invoice Records are customized by YBP to meet KSUL cataloging specifications for order and invoice data. 9xx fields were appended to generate order records. Pertinent data includes a vendor code, a DDA fund code to track expenditures, a matching fund code mapped from LC print approval plan, and price. The Batch MARC Load program further modifies these records during the load process. This process closely resembles the library's process for receiving WorldCat Cataloging Partners records for YBP print materials. Table 6.2 provides a complete list of designated MARC codes for order and invoice data and shows how the load script reformats the point of invoice records for inclusion in Innovative Interfaces, Inc. Millennium ILS.

TABLE 6.2

MARC data field specifications.

\textbf{KSUL constant data appended to bibliographic record}			
Tag	*Subfield*	*Data value*	*Description*
910	a	YBP DDA	Facilitates potential for batch removal or edit by presence in all
960	a	t	Order acquisitions type
	g	e	Order physical form of item
	k	a	Order receiving location
	l	a	Order billing location
	m	1 (numeral 1)	Financial encumbering / disencumbering status
	v	ybpdd	Order vendor code
961	m	5266-52	Order subaccount number
981	a	ybpdd	Order vendor code
	b	ddaeb	Order vendor code
	c	onlin	Order location
	o	r	Order type
999	a	kentc	Bibliographic location code
	c	- -	Cat date. Controls application of authority control processing and cost. The syntax is [blank][blank]-[blank][blank]-[blank][blank]
	e	3	III material type
	f	z	III display value (z = suppress from OhioLINK)
\textbf{KSUL local variable data appended to bibliographic record}			
Tag	*Subfield*	*Data value*	*Description*
961	c	Fund code from approval plan	Order Note. Department fund code assignment transferred from print approval plan
	m	5266-52	YBP approval sub-account number
980	a	[yymmdd]	Invoice date
	b	[implied decimal]	Invoice list price
	c	[implied decimal]	Invoice tax exempted
	e	[implied decimal]	Invoice net price
	f	[numeric value]	Invoice number
	g	[numeric value]	Invoice quantity

FUTURE DIRECTIONS FOR DDA

KSUL analyzed data collected after the 2012 calendar year of DDA purchases, a period that included the six months' pilot project and the first half year of fiscal year 2013. (See table 6.3.) Within that period the total number of DDA e-books purchased totaled 896, with the total number of user sessions recorded as 3,460. The cost of a single DDA e-book averaged $96 while the cost of a single user session was $12.00. With these numbers in mind KSUL librarians evaluated the cost-effectiveness of DDA. Even though e-books provide users with on-demand access, an e-book that enjoyed one user session is costly. Examining title lists and subject breakdown may provide clues for fine-tuning the DDA to see more return on investment. Similar DDA models include provision for short-term loans, where after a set number of loans are triggered, the e-book is then purchased. Because the cost of the short-term is relatively low and actual purchases are reserved for high-demand e-books, this may be an effective way to achieve cost savings.

Collection budgets are affected by changing acquisition models. The transition of expenditures for print books to DDA and continuing expenses for e-books leasing and hosting fees may warrant the redistribution of central collection funds to targeted department funding. Because the print approval fund codes are included in the data collection for DDA trigger purchases, collection managers can also use this information to examine purchasing patterns. Examining subject distribution for triggered purchases and for broad areas of content that were never accessed may provide insight into how dollars can be reallocated in an equitable manner.

TABLE 6.3
DDA data 2012.

DDA outcomes for calendar year 2012	
Total titles in discovery pool 1/1/2012	22,555
Total titles in discovery pool 12/31/2012	32,000
Total cost of triggered e-book purchases	$86,100
Average cost per DDA e-book	$96
Number of triggered e-book purchases	900
Number of e-books used	2,656
Number of e-books used but not purchased	1,756
Total user sessions for all titles in DDA discovery pool	7,178
Cost per user session of all DDA discovery pool	$12

Based upon usage reports, KSUL determined that the default for single simultaneous user access appeared adequate for the majority of books triggered. However, for high-demand e-books that show a number of turn-aways or wait queue instances, the library may look for ways to provide better service for these resources. One way to respond to high demand is automated upgrade to multiuser access, provided a multiuser license is available. If the multi-user option is not available, then the purchase of additional single-user-only perpetual licenses for a single title may be an alternative.

Another consideration for future DDA programs could be the incorporation of additional e-book suppliers for a multi-vendor demand-driven acquisitions program. The advantage of adding additional e-book providers is the provision of more unique content, platform choice, and possible cost savings. Any changes in DDA protocol will require workflow adjustment to make sure records are accurate and current.

For a long-term continuing DDA program, librarians will need to formulate parameters for weeding unused DDA-eligible content. Factors such as older publication date and superseded editions may be targets for periodic weeding. Changing focus in curriculum may also prompt the librarians to reevaluate DDA subject parameters in tandem with the print approval plan.

During the pilot KSUL continued to receive orders from selectors for e-books, but KSUL decided to hold these orders until the conclusion of the DDA to see if any of these would be triggered by use. Subsequent analysis of these order revealed that 80 percent had records in the DDA discovery pool but most were not triggered for purchase. Going forward, KSUL decided to purchase requested e-books whether or not they were accessible via the DDA in order to provide stable access to these e-books in the event the publishers withdrew their e-books from the discovery pool.

Although KSUL will continue to look for opportunities to acquire e-books through consortia DDA or other shared e-book deals, the existing local DDA offers on-demand service and useful information about e-book use at KSU. DDA models for the e-book publishing and trade industry are rapidly evolving with the increased market and consumer demand. Although there are aspects of the DDA program that can be improved upon, the overall outcome is considered successful. Book jobber–mediated DDA provides clear advantages as it can be integrated into existing acquisitions workflow, it provides LC control over DDA-eligible content, maintains predictable expenditures, and improves e-book services for library users.

REFERENCES

Anderson, Kristine J., Robert S. Freeman, Jean-Pierre V. M. Herubel, Lawrence J. Mykytiuk, Judith M. Nixon, and Suzanne M. Ward. 2002. "Buy, Don't Borrow:

Bibliographers' Analysis of Academic Library Collection Development through Interlibrary Loan Requests." *Collection Management* 27 (3–4): 1–11.

Currie, Lea, and Kathy Graves. 2012. "A New Model for Demand-Driven Acquisition." *CULS Proceedings* 2:12–16.

Doyle, Greg, and Cory Tucker. 2011. "Patron-Driven Acquisition—Working Collaboratively in a Consortial Environment: An Interview with Greg Doyle." *Collaborative Librarianship,* 3 (4): 212–16.

Fischer, K. S., M. Wright, K. Clatanoff, H. Barton, and E. Shreeves. 2012. "Give 'Em What They Want: A One-Year Study of Unmediated Patron-Driven Acquisition of Ebooks. *College & Research Libraries* 73 (5): 469–92.

Hodges, D., C. Preston, and M. J. Hamilton. 2010. "Patron-Initiated Collection Development: Progress of a Paradigm Shift." *Collection Management* 35 (3–4): 208–21. doi:10.1080/01462679.2010.486968.

JARED L. HOWLAND, REBECCA
SCHROEDER, AND TOM WRIGHT

7

Brigham Young University's Patron-Driven Acquisitions

Does It Stand the Test of Time?

FOR MANY YEARS, WE AT BRIGHAM YOUNG UNIVERSITY (BYU) have used patron-driven acquisition (PDA) strategies in our overall collection development plan. This approach includes faculty and student research requests and patron suggestions. We also rely on our users to drive the purchase of additional copies of owned materials by buying books with multiple holds. In the last several years, we added an interlibrary loan (ILL) purchase program for items too new to borrow and e-book patron-driven acquisitions to our existing patron-initiated purchasing plans. We use these programs in an effort to better utilize the acquisitions budget while still providing our patrons with access to needed materials.

BRIGHAM YOUNG UNIVERSITY

BYU is primarily an undergraduate institution with selected PhD and master's programs. The Harold B. Lee Library, which is the library for all of campus except the law school, has an operating materials budget of $10 million. As

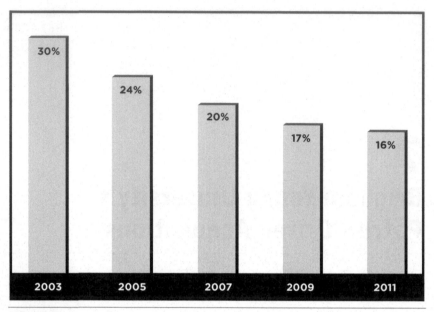

FIGURE 7.1
The percent of the library's collection that circulates in a given year
(of materials that are in circulating collections).

with most academic libraries, the majority of this budget is allocated toward continuing subscriptions to academic journals and databases. Over the years, the pressure to maintain these continuations has eaten away at our monograph budget and continues to be a major issue as we seek more effective ways of providing the best information resources for our users.

BYU started using patron-driven models based on two realities. One is the continuing pressure on material budgets. We have basically maintained a flat budget for the last six years and have made serious adjustments to our purchasing priorities. The second reality is the declining use of our print monograph collection, a trend mirrored around the country. As a percent of the total circulating collection (2.4 million), use has declined from 30 percent to 16 percent in the last decade (figure 7.1).

In 2009 we completed a retrospective ten-year analysis comparing our monograph acquisitions to their circulation activity. The findings of this analysis were helpful as we examined our purchasing patterns. A book purchased in 1999 had a 50 percent chance of circulating in ten years. Put another way, of all books purchased in 1999 (55,490) only 50 percent had circulated by 2009. Only 34 percent of books purchased in 2008 had circulated by the end of 2009. Even after allowing for ten years, half of our books are not used. Perhaps a better model for acquisitions was needed.

There is another dynamic that is changing the way we look at our collections. Collection development has been transformed by the introduction of the network and ubiquitous computing to the academic library world. Whereas librarians previously worked from set criteria like authoritative bibliographies to build isolated static collections, we now have opportunities to share collections, turn access on or off at will, and decide whether we should own or just provide access to content.

Although there are many ways to measure PDA's effectiveness, we began to evaluate the success of our various models in 2011 using a cost-per-use (CPU) metric. In that study we measured the use, cost, and CPU of each of our PDA models and found that, overall, using PDA models was a much more cost-effective way of acquiring library resources than the traditional just-in-case models.[1]

So it is natural that, as we continue to expand these programs, we wanted to have a better sense of their long-term success. Were the initial uses of PDA materials just that? Or was there an indication that the user-driven model is successful in predicting future demand as compared to the more traditional form of just-in-case collection building? This chapter revisits the previous study and uses that data to extend the time line and track these purchases over time to determine if the initial success of the various PDA models has been sustained.

BYU'S PDA MODELS

BYU employs five PDA models to acquire monographs: faculty-expedited orders, ILL requests, suggest-a-book online requests, multiple holds trigger, and e-books. A faculty-expedited order is simply the timely acquisition of a faculty request without subject librarian mediation. Faculty can initiate a request via a link on the library web page. The library seeks to order, process, and deliver this book within ten working days. Since these acquisitions support the curriculum and research needs of the university, the books are charged to the appropriate subject librarian's materials budget.

Suggest-a-book requests are also initiated through a link on the library web page. Such a request differs from a faculty-expedited book order in that a subject librarian mediates it. The acquisitions department collects the suggestions and forwards them to the appropriate librarian. If the librarian decides to purchase, the books are charged to his or her collection budget. This is a patron-driven process but there is no rush order or patron notification upon receipt.

Too-new-to-borrow ILL requests are another purchasing method that fits the PDA model. Often, libraries are reluctant to loan newly published monographs. ILLiad requests for items in that category, and that fit other predetermined criteria, are rush ordered and paid for through a budget designated for this purpose. At BYU, we limit these orders by language (English) and price ($50 threshold for student requested nonfiction; $80 for all staff and faculty requests).

Holds placed on a book are reliable indicators of demand for that book. When patrons place multiple holds on items, BYU will often purchase multiple copies. This practice is librarian-mediated after a threshold of three holds per copy has been reached. If the librarian decides to proceed, additional copies are rush ordered and, upon receipt, checked out to the next patron in the holds queue. These books are funded by a designated budget created for this purpose. These tend to be popular literature titles.

The electronic e-book PDA model is by far our largest patron-driven endeavor. A pilot was initiated in 2009, and we have continued to expand its scope. PDA for e-books was introduced as a volunteer program wherein selectors were allocated funds outside their traditional budgets. Participation has increased each year, and in 2014 all purchases will be integrated back into individual budgets so that all PDA e-book purchases will be funded entirely through selectors' traditional budgets. This model allows us to load thousands of bibliographic records into our catalog that meet the academic profile established with our book vendors. This effort is coordinated through the library's acquisition unit, the book agent, and a third-party e-book vendor. The library's approval profile is used to govern what records are placed in the catalog. Once loaded into the catalog, a purchase is triggered when a predetermined number of pages are viewed in conjunction with time spent in the book per use. BYU is not charged until these limits are reached for any individual book. Users view all these titles as part of the library collection. They are not aware of the purchasing process, and the process is largely seamless to the patrons.

METHODOLOGY

For this study, we compared the cost, circulation or use, and the cost-per-use of titles in each of the print and electronic PDA models. For print PDA, we examined the titles that were either purchased or selected during fall semester 2009. We used reports from our Integrated Library System (ILS) to generate the title list and the cost of the individual books. To measure the use of each item, we counted each checkout and in-house use. The statistics showed us the monthly uses, allowing us to measure the use for a full twenty-six months from the time a book was available to our patrons. CPU was calculated by dividing the total price of the items by the total number of uses they had. The mean and median were calculated from the CPU results. These statistics were then compared to a sample of traditionally purchased titles that were acquired during the same period of time.

TABLE 7.1

Summary of random samples.

	Total purchased (*n*)	Total cost ($)	Mean (median) cost ($)
Print			
Faculty-expedited	38	1,568.19	41.27 (32.50)
Suggest-a-book	33	1,215.03	36.82 (24.56)
Interlibrary loan	55	1,577.11	28.67 (21.60)
Holds queue	35	531.43	15.18 (16.19)
Traditional	217	8,199.54	37.79 (27.23)
Electronic			
Patron-driven	324	24,828.92	76.63 (74.95)
Traditional	163	17,033.55	104.50 (90.00)

The title list used in our current study was slightly different than the list used in the previous study. A few print titles have been lost since the previous study and were therefore deleted from the current study. Several other titles that had erroneously been included in the original analysis were identified and removed from the new study. Table 7.1 includes statistics describing the various samples used for this study.

For electronic PDA, we measured the use of titles that were triggered and purchased during our PDA pilot. Our partners for the pilot were YBP Library Services (YBP) and ebrary and ran during the months of December 2009 through July 2010. For our study, we gathered the COUNTER statistics and the e-book cost from the vendor's reports and website. As with the print measurements, the CPU was calculated by dividing the total cost of the books by the total number of uses. These statistics were then compared to a sample of traditionally acquired e-books selected during the same period of time.

In comparing our previous analysis with the current usage and CPU of e-books, we found that there were minor inconsistencies in the way our vendor made adjustments to their usage statistics. Another challenge that surfaced was that ebrary's COUNTER statistics are full-text section requests, known as COUNTER report #2, whereas electronic book library (EBL) numbers are for full-text title requests, known as COUNTER report #1. Therefore the EBL statistics are slightly lower compared to the ebrary materials. Most of the titles used in this study were ebrary but we did have a few EBL titles in the traditionally acquired sample. There is no way for us to adjust those numbers so we decided to keep the titles despite the inconsistencies on the basis that there are so few of them that the difference in the final analysis would be negligible.

Because of the problems described above, we recalculated the usage from the previous study using the newer methodology so that accurate comparisons could be made. This changed the numbers from what was previously reported but the conclusions and findings remain unchanged.

RESULTS

Print Patron-Driven Acquisitions

On a strictly CPU analysis, PDA models are the clear winner. Table 7.2 shows the circulation and CPU data of each of the five BYU print PDA models. The models are listed in order of least to most effective, with faculty-expedited orders as the least effective model followed by suggest-a-book orders and interlibrary loan orders. The most cost-efficient model is the holds queue order. Our original analysis with four months of data indicated that the least effective PDA model had a 51.7 percent lower CPU than the traditional model. After twenty-six months of use, the least effective PDA model still had a 34.7 percent lower CPU on average than the traditional model and received an average of 168.8 percent more uses. The most effective PDA model had, on average, a 93.1 percent lower CPU after four months and a 95.4 percent lower CPU after twenty-six months and received 871.9 percent more uses on average than the traditional model.

TABLE 7.2

Cost and circulation data for print acquisitions.

	Total circulations		Mean (median) circulations		Mean (median*) cost-per-use ($)	
	4 months	*26 months*	*4 months*	*26 months*	*4 months*	*26 months*
Faculty-expedited	59	206	1.6 (1.0)	5.4 (1.0)	26.58 (22.69)	7.61 (20.00)
Suggest-a-book	47	221	1.4 (1.0)	6.7 (3.0)	25.85 (12.50)	5.5 (7.45)
Interlibrary loan	135	430	2.5 (2.0)	7.8 (3.0)	11.68 (12.88)	3.67 (6.24)
Holds queue	140	978	4.0 (4.0)	27.9 (30.0)	3.80 (3.60)	0.54 (0.55)
Traditional	149	703	0.7 (0.0)	3.2 (1.0)	55.03 (19.42)	11.66 (13.00)

*For titles that had use

These statistics also show that findings from the previous study are corroborated and the longer books are available to patrons, the CPU generally decreases. This holds true for both PDA and traditionally acquired books. The change over time of the average CPU of the various print PDA models can be seen in the slope graph shown in figure 7.2. The most striking portion of this graph is the traditional acquisition model. The average CPU of traditionally acquired materials drops at a significantly faster rate than the PDA materials. This dramatic slope is exaggerated by the low initial use of traditionally acquired materials. The increased usage of traditionally acquired materials over longer periods of time explains why the average CPU for the least effective PDA model went from 51.7 percent lower to only 34.7 percent lower than traditional models.

When comparing acquisition models, the comparison of the number of titles that received use to the number of titles without any use is an interesting exercise. Almost all PDA titles had use, and their use increased over time. The suggest-a-book model had a higher number of items that did not circulate, which shows the library's policy to not notify the patron of the purchase could be a problem and suggests a need for process improvement. Even with this oversight, the suggest-a-book model only yielded 15.2 percent of titles without use while 44.7 percent of traditionally acquired materials received no use. With the other PDA models, there was only one book that did not get a use. So not only are there more uses for PDA-acquired materials, but a much higher percentage of these materials get used. (See table 7.3.)

TABLE 7.3
Comparison of print circulation across purchasing models.

	Percent (%) of titles with no circulation (*n*)	
	4 months	*26 months*
Faculty-expedited	5.3 (2)	2.6 (1)
Suggest-a-book	42.4 (14)	15.2 (5)
Interlibrary loan	1.8 (1)	0.0 (0)
Holds queue	5.7 (2)	0.0 (0)
Traditional	67.7 (147)	44.7 (97)

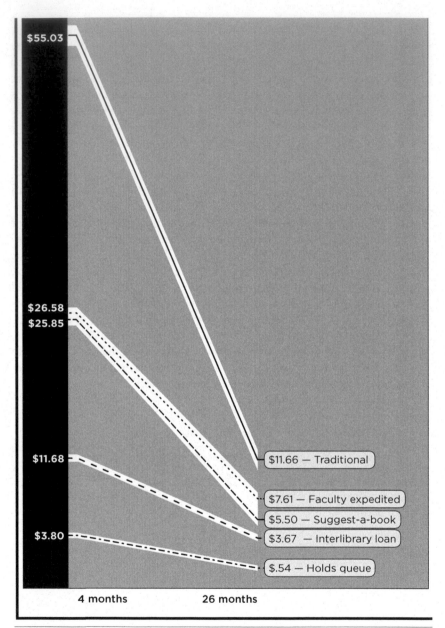

$55.03

$26.58
$25.85

$11.68

$11.66 — Traditional

$7.61 — Faculty expedited
$5.50 — Suggest-a-book
$3.80

$3.67 — Interlibrary loan
$.54 — Holds queue

4 months   26 months

FIGURE 7.2

Slope graph comparing mean cost-per-use of 4 months of data to 26 months of data for various print acquisition models.

ELECTRONIC PATRON-DRIVEN ACQUISITIONS

Electronic purchases show similar trends to what we saw with print acquisition models. As shown in table 7.4, PDA models were 94.4 percent cheaper on average and received 1,301.1 percent more uses on average than the traditional model. All PDA materials received at least eleven uses, so comparing use or nonuse of PDA titles is not as meaningful for electronic materials. However, there were a fair number of them that received no use after the month in which a purchase was triggered. To compare, 66.9 percent of traditionally acquired electronic content received no use at all while 29.9 percent of patron-driven acquired materials received no use after the month the purchase was triggered. (See table 7.5.) Curiously, some titles received significant early use, and then no more uses during the period of this study. One title received 991 COUNTER uses in one month and then no uses for the following twenty-five months.

TABLE 7.4

Cost and use data for electronic acquisitions.

	Total use[a]		Mean (median) use[a]		Mean (median[b]) cost-per-use ($)	
	4 months	*26 months*	*4 months*	*26 months*	*4 months*	*26 months*
Patron-driven	35,148	77,562	108.5 (54.0)	239.4 (86.5)	0.70 (1.09)	0.32 (0.71)
Traditional	165	2,999	1.0 (0.0)	18.4 (0.0)	103.23 (7.50)	5.68 (6.80)

a. COUNTER-compliant uses.
b. For titles that had use.

TABLE 7.5

Comparison of electronic uses across purchasing models.

	Percent (%) of titles with no use[a, b] (*n*)	
	4 months	*26 months*
Patron-driven	61.1 (198)	29.9 (97)
Traditional	89.0 (145)	66.9 (109)

a. COUNTER-compliant uses.
b. For patron-driven, we looked at titles that received no use after the month the purchase was triggered.

DISCUSSION

Patron-driven acquisition models, when compared to traditional acquisition methods, lead the way in both use and cost-effectiveness. This seems to suggest that librarians should do more to solicit patron feedback and suggestions regarding how collections are built. The more patron-driven outlets are available for purchasing, the more relevant our collections will become. Of course, this must be carefully balanced with an academic library's mission to archive and preserve information for future generations. Patron-driven cannot be the only purchasing mechanism available to a library or we risk losing our long-term research relevance.

An interesting fact uncovered by this study is that for all but the faculty-expedited orders, the PDA-acquired titles were all much cheaper, on average, than the traditionally purchased materials. This is likely due to several factors. For one, we place restraints on the type and cost of materials for the too-new-to-borrow interlibrary loan books. The remaining print acquisition models, however, have no such restraints. This tends to direct our PDA purchases to less expensive books than those librarians buy for their collections.

In an effort to better support patrons and their needs, we have recently undertaken a project to consolidate all of our various options for requesting materials. For example, in our catalog, patrons can place a hold on items that have been checked out for less than three weeks, place a recall on items that have been checked out for longer than three weeks, or request an item through interlibrary loan. Each of these is a separate function and requires extensive library knowledge to successfully navigate the system to request materials. Rather than make patrons learn the intricacies of how the library operates, we hope to replace these various options with one button: "Get this item."

This presents a powerful opportunity for us to completely overhaul the way we purchase materials in our library. Many vendors are now offering a print PDA model. Combining this print PDA with the "Get this item" button, which would obscure the fact that we have not yet purchased the item for the patron, has the potential of overturning the way we purchase materials for the library. It could supplement, or completely replace, our traditional approval purchasing program. This new program would guarantee that every item requested by patrons is used at least once, unlike the current situation shown in table 7.2.

Historically, only 50 percent of the circulating materials we purchase are used within ten years. If they do not circulate in the first ten years of being available, the odds of them ever circulating drops precipitously. Contrast this to the 100 percent usage of the e-book PDA model and you have a strong case for change. The e-book model also offers 24/7 access and short turn-around times for users, which is a key factor in the higher use levels of these purchases. This suggests that we have been inefficiently allocating some of our collection resources for a very long period of time. We spend approximately $1.7 annually on monographs, meaning about $850,000 worth of materials are never used. That is money spent annually on resources that could perhaps be reallocated for more targeted purchases to meet the needs of our students and researchers.

Additionally, some librarians express the concern that PDA removes them from the selection process. This is simply not true. Or, at least, it is no more true than the traditional approval model already has removed them from the process. PDA purchases allow librarians to set up a profile of the types of materials they would like to make available to users. This profile can exactly mirror the existing approval profile used for current approval purchases. Librarians can manipulate, manage, and revise their profiles for PDA just as they always have, the sole difference being that libraries do not own any of the materials until a PDA purchase is triggered. Looking at it this way, there seems to be little reason for continuing with traditional approval programs as currently constituted. There is always some value in having materials available just in case, but it is to our economic benefit to keep that just-in-case inventory as marginal as possible.

Another issue that libraries must face with electronic PDA models is the period of time untriggered records are left in the catalog. At BYU we have opted to leave records in the catalog indefinitely. This actually resembles a virtual just-in-case collecting model discussed earlier. However, this one still links expenditures to demand. Of course, increasing the number of just-in-case records in the catalog certainly raises the potential for increased expenditures over longer periods of time.

The allocation of usage between PDA and traditionally acquired materials is also a point of interest. Traditionally acquired materials are less likely to circulate. However, even when circulated, on average they received a lot fewer circulations than PDA materials. A PDA item is not only more likely to circulate; it is more likely to circulate a lot.

Finally, all of the evaluated purchasing models are trending to a lower CPU and show few signs of asymptotically trailing off anytime soon (see figure 7.2). This indicates that further, even longer-term study is warranted before anything definitive can be said about the economics surrounding PDA compared to traditionally acquired materials. Out of the gate, there is plenty of evidence to suggest that PDA should be used by libraries more than they are right now. Over the first few years, PDA models are more cost-effective, but traditionally acquired materials make up ground over longer periods of time. How much ground is made up over longer periods of time should be studied more carefully, thus helping us determine the appropriate mix of PDA and traditional acquisitions.

CONCLUSION

BYU has used several different patron-driven acquisition models for a number of years. With the advent of PDA for e-books, we have engaged in studies to determine the cost benefit of these models. This study followed in the steps of an initial four-month look at cost and use of the library's PDA models. It found that the favorable CPU numbers of the first study, in comparison to traditional collecting models, continued over a 26-month period. PDA purchases were essentially guaranteed at least one use and tended to have more significant use over time, confirming the assertion that initial demand is a predictor of future use.

The CPU of traditionally purchased titles did decline over the 26-month period but did not approach the efficiencies of the other models as the majority of items had still not been used. A longer time frame is needed to determine the long-term CPU of the traditional model in relation to the PDA purchases. However, given our own internal studies that show a ten-year span is needed to reach 50-percent circulation, it is not anticipated that the traditional group will reach the patron-driven one in cost efficiencies.

We propose an expanding profile for patron-driven acquisitions as a better use of collection funds to support a more relevant collection. However, for the foreseeable future, we will need to find the proper balance between these and traditional models for a number of reasons. Until all publishing is digital and the concept of out of print is obsolete, we will continue to pursue this balance.

NOTE

1. Rebecca Schroeder, "When Patrons Call the Shots: Patron-Driven Acquisition at Brigham Young University," *Collection Building* 31, no. 1 (2012): 11–14.

MAURA VALENTINO

8
Patron-Driven Digital Collection Development in Archives

DIGITAL COLLECTION DEVELOPMENT IN ARCHIVES DIFFERS from traditional collection development in that it does not involve the acquisition of a new item but is based on a procedure performed on items already existing in the library collection. Librarians have begun to study how patron-driven development of collections can reduce costs while at the same time adding meaningful objects to the collection. In support of these efforts, many libraries have begun to use a just-in-time model of collection development rather than a just-in-case model. This chapter will examine a case of digital patron-driven collection development and discuss its advantages.

BACKGROUND

The Special Collections and Archives Research Center (SCARC) at Oregon State University (OSU) maintains many digital collections. One of these collections, the Best of the OSU Archives collection, consists of a large number of historical photographs related to the history of OSU. As with many digital collections, the collection was in use for some time before efforts were made to digitize the collection. Before digitization, if a patron wanted a copy of a particular image, a photographic negative was created from that image and then a print copy was made for the patron. Once a photographic image had been requested and the negative made, the same negative was used if another patron requested the same image. When scanners became available, images were scanned and stored as tagged image file format (TIFF) files. From these files an image was printed for the patron or the file was transmitted to the patron in electronic form.

When it was decided SCARC would create an online version of the collection, a determination had to be made with regard to which objects in the collection to digitize. Upon analysis of activity related to the collection it became apparent that the same images were often requested multiple times. These images were selected for inclusion in the digital collection. Other images were selected by SCARC staff members for inclusion in order to ensure that the digital collection would be representative of the image collection as a whole. In this way an analysis of patron use, combined with determinations made by staff members, determined which objects were added to the digital collection.

SCARC's Gerald W. Williams collection was also developed through the use of patron-driven collection methodologies. This collection is comprised of a wide variety of images related to the history of the state of Oregon. When it was determined that this collection should be digitized, SCARC relied on a particular patron to develop the collection. This patron, Oregon Public Broadcasting, selects images from the collection for use on the television series *Oregon Experience* or for another of their television programs. Once a representative from Oregon Public Broadcasting selects an image for use, Oregon Public Broadcasting scans the image using standards determined by SCARC. The image is then included in the digital collection. In this way a particular patron determines which objects are added to the digital collection. By allowing patrons to assist in determining which objects should be added to their digital collections, SCARC has realized savings in cost and other resources while developing two of the most widely accessed digital collections maintained by OSU Libraries and Press (OSULP).

Allowing patrons to influence purchasing decisions is not a new concept. The "just-in-case" model of collection development in which collection librarians use knowledge of their patrons to choose materials has several shortcomings, among which are funds used to obtain materials that never circulate (Tanner 2011, 1). Although the costs associated with digitizing an object and adding it to a digital collection differ from those related to a traditional purchase, digital collections are subject to cost and resource limitations as well. In both cases, inefficient use of resources may result if objects are added to a collection but never accessed by patrons.

While librarians in both public and academic settings see the value of allowing patrons to choose which objects are added to their collections, they also see disadvantages to collection development efforts that are solely patron-driven. For example, patrons are typically only interested in their own needs, whereas librarians have the needs of all of their patrons in mind when making collection development decisions. One solution to this problem is to employ a combined approach balancing traditional and patron-driven collection development as was done in the case of SCARC's Best of the OSU Archives collection. In the case of this collection, too narrow a focus was avoided by choosing images that were requested by multiple patrons and by including images selected by SCARC staff members to ensure the collection would be representative and meet the needs of a diverse group of patrons.

Other potential difficulties with patron-driven collection development efforts have also been encountered. For example, a patron may request an item be purchased and added to the collection only to determine that it is not useful once the item has been obtained (Tyler 2011, 1). This leads to wasted funds and other resources. However, this problem is mitigated in many digital collections where the patron will have already viewed the image or object in its entirety in person. Another potential issue with patron-driven collection development is that patrons have no knowledge of the library's budgetary and other resource-related concerns and therefore may not reflect these realities in their selections (Reynolds et al. 2010, 246). Once again, by their nature digital collections help to mitigate this problem. For example, in many cases when a patron requests a copy of an image, the patron is charged a fee to cover the production of the copy they require. So, careful management of funds is built into this scenario. As can be seen, careful crafting of patron-driven collection development efforts, combined with some of the advantages inherent in digital collections themselves, can enable libraries to reap many of the benefits of patron-driven collection methodologies while mitigating some of their disadvantages.

COLLECTION PERFORMANCE VS. COST

Several researchers have tried to quantify the costs of creating a digital collection. Charles Hamaker laments the lack of a formula for making traditional collection development decisions, but Michael Boock and May Chau have created just such a model for use in digital collection development decisions. David Tyler also offers ideas on reducing costs.

Boock and Chau use the theory of value engineering to provide a structured methodology for choosing collections for digitization. The key measure in their methodology is the equation Value (of a collection) = Performance/

Cost. They define performance as significance to internal and external stakeholders, uniqueness, and resulting exposure. Based on this type of analysis, the potential performance of a patron-driven digital collection is high. The following discussion will examine how the SCARC collections described earlier fare when subjected to this type of evaluation criteria.

SIGNIFICANCE FOR INTERNAL STAKEHOLDERS

First let us examine the SCARC collections' significance for internal stakeholders. According to Boock and Chau, a collection receives the highest score for significance if it provides significant information related to the institution's area of focus and supports the university's strategic plan. The SCARC collections support both the OSU mission statement as well as the OSULP's mission statement. In addition, the collections also support the mission statement of SCARC. Let us examine each of the areas in turn. See appendix 8 for the text of the three mission statements.

First, let us consider the ways in which OSU's patron-driven collections support the university's mission statement. The Oregon State University mission statement calls for student engagement and for providing research opportunities. By creating a patron-chosen collection of historical photographs and by making these photographs available to patrons online, it is hoped that students will use the objects in the collection as primary research materials. It is also believed that the collection, consisting as it does of compelling, interesting, and entertaining images related to the university, will encourage student engagement. As the included objects were selected by patrons, the photographs have a high "fun" factor in many cases. For example, figure 8.1 provides an interesting look at the clothing worn by women basketball players in 1903. Figure 8.2 provides another example of such a photograph contained within the collection and one that is likely to provoke the question, "Why did the librarians wear so much fur in the 1920s?" On a more serious note, such photographs, even if not used in connection with scholarly research, provide students with exposure to the types of collections maintained by SCARC and may provide an introduction to SCARC, thus promoting the use of SCARC's collections in future research. As students spend increasing amounts of time online, exposure to SCARC's patron-driven digital collections can encourage students to seek out other online resources hosted by OSU and by other organizations which may assist them in their research endeavors.

Next let us consider how OSU's patron-driven collections help OSULP to meet the goals set forth in its mission statement. OSULP's mission includes building gateways to unique resources. These two collections meet that goal as they are unique collections. Another key aspect of the OSULP mission is to engage with the community at large. As members of the community at

FIGURE 8.1
Oregon Agricultural College (now OSU) women's basketball team, 1903.

FIGURE 8.2
Library staff on north steps of library circa 1920–1929.

large use the images in the collections and assist in selecting which images are included in the collections, both collections support the goal of encouraging engagement between the community and OSULP.

Last, let us consider how the collections support the mission statement of SCARC itself. As determined by its mission statement, one of SCARC's defined collection areas is the history of OSU. Comprised as it is of photographs related to the history of the university, the Best of the OSU Archives collection clearly supports SCARC's mission to create collections related to the history of OSU. In addition, the mission statement directs SCARC to provide online access to and discovery of its collections. Pursuant to this directive, both collections may be accessed online. Online availability improves discovery, particularly when compared to collections that are accessible only through in-person visits. In fact, digital collections generally empower discovery by eliminating or reducing the need for in-person visits to special collections and archives facilities to discover and access the collections. Digital collections also generally preserve and disseminate knowledge, which is another goal stated in the SCARC mission statement. In the case of the SCARC collections, historical photographs are preserved when they are scanned to a persistent electronic format (TIFF), and they are disseminated when they are placed online for easy patron access. Another goal mentioned in the SCARC mission statement is to provide "responsive, personable and expert public service." By having images that were requested many times and presumably would continue to be requested already available online, staff time can be spent serving patrons in other ways. Finally, by adding representative images to the collection based on the expertise of staff members, SCARC has improved the relevance and depth of the collection, which should lead to improved discovery of the collection as a whole.

SIGNIFICANCE FOR OUTSIDE STAKEHOLDERS

Boock and Chau also submit that a digital collection should be of interest to outside stakeholders. An examination of user access statistics reveals that the Best of OSU Archives digital collection has been accessed by numerous users not directly connected with the university from locations as diverse as Lisbon, Honolulu, Nanjing, Seattle, and Berlin. Boock and Chau also rate a collection's usefulness for outside stakeholders by analyzing the collection's historical interest to researchers. Given the high level of user access to the collections, the SCARC patron-driven digital collections also score high in this regard. Additionally, the objects in the Gerald W. Williams collection were selected by outside researchers, thus providing an additional confirmation of their interest to research professionals.

COLLECTION UNIQUENESS

Boock and Chau also describe uniqueness as "content [that] is held uniquely by the institution and extremely unlikely to be digitized by another institution." The Best of OSU Archives collection focuses on materials directly related to OSU, and these materials are not included in the digital collections of other institutions, nor are they likely to be. Similarly, the Gerald W. Williams collection contains objects that are not represented in the digital collections of other institutions. While individual objects contained within the two collections may be held in the collections of other individuals or institutions, the collections are generally unique.

COLLECTION EXPOSURE

The last part of Boock and Chau's significance variable is the exposure that results from the existence of the digital collection. The continued popularity of both collections infers exposure to the university, OSULP, and SCARC. While user statistics collected based on website traffic have limitations, one can clearly see that the two patron-driven collections discussed here are consistently the most used over time. The monthly visits for the five most accessed OSU digital collections have been averaged over the past two years, and as seen in figure 8.3, the two patron-driven collections are the most popular. However, it cannot be determined from these statistics alone why an

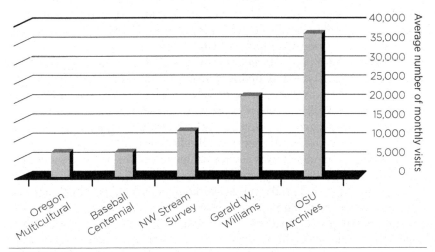

FIGURE 8.3
Five most popular collections.

object is being accessed. For example, is a patron accessing the collection for serious research purposes or are they just indulging a curiosity? Institutions needing such information might consider conducting a user survey to help determine why certain objects in the collection are accessed and for what purpose. In addition, the presence of photographs from the Gerald W. Williams collection in programming presented by Oregon Public Broadcasting creates a synergistic effect. Individuals who are exposed to the collection's images during a television program may seek out the source of the images. In this way exposure of the collection may be increased.

COST

The costs associated with the development of these patron-driven digital collections were very low. The required software and other technical infrastructure for the digital collections were already deployed, and many of the ongoing costs of this infrastructure were unaffected by the addition of these two collections. Costs were also reduced due to the fact that the copyrights to the photos in the collection were owned by OSU. This eliminated the need for costly and time-consuming research relating to copyright issues, often a concern when creating digital collections of photographic objects.

In 2006, Tanner in his "Handbook on Cost Reduction in Digitisation" posits that libraries need to squeeze every last drop of value from their available resources in order to remain viable in the current cost-cutting environment (7). Reusing digital files from already scanned photographs to create a digital collection, as was done in the case of the Best of OSU Archives collection, provides an example of efficient use of limited resources. Tyler notes, "The rule for cost reduction is to look at every stage that requires human intervention and either remove it, reduce it or make it as efficient as possible." To this end he suggests dividing digitization efforts into separate activities and training the lowest-paid worker possible to complete each task. In the case of the Gerald W. Williams collection, patrons from Oregon Public Broadcasting selected the images for inclusion in the collection, reducing demands on library staff resources. In the case of both collections, the selection of objects and scanning of the objects was already complete and the necessary metadata already existed. Therefore, the manipulation of existing files and the repurposing of metadata required a simple workflow that could be assigned to student employees, reducing personnel costs and freeing library staff to focus on other initiatives. In conclusion, the creation of digital collections based on items that are already in digital form due to earlier patron requests is typically cost-efficient. Institutions that currently maintain no digital collections but have been digitizing items for individual patrons might consider these objects as the basis for their first, cost-effective digital collection development efforts.

ISSUES OF POPULARITY

One consideration in traditional collection development is that a popular book may circulate so many times that it deteriorates and must be weeded from the collection or replaced. At the University of Oklahoma Libraries conference in 1991, Charles Hamaker discussed this issue at length yet failed to come up with an algorithm to determine earlier in the life cycle of a particular title if additional copies should be purchased. With digital collections, this is not an issue. A digital item does not deteriorate based on the number of people who access the object. In fact, a digital repository following best practices will always keep a preservation copy of the object that is not accessed by the public. Therefore, with proper digital preservation, deterioration of the object from repeated access is not an issue. Hamaker also worried that new models of collection development and patron access would not necessarily meet patron demands. As has been discussed, using a patron-driven collection development model for digital collections leads to collections that meet the patron's needs as demonstrated by the high rate of patron access to such collections as discussed above.

Another issue often encountered in collection development relates to an object's cost versus the number of times the object is accessed. Brian Adams and Bob Noel argue that if an inexpensive book only circulates a few times, it was still worth the purchase, but a more expensive book would have to circulate many times to justify its cost. While costs to initially digitize an object may vary based upon its size, condition, and other factors, once digitized any activities relating to objects in a digital collection share a similar cost per item, reducing the complexity of this type of analysis.

CUSTOMER SERVICE AND COLLECTION DEVELOPMENT

Patron-driven digital collections can help to improve customer service. In discussing a customer service project in the United Kingdom, Elizabeth Smith compresses several business-related ideas on customer service and relates them to the activities of institutional archives. Her conclusion is that customer service is giving the customer what they want as they determine they want it. In the traditional just-in-case collection development model a librarian endeavors to give patrons what the librarian perceives they may want. With patron-driven digital collection development as used in developing the Best of the OSU Archives and Gerald W. Williams collections, patrons are given easier access to objects they have already requested. This provides a greater degree of certainty that the patron's customer service needs, as defined by Smith, will be met.

LIMITATIONS OF PATRON-DRIVEN DIGITAL COLLECTION DEVELOPMENT

A patron-driven collection may not have the focus of a librarian- or archivist-selected collection. The focus may be wider or the selection so diverse as to not have a focus at all. However, it is important to consider that additional digital collections can be created from the underlying objects that form a patron-driven collection. For example, in the case of the Best of the OSU Archives collection a group of lantern slides used for educational purposes in the 1930s had been added to the collection. While these are interesting images worthy of preservation and inclusion in a collection, they are somewhat out of place in a collection focused on historical photographs. However, it was a simple undertaking to include these objects in a separate dedicated collection focused on the lantern slides themselves. Such collections can be created as needed in most patron-driven digital collection scenarios.

Including objects that have been requested by more than one patron in a digital collection for additional online access is a strategy that is appropriate for many collections. However, some institutions may wish to control which objects are available for online dissemination for a variety of reasons including financial, copyright, technical, organizational, or other concerns. While allowing various levels of access can be controlled with technology, these issues must be addressed as part of the collection development process by the affected stakeholders.

Another potential pitfall encountered in the development of digital collections relates to the fact that users of a digital collection may not realize that the collection is only part of a larger digital or physical collection. This is a potential limitation of any digital collection used as a representation of a physical collection. Often users access only an individual object in a collection found using an online search engine. While viewing such an object the user may be unaware of the extent of the digital or physical collection to which the object belongs. Effective user interface design and metadata can help to mitigate this problem. For example, the entire physical collection upon which the Best of the OSU Archives digital collection is based consists of over 600,000 images. Some of these are contained on glass negatives or lantern slides which are fragile and take great care to digitize. Due to factors such as these and the large size of the collection it will be some time before all of the objects in the physical collection can be represented in the digital collection. In the interim, it is hoped that by providing access to the most interesting objects through the digital collection, patrons will be encouraged to explore the physical collection in greater depth.

CONCLUSION

While digital collection development is a new and evolving undertaking for many institutions, the use of patron-driven, just-in-time collection development is proving effective in many scenarios. While studies of such efforts are still in their infancy, the examples provided by OSULP's Best of the OSU Archives and Gerald W. Williams collections demonstrate how such a methodology can help to develop collections that successfully meet the needs of library patrons while conserving the hosting institution's time, funds, and other valuable resources. These advantages, combined with the high collection utilization evident in these projects, should encourage librarians to consider using such methodologies as they develop, implement, and improve their digital collections today and in the future.

REFERENCES

Adams, Brian, and Bob Noel. 2008. "Circulation Statistics in the Evaluation of Collection Development." *Collection Building* 27 (2): 71–73.

Boock, Michael, and May Chau. 2007. "The Use of Value Engineering in the Evaluation and Selection of Digitization Projects." *Evidence Based Library and Information Practice* 2 (3): 76–86.

Hamaker, Charles. 1991. "Some Measures of Cost Effectiveness in Library Collections." *Journal of Library Administration* 16 (3): 57–69.

Reynolds, Leslie, J. Carmelita., C. Pickett, Wyona Vanduinkerken, Jane Smith, Jeanne Harrell, and Sandra Tucker. 2010. "User-Driven Acquisitions: Allowing Patron Requests to Drive Collection Development in an Academic Library." *Collection Management* 35 (3–4): 244–54.

Smith, Elizabeth. 2003. "Customer Focus and Marketing in Archive Service Delivery: Theory and Practice." *Journal of the Society of Archivists* 24 (1): 35–53.

Tanner, Simon. 2006. "Handbook on Cost Reduction in Digitisation," Minerva Project, www.minervaeurope.org/publications/CostReductioninDigitisation_v1_0610.pdf, p. 14.

Tyler, David C. 2011. "Patron-driven Purchase on Demand Programs for Printed Books and Similar Materials: A Chronological Review and Summary of Findings." Library Philosophy and Practice, www.webpages.uidaho.edu/~mbolin/tyler.htm.

APPENDIX 8
Mission Statements

Mission Statement of SCARC

The OSU Libraries Special Collections and Archives Research Center (SCARC) stimulates and enriches the research and teaching endeavors of Oregon State University through primary sources. As part of the University's land grant mission, SCARC makes these resources available to the OSU community, Oregonians, and the larger community of scholars and independent researchers. As the repository for and steward of the Libraries' rare and unique materials, we build distinctive and unique collections in our signature areas: natural resources, the history of science, university history, and Oregon's multicultural communities. These collections encompass manuscripts, archives, rare books, oral histories, photographs, ephemera, audio/visual materials, electronic and born digital records.

To achieve this mission, the Special Collections and Archives Research Center:

- Provides unique opportunities for teaching and learning
- Facilitates discovery through online access to SCARC collections
- Provides responsive, personable, and expert public service
- Assists communities in collecting, managing, preserving, and making their histories accessible
- Promotes access to and preservation of SCARC collections by collaborating within the OSU Libraries, the University, and regional primary resource communities
- Engages high achieving students through experiential learning opportunities

The Mission Statement of OSU Libraries and Press (OSULP) reads as follows:

> The OSU Libraries and Press cultivate superior scholarship and creativity, empower discovery, and preserve and disseminate knowledge. We develop user-focused services, share our expertise through teaching and research, and build gateways to unique resources to further the growth of the University, the people of Oregon, and the global scholarly community. We advance OSU's land grant mission by contributing to learner success, scholarly excellence, and community engagement.

Mission Statement of Oregon State University

As a land grant institution committed to teaching, research, and outreach and engagement, Oregon State University promotes economic, social, cultural and environmental progress for the people of Oregon, the nation and the world. This mission is achieved by producing graduates competitive in the global economy, supporting a continuous search for new knowledge and solutions, and maintaining a rigorous focus on academic excellence, particularly in the three Signature Areas: Advancing the Science of Sustainable Earth Ecosystems; Improving Human Health and Wellness; and Promoting Economic Growth and Social Progress.

JEANNE HARRELL, CARMELITA
PICKETT, SIMONA TABACARU,
JEANNETTE HO, ANA UGAZ,
AND NANCY BURFORD

9

PDA in a Multi-Library Setting

Challenges, Implementation, and Outcomes

BUDGET CONSTRAINTS ARE A CONSTANT CONCERN FOR ACA-demic and academic health sciences libraries attempting to provide access to critical scholarly resources in support of evolving curricula and user expectations. The Texas A&M University (TAMU) library system includes an academic library with four on-campus facilities (TAMU Libraries) and a medical library (Medical Sciences Library). These libraries have separate budgets and catalogs, but collaborate closely in collection development and use the same integrated library system (ILS), Voyager. In 2006, the TAMU Libraries began transforming their funding structure and incorporating measures to ensure the libraries' collaboration with their user community. This transformation included the elimination of over 200 individual subject-based fund accounts and the development of acquisitions programs with dedicated allocations to support a new initiative: "Suggest a purchase," a patron-driven acquisitions (PDA) model (vanDuinkerken et al. 2008). Expanding this print user-driven acquisitions model to align with current national e-book trends would include an evaluation of the existing acquisitions model with a close eye toward the e-book marketplace and approval plan services.

In 2010, the TAMU president requested that vice presidents and deans begin to plan for a $60-million reduction/reallocation (Ammerman 2010). This reduction translated to a $3.1-million reduction for the TAMU Libraries. Library administration determined that two-thirds of the budget cut for the libraries would be achieved by reducing the libraries' materials budget. As collections personnel began planning for a $2-million reduction, they took the opportunity to review existing e-book purchasing models with the idea of moving to a PDA e-book model. The library's previous acquisitions model for e-books would be reassessed to mitigate duplication and incorporate additional oversight. Since the budget reduction was inevitable and with no prospects of additional funding to expand the existing print PDA to e-books, the only alternative to support an e-book PDA program would include reallocating funds from existing e-book initiatives (Pickett, Tabacaru, and Harrell 2012). There were numerous factors that could make a success of the expansion of the existing PDA into e-books. These factors include the approval plan, which used the publishing industry with its ability to integrate e-books, partnerships between e-book aggregators and approval plan vendors, publishers' response to technological advances (mobile devices), and TAMU campus acceptance of digital content (Cook and Maciel 2010).

In preparation for the library's materials budget reduction, collections personnel began a careful review of the approval plan and existing e-book deals with aggregators and publishers. As a result of the review, the director of collection development transitioned the library from comprehensive e-book package arrangements with Elsevier, Springer, and Wiley to more title-by-title e-book purchasing. Some of these comprehensive deals were problematic, requiring additional acquisitions and technical services resources to verify titles and access in the local ILS and vendor platforms. The evaluation also yielded additional measures by which the library could mitigate further duplication and cost; 167 publishers available on the approval plan were modified for notification rather than automatic purchase of titles, while 30 publishers were blocked from the approval plan. Of the 167 publishers, 132 became notification-only publishers because no discount was given. This evaluation positioned the libraries for a successful e-book PDA pilot.

LITERATURE REVIEW

Academic libraries have implemented on-demand acquisitions programs since early 1990. Initially, these on-demand programs were introduced for print books when libraries started purchasing titles requested by patrons through interlibrary loan (ILL). In September 1990, Bertrand Library at Bucknell University was among the first libraries in United States to initiate an on-demand acquisition program based on patrons' ILL requests (Perdue and Van Fleet 1999). Such on-demand purchase programs are discussed in the library literature as variations of PDA programs. Several studies describe PDA programs based on ILL requests. Purdue University Library started its program in 2000 (Anderson et al. 2010). University of Nebraska-Lincoln Libraries implemented their program in 2003 (Tyler et al. 2010). University of Florida Libraries initiated a Books on Demand pilot program in 2006 (Carrico and Leonard 2011). Ohio State University Libraries started their program in 2008 (Hodges, Preston, and Hamilton 2010a), and University of Mississippi Libraries began a patron-initiated purchasing program in 2009 (Herrera and Greenwood 2011). TAMU Libraries have purchased monographs requested through interlibrary loan since the late 1990s, and by fiscal year 2007 the libraries adopted a "Suggest a Purchase" plan with funds specifically allocated for the purchase of monographs based exclusively on patron requests with little library staff prepurchase evaluation of materials (Reynolds et al. 2010).

The first PDA option for e-books was introduced by NetLibrary in 1998 (Hodges et al. 2010b; Walker 2012). PDA programs, also known as demand-driven acquisition (DDA) programs, grew rapidly in the 2000s. According to a survey conducted by the Publishers Communication Group, in 2010 there were 32 academic libraries with active PDA programs, 42 planned to implement PDA within the next year, and an additional 90 research libraries were projected to adopt PDA within three years (Lenares and Delquie 2011). Current PDA models allow library patrons to discover print and e-books that are not owned by the library in the Online Public Access Catalog (OPAC). Patrons can initiate a purchase by simply using or requesting a title.

While some academic libraries such as the Ohio State University Libraries and University of Florida Libraries implemented more than one PDA program for both print and e-books (Hodges et al. 2010a; Carrico and Leonard 2011), many research libraries have adopted PDA for e-books only (Southern Illinois University, see Nabe, Imre, and Mann 2011; University of Iowa Libraries, see Fischer et al. 2012; University of Texas Libraries, see Macicak and Schell 2009; and University of York, see Sharp and Thompson 2010).

Partnerships between e-book aggregators and approval plan vendors enabled academic libraries to initiate PDA programs through their approval plan vendors. This created opportunities for academic libraries to use their existing approval profiles for PDA program implementation, enabling duplication control and streamlined workflows. One example is the University of Minnesota Libraries, which implemented "a fully integrated demand-driven ebrary eBook acquisition program with YBP" (Walker 2012). Encouraged by the positive impact of the "Suggest a Purchase" user-driven acquisition program, and taking advantage of the existing YBP approval plan services, the TAMU Libraries began to investigate a PDA pilot program in the fall of 2011.

INITIAL STEPS

Since there are multiple options when PDA plans are being considered, collection development/acquisitions personnel researched various options. In June 2011 the coordinator of monograph and automated acquisitions, who was charged with implementing the PDA pilot, attended an American Library Association (ALA) pre-conference held in New Orleans. This Association for Library Collections and Technical Services (ALCTS) pre-conference offered an excellent overview of providers, and attendees heard firsthand experiences from librarians who had worked with the various PDA providers.

E-book aggregators, such as ebrary and EBL, provide PDA programs. Ingram/Coutts offers a different model by providing an exclusive product that does not incorporate e-book content from other sources. Approval-plan vendors, such as YBP and Rittenhouse, also offer e-book PDA plans. Since the TAMU Libraries could no longer financially support purchasing large quantities of books "just in case," they needed to begin purchasing titles "just in time" for research and instruction. With PDA plans, purchases are not made until the book is actually used or requested, so the initial decision was that a PDA plan might support user needs as well as the library's need to cut costs. Although print PDA plans are available, TAMU Libraries decided to limit the PDA pilot program to e-books only.

VENDOR DEMONSTRATIONS

In the summer of 2011, the coordinator of monograph and automated acquisitions contacted the major e-book PDA vendors to invite them to demonstrate their product features to library staff. These presentations took place between September 20 and September 28, 2011. Prior to the demonstrations, TAMU Libraries sent the vendors a list of questions (appendix 9) to facilitate comparisons among the different products and vendors. Internal invitations to attend the demonstrations included subject librarians and other user services staff to help them understand the e-book PDA pilot from the beginning of the project.

IMPLEMENTATION PLANS

With the decision made to initiate an e-book PDA pilot project at the TAMU Libraries, it was important to include all the stakeholders. Since TAMU has both academic and academic health sciences libraries on the same campus, and the libraries collaborate closely with print collection development, the

Medical Sciences Library was invited to participate in the pilot. With the Medical Sciences Library acceptance, both libraries needed to be represented on the implementation group. Bibliographic records would need to be added to both of the libraries' catalogs, so the implementation group needed to include cataloging and integrated library system personnel who could plan how and when the records would be added and perhaps later removed from the catalogs. After consultation, the coordinator of monograph and automated acquisitions identified the following as stakeholders to include in the implementation group. From the TAMU Libraries, representatives included the director of collection development operations and acquisitions services, the coordinator of monograph and automated acquisitions, the development relations specialist, the head of cataloging, and the head of consortia systems. Medical Sciences Library members were the onsite collections librarian and the collection development and strategic initiatives coordinator.

The first meeting of the group, held on October 28, 2011, confirmed that the pilot would move forward with $100,000 designated from the TAMU Libraries budget and $25,000 from the Medical Sciences Library budget. It also confirmed that the PDA plan would be an e-book only plan. After discussion of the various vendors, the group decided to implement the e-book PDA plan demonstrated by YBP. Since YBP is TAMU Libraries' major approval vendor, it would be possible to set the PDA plan to send records for titles marked as approval plan notifications and would supplement the e-preferred approval plan set up by the TAMU Libraries in fall 2010. In this way, the PDA would enhance both libraries' collections while overall basic collection needs would continue to be supplied by the approval plan and its detailed profile.

After a short time, the group reached several significant decisions. With the advantage of many years of experience with various automated library systems, the head of consortia systems advised the group that MARC records could be loaded into the catalogs and could remain indefinitely. She advised that a single location code should be used for the PDA records so they could be globally suppressed or removed from the catalogs, should it become necessary. Other specific cataloging decisions and workflow details are discussed in the cataloging section of this chapter.

Another decision for the group was the source of the e-books that would be identified by YBP using the approval plan profiles. At the time, YBP allowed e-books to be acquired from only two aggregator sources, ebrary or EBL. At the request of the group, YBP performed an analysis to determine the number of e-book titles available from each aggregator based on both libraries' approval profiles for notifications. The report revealed that 94 percent of the total available titles could be supplied by ebrary, while 72 percent could be supplied by EBL. After seeing the analysis, the implementation group decided to select ebrary as the e-books aggregator, using the existing YBP approval profiles.

The implementation group participated in multiple conference calls with both YBP and ebrary representatives during the following months to work through implementation decisions. One of the first decisions caused a lengthy delay, but proved to be a good decision that would offer more options to test during the pilot. Although supported by a separate collections budget, the approval profile for the Medical Sciences Library was part of the main TAMU Libraries' YBP approval plan account as a sub-account. This arrangement facilitated close collection development collaboration to minimize campus duplication and to ensure adequate coverage for all research disciplines. However, the implementation group discovered that to maintain the existing division of responsibilities between the libraries, both financial and intellectual, it would be necessary to create separate ebrary channels, and in order to bill the separate ebrary channels, YBP needed a completely separate account for the Medical Sciences Library. With the existence of separate catalogs, each library wanted only those records loaded for which they would be financially responsible, and this would not have been possible with the existing YBP account structure. This decision allowed the Medical Sciences Library to trial the short-term loan (STL) model; this model offered the option of a seven-day loan rather than immediate purchase. Triggers for STL and purchase of a title were significant use, defined by ebrary as ten minutes of use, printing, or downloading of content.

While YBP worked on separating the accounts and duplicating the approval profile onto the new account, a process that would not be completed until February 2012, the implementation group continued planning other workflows related to the PDA pilot. One of the main workflows would require the expertise of cataloging personnel to be sure that the records loaded would meet cataloging standards for uploaded MARC records.

CATALOGING

There are two categories of records in YBP's PDA service: discovery records and point-of-invoice records. In the first category, "discovery" records are delivered for PDA titles that libraries do not own, but want to make discoverable and accessible through their catalogs. According to documentation provided by YBP, they are derived from existing MARC records for the print version of a PDA title when available, conform to Program for Cooperative Cataloging (PCC)'s *MARC Record Guide for Monograph Aggregate Vendors* (2009), and contain Library of Congress Classification numbers and site-specific URLs that link to the full text of the resource. When a record for the print version of a title is not available, software is used by YBP to assemble bibliographic data provided by e-book aggregators or publishers, including Baker and Taylor, to create a "machine-generated" record. In the second category, "point-of-invoice" records are delivered after a title is triggered for purchase in an institution's local catalog after significant use of a particular title.

At the TAMU Libraries, the implementation team decided to receive discovery records from YBP, but not point-of-invoice records. Point-of-invoice records, created internally at YBP, lack OCLC numbers, and the team wanted to have both libraries' holdings for titles they owned be reflected as accurately as possible in OCLC's WorldCat database. The benefits of setting holdings information in OCLC described by Kristin E. Martin (2007) include more accurate information for interlibrary loan purposes, greater ability to mine OCLC data for data regarding holdings, and greater sharing of catalog records among libraries. Moreover, both libraries would benefit if a future decision was made to migrate to a product that would require accurate holdings in the WorldCat database, such as WorldCat Local. As Wu and Mitchell (2010) state, the holdings reclamation process of reconciling records that are purely local with records in WorldCat and retrospectively updating holdings in this database can be a "complex and expensive process" (p. 173). Based on these reasons, it was decided it was preferable to use records from OCLC to overlay the discovery records for titles that were triggered for purchase, and to update the OCLC records with the libraries' holding symbols during this process (TXA for the TAMU Libraries, TMV for the Medical Sciences Library).

VENDOR RECORD CUSTOMIZATIONS

One of the value-added services offered by YBP was discovery record customizations for an annual fee of $2,500. (This cost does not include customizations to the 001 field and the 856 field, which can be customized at no charge.) The head of cataloging at the TAMU Libraries requested a sample of records and reviewed them with the help of two cataloging librarians to determine if any customizations should be requested. A file containing 115 sample MARC records was received from YBP in December 2011. Based on this review, the head of cataloging requested that YBP perform the following customizations:

- Replace the YBP number (e.g., 001 ebd4190954 with the ebrary
  ID number (e.g., ebr10589877). As the documentation provided
  by YBP representatives stated, the 001 contains the YBP number.
  Cataloging personnel decided that it would be beneficial to replace
  it with the ebrary ID since this would help the libraries identify
  PDA titles from ebrary that could potentially duplicate titles that
  were independently selected by subject librarians and subsequently
  purchased from the same vendor. Such titles that were purchased
  would have records with ebrary ID numbers in them.

- Code the 008 MARC21 fixed-length data character position 23 ("Form of item") with the value "o" for "online resource." The 008/23 field was mostly coded with "o" for "online resource," but a few were coded "s" for the broader category of "electronic resource" (*MARC 21 Format for Bibliographic Data* 1999). It was the TAMU Libraries local cataloging policy to always code for the more specific aspect since this was useful in distinguishing records for electronic resources that were online versus those that were not online (e.g., a CD-ROM).
- Delete the 533 MARC field. Although the descriptive information in these records appeared to be based on the online manifestations of the titles, they nevertheless contained a 533 field for electronic reproductions. This followed the Library of Congress Rule Interpretation (LCRI) 1.11A, which instructed catalogers to base the description on the original print record of the same title and record all details about an electronic reproduction in a 533 field (2010). As this was incorrect according to the current PCC "provider-neutral" guidelines for cataloging monographic electronic resources, cataloging personnel requested that YBP delete the 533 field for discovery records it delivered for this pilot (2009).
- Add a local form/genre term "Electronic books" in the 655 field. The records in the sample lacked any genre/form headings that would indicate that the resources being described were electronic books. It was the TAMU Libraries' local policy to always include a local genre/form term (e.g., 655 _7 Electronic books. $2 local). This particular term is used in both the TAMU Libraries OPAC and the campus-wide Primo discovery interface (where it appears as a faceted genre category) to enable users to limit their searches to electronic books. The local 655 was added to the customization list to maintain that capability.
- Code the first indicator of the 776 field with the value "1." The records in this sample file contained 776 linking fields with ISBN numbers and Library of Congress record number for the print versions of the titles with both indicators blank. Although this information would not display if both indicators were blank, this request served as a precaution in the event that PDA discovery records were later delivered with indicators that would cause this information to display as a hyperlink in both libraries' OPACs with the label "Available in other form." If users clicked on this hyperlinked information, they would not retrieve any results.

- Add a prefix to the URL in the 856 field subfield $u that would allow remote access to the content of a resource through the Libraries' EZ Proxy server.
- Add a public message in the subfield $z of the 856 field: "Connect to the full text of this electronic book."
- Add a 955 field with the phrase "PDA YBP record"
- Add a 945 field with the term "machinegen" for machine-generated records only. In the sample that was reviewed, records that fell into the "machine-generated" category contained minimal information and lacked call numbers and subject headings. The letters in the titles for these records in this sample also were entirely capitalized. The above customization was requested in order to help cataloging staff identify these records in order to locally enhance them to improve their discoverability.

Example:

245 00 $aMARGINALIZED STUDENTS $h[electronic resource].
260 \\ $aSAN FRANCISCO: $b JOSSEY-BASS $c 2011.
300 \\ $a1 online resource.
533 \\ $aElectronic reproduction. $b Palo Alto, Calif. $n Available via World Wide Web.
710 2\ $a ebrary, Inc.
856 40 $u http://ezhost.panam.edu:2048/login?url=http://site.ebrary.com/lib/utpa/Top?id=10504232

Another customization, that was not requested of the vendor but made locally, was the creation of a new location code "pda" in both catalogs for the holdings records of discovery bibliographic records. This code would display the same message as the "www" code in the OPACs for both libraries as well as in their unified Primo discovery interface: "Available online." The reasoning for the latter was that users would not need to know if the libraries owned a particular resource as long as they could access the content online.

Finally, it was decided not to implement YBP's record enrichment service of discovery layer records (e.g., addition of tables of contents, summaries, author biographical/affiliation information). This service would cost an additional $1,000 beyond the $2,500 charge for YBP record customizations. The offered enrichments did not seem worth this cost, as many of the locally reviewed discovery records already contained tables of contents, and the implementation team judged that other enrichments (e.g., summaries and author biographical/affiliation information) offered by YBP were not necessary. The implementation team questioned the quality of the summary notes, since the sample provided by YBP appeared to use promotional language rather than objectively summarize the content.

IMPLEMENTATION OF THE PDA PILOT IN APRIL 2012

There were two initial test loads of a limited number of records beginning on April 12, 2012 to be sure the workflow was working properly before a retrospective load of 5,871 profiled notification titles were loaded into the TAMU Libraries OPAC, covering 2008 through 2011. The retrospective record load for the Medical Sciences Library catalog for the same time period totaled 1,724.

Keeping subject librarians informed about the progress of the implementation was important. They needed to know what the OPAC records would look like, how to work with acquisitions staff, and what impact the PDA e-book records might have. The subject librarians were encouraged to ask questions and were notified periodically about titles that triggered purchases on the PDA pilot.

RECORDS REVIEW DURING IMPLEMENTATION

When the libraries implemented the e-book PDA service in April, the head of cataloging and two cataloging librarians at the TAMU Libraries spot-checked records loaded in the TAMU Libraries' test server prior to being loaded in the production server of the catalog. They discovered a few records contained errors that would negatively impact users' ability to retrieve them. For example, the General Material Designation (GMD) appeared incorrectly in the 245 of one of the records (e.g., 245 $a Trade Promotion Strategies $h [electronic resource] $b Best Practices). In addition, they discovered that the place of publication was sometimes missing from the 260 field, and publisher names sometimes appeared incomplete (e.g., 260 $b Business Expert Pr $c 2011). Other observations included missing series numbers, invalid characters, and incorrect coding in indicators. In addition, some of the new YBP PDA titles duplicated ebrary titles that already had records in the catalog. Since these problems occurred on only a few of the reviewed records, it was decided that it would not be too much work for cataloging staff to identify and correct errors in problematic records after the consortia systems unit loaded the file in the catalog. In particular, those records would include the machine-generated records that lacked subject headings and call numbers and were supposed to represent only one percent of all discovery records, according to YBP's documentation.

CATALOGING WORKFLOW AT THE TAMU LIBRARIES

At the TAMU Libraries, the head of cataloging and a cataloging staff member established a workflow for (1) checking the quality of discovery layer records and correcting errors in them after they were loaded each week, and (2) cataloging titles from the YBP PDA program that were triggered for purchase.

Every week, the head of cataloging and a staff member received e-mail notifications informing them that a new file containing PDA discovery records had been bulk loaded into the local Voyager systems. After receiving this message, the staff member logged into the library's WinSCP server where the MARC files were stored, navigated to the directory where the latest file was saved, and downloaded a copy to the cataloging unit's shared folder on the library's network. From this location, the downloaded file was opened using MARCedit, a free MARC record editing program, and exported to an Excel spreadsheet as a tab-delimited file. This allowed the data from each record to appear in separate columns for each MARC field (see figure 9.1).

Using this spreadsheet, the staff member examined the data in the records on a field-by-field basis, looking for instances where the coding was incorrect, titles in the 245 field and publisher information in the 260 field that had errors in them, and for machine-generated records that had a 945 field in them with the word "machinegen" that needed subject headings or other corrections. The cataloging staff member retrieved the records in the catalog and manually corrected these errors. For machine-generated records that lacked subject headings, the staff member searched for headings on an existing record for the same title (either print or electronic) in OCLC Connexion and added them to the YBP PDA record in the catalog. If a matching record for the online version of a title existed in OCLC, the staff member imported the record and used it to overlay the PDA record in the catalog but did not update it in OCLC with the library's holdings symbol, as the library did not yet own this particular e-book. If no record was found for the title on OCLC, the staff member would contact a cataloging librarian who would then assign subject headings and a call number for the YBP PDA record in Voyager. After the record was corrected, the 945 "machinegen" field was deleted so that it would no longer be retrievable as a problematic record in need of corrections.

The cataloging staff member also received e-mail notifications of YBP PDA titles that were either "triggered" (i.e., titles that will be purchased based on the PDA trigger the next time that PDA orders are processed) or purchased each week. For both categories of titles, the cataloging staff member would search OCLC for a matching record. If a record for the electronic version was found, it was exported from OCLC Connexion into the local catalog where it

A	B	C	D	E	F	G	H	I
1	6	7	8	35	100	245	260	300 44(
ebr10661079	m\\\\\o\\d\cr\-n-||||	\\ob\\\\001\0\eng\d	130202s2013\\\\onc\\\		1\SaMcIver, Don.	10$aEnd of the line$h[electronic resource] :$bthe 1857 train wreck at the Desjardins Canal Bridge /$cDon McIver.	\\SaToronto ;$aTonawanda, NY :$bDundurn,$cc2013.	\\Sa1 online resource.
ebr10623005	m\\\\\o\\u\cr\cn||||	\\ob\\\\001\0\eng\d	121130s2013\\\\enka\			00$aCanonical morphology and syntax$h[electronic resource] /$cedited by Dunstan Brown, Marina Chumakina, and Greville G. Corbett.	\\SaOxford :$bOxford University Press,$c2013.	\\Sa1 online resource.
ebr10662048	m||||||||d\cr||n||||	\\ob\\\\001\0\eng\d	130325s2013\\\\gw\a\		1\SaCorbari, Eliana.	10$aVernacular theology$h[electronic resource] :$bDominican sermons and audience in late medieval Italy /$cEliana Corbari	3\SaBerlin ;$aBoston :$bDe Gruyter,$cc2013	\\Sa1 online resource.

K	L	M	N	O	P	Q	R	S
490	533	655	710	830	856	650	945	
	\7$aElectronic books.$2local	2\Saebrary, Inc.			40$uhttp://lib-ezproxy.tamu.edu:2048/login?url=http://site.ebrary.com/lib/tamu/docDetail.action?docID=1066107 9$zConnect to the full text of this electronic book	\0$aRailroad accidents$zOntario$zHamilton $xHistory$y19th century.		
1\SaOxford linguistics	\7$aElectronic books.$2local	2\Saebrary, Inc.	\0$aOxford linguistics.	40$uhttp://lib-ezproxy.tamu.edu:2048/login?url=http://site.ebrary.com/lib/tamu/docDetail.action?docID=1062300 5$zConnect to the full text of this electronic book	\0$aGrammar, Comparative and general$xMorphology.;\$aGrammar, Comparative and general$xSyntax.	\\Samachinegen		
1\SaTrends in medieval philology ;$vv. 22	\7$aElectronic books.$2local	2\Saebrary, Inc.	\0$aTrends in medieval philology ;$vv. 22.	40$uhttp://lib-ezproxy.tamu.edu:2048/login?url=http://site.ebrary.com/lib/tamu/docDetail.action?docID=1066204 8$zConnect to the full text of this electronic book	\0$aSermons, Latin$zItaly$xHistory.;\0$aSermons, Italian$zItaly$xHistory.;\0$aTheology$zItaly$xHistory.			

FIGURE 9.1

Example of the Excel spreadsheet used to spot-check PDA records for errors.

would overlay the existing YBP PDA record for the same title. The 955 field was not retained during this process. The location code on the holdings record was changed from "pda" to "www" to indicate that the record was now owned by the libraries. If no record for the resource was found in OCLC (either of the online version or a print version to derive a record from), the staff member sent the title to a cataloging librarian who would create an original record for the title in the OCLC database. (See figure 9.2.)

Finally, cataloging staff would sometimes encounter duplicate YBP discovery records in the TAMU Libraries catalog when cataloging new electronic books that the libraries purchased or licensed from other vendors (e.g.,

	ebrary DocID	ISBN Print	ISBN Electronic	Title	Trigger Date	Trigger Event	Purchase Date	Order Number	Order Name	Purchase License	Single User List Price	Purchase Multiplier
2	10522398	9781409435471	9781409435488	Inquisitor in the Hat Shop : Inquisit	2012/04/11	View	2012/04/18	152049	PDA_tamu_2012Apr18	MUPO	$124.95	150%
3	10522405	9781409435426	9781409435433	Central and Eastern European Med	2012/04/12	View	2012/04/18	152049	PDA_tamu_2012Apr18	MUPO	$99.95	150%
4	10541069	9781591581772	9781610692359	Genreflecting Advisory Series : Rom	2012/04/14	Chapter Download	2012/04/18	152049	PDA_tamu_2012Apr18	MUPO	$55.00	150%
5	10545359	9780313397769	9780313397776	Educated Parent 2 : Child Rearing i	2012/04/16	Copy	2012/04/18	152049	PDA_tamu_2012Apr18	MUPO	$48.00	150%
6	10274098	9780710313409	9780203883181	Scientific Research in World War II	2012/04/24	View	2012/04/27	154396	YBP_EBR0000034405	SUPO	$150.00	100%
7	10331465	9781576755778	9781576755877	Introverted Leader : Building on Yo	2012/04/23	Chapter Download	2012/04/27	154396	YBP_EBR0000034405	SUPO	$29.95	100%
8	10335233	9780749456528	9780749458409	Successful Interview Skills : How to	2012/04/24	View	2012/04/27	154396	YBP_EBR0000034405	MUPO	$15.95	150%
9	10351563	9781606234624	9781606234792	Procrastinator's Guide to Getting T	2012/04/18	View	2012/04/27	154396	YBP_EBR0000034405	SUPO	$40.00	100%
10	10382444	9780415774987	9780203851555	Logic : The Basics	2012/04/19	View	2012/04/27	154396	YBP_EBR0000034405	SUPO	$90.00	100%
11	10392132	9780521518321	9780511726156	English Grammar : Understanding	2012/04/21	View	2012/04/27	154396	YBP_EBR0000034405	SUPO	$110.00	100%
12	10439521	9780815316596	9780203834473	Dante Encyclopedia	2012/04/19	View	2012/04/27	154396	YBP_EBR0000034405	SUPO	$290.00	100%
13	10445762	9780230271678	9780230293168	Russian Foreign Policy in the 21st C	2012/04/26	View	2012/04/27	154396	YBP_EBR0000034405	SUPO	$89.00	100%

	Purchase Total	OCLC Number	Publisher	Imprint	Year Published	Library of Congress Call Number	Primary BISAC Category	Primary BISAC Subcategory	Available License
2	$187.43	772519325	Ashgate Publish	Ashgate Publishing Gro	2012	BX1723.B37 2012eb	HISTORY	Modern / 16th Century	SUPO MUPO
3	$149.93	772514236	Ashgate Publish	Ashgate Publishing Gro	2012	P92.E93.C47 2012eb	POLITICAL SCIENCE	Public Policy / Social Pol	SUPO MUPO
4	$82.50	787848514	ABC-CLIO	Libraries Unlimited	2012	Z1231.L68.R37 2012	LANGUAGE ARTS & DI	Library & Information S	SUPO MUPO
5	$72.00	787851014	ABC-CLIO	Praeger	2012	HQ755.8.S362 2012eb	FAMILY & RELATIONSH	Parenting / General	SUPO MUPO
6	$150.00	646794074	Kegan Paul	Kegan Paul	2008	Q141.S35 2009eb	HISTORY	Military / World War II	SUPO
7	$29.95	646832861	Berrett-Koehler	Berrett-Koehler Publish	2009	BF637.L4.K27 2009eb	BUSINESS & ECONOMI	Leadership	SUPO
8	$23.93	646836502	Kogan Page	Kogan Page Ltd.	2009	BF637.I5.T44 2009eb	BUSINESS & ECONOMI	Careers / Job Hunting	SUPO MUPO
9	$40.00	646875796	Guilford Press	Guilford Publications	2009	BF637.P76.B37 2010eb	PSYCHOLOGY	Applied Psychology	SUPO
10	$90.00	647917748	Routledge	Routledge	2010	BC108.B347 2010eb	MATHEMATICS	General	SUPO
11	$106.00	649908910	Cambridge Univ	Cambridge University	2006	PE1112.A48 2010eb	LANGUAGE ARTS & DI	Grammar & Punctuation	SUPO
12	$290.00	704518577	Routledge	Routledge	2010	PQ4333.D36 2010eb	LITERARY CRITICISM	European / Italian	SUPO
13	$85.00	706425661	Palgrave Macmi	Palgrave Macmillan	2010	DK510.764.R865 2010eb	POLITICAL SCIENCE	International Relations	SUPO

FIGURE 9.2

Example of a weekly PDA Trigger Report.

CRCnetBASE, etc.). When this occurred, they deleted the discovery records and notified the coordinator of monograph and automated acquisitions so that YBP would be informed about the duplication and have the title removed from the ebrary PDA channel.

ISSUES IDENTIFIED AND ADDRESSED

The initial split of the YBP profile by pulling out the Medical Sciences Library profile caused a delay that was resolved in February 2012. The first attempt at the retrospective loads resulted in duplication of a substantial number of e-book records already in the catalogs. To address this, the libraries extracted all ISBNs in all unsuppressed bibliographic records in both catalogs; those ISBNs were uploaded into GOBI3 (YBP's online database of titles) to allow YBP to de-duplicate records prior to assembling the retrospective files. The second retrospective load did not result in the large number of duplicate records.

Although the TAMU Libraries transitioned away from comprehensive e-book packages from the major publishers, specific subject collections were still purchased. Titles published by Morgan Claypool were included in the first PDA loads, but those titles were purchased directly from the publisher. On request, YBP removed this publisher from the PDA profile in YBP and ebrary. A similar issue arose with CRC titles. The TAMU Libraries purchased several CRC e-book subject collections, but not all of them so CRC could not be blocked on the PDA. The solution to this issue was to periodically create a list of PDA records that duplicated CRC e-book records; library staff notified YBP of the duplicate titles and requested that the titles be removed from the PDA profile in ebrary. This has proven to be an effective workflow.

Another issue was the lack or scarcity of PDA coverage for certain publishers, such as Elsevier and Springer. There is still not as much content available from those publishers as would be preferred, but discussions continue.

MEDICAL SCIENCES LIBRARY EXPERIENCE WITH PDA MODEL

In considering a PDA program, the option for short-term loans (STL) held significant promise for the Medical Sciences Library. Analysis of the use of print titles in the collection showed that 20 percent of those titles were never used; of those that were used, a significant number were used three times or less. The short-term loan aspect of a PDA program presented the opportunity to observe the number of titles that exceeded one loan. Assessment of the titles loaned could also reveal subject areas for further collection development.

After the initial retrospective load, an average of 20–30 discovery records were added to the Medical Sciences Library catalog on a weekly basis. In selecting the library's current approval plan vendor it was expected that the previously established approval plan profile for print books would guide the mix of e-books that were loaded into the catalog. There was also the expectation that records would not need to be reviewed after loading, but the small number of discovery records added the possibility for reviewing records to ensure appropriateness. This proved a wise strategy as the Medical Sciences Library also acquired e-books from other vendors; some of these e-books lacked an ISBN matching point, which led to duplicate records. There were other titles coming in on the weekly record loads that the library wanted to purchase immediately rather than incur a succession of loans; library staff purchased those titles and requested that YBP have them removed from the ebrary channel. It was also found that some discovery records did not result in a successful link at the e-book vendor site. Representatives with the e-book vendor had to be contacted to resolve a few of these access issues. After several months, review of weekly discovery records dropped down to spot-checking.

An analysis of the program from April through December 2012 revealed that a significant savings was realized in selecting the short-term loan option. A total of $1,600 was spent on STL, as opposed to paying list price for the same e-books totaling approximately $5,900. Of the 67 titles incurring a loan, 52 (77 percent) were loaned just once, 8 (12 percent) loaned 2 times, 4 (6 percent) loaned 3 times, and 3 titles (5 percent) exceeded the loans to result in a purchase. True to the proposal made by the PDA vendor, not all publishers permit STL on their titles so the Medical Sciences Library paid the cost of those e-books with the first use. There were eighteen e-books that fell into this category, totaling approximately $1,900.

For the Medical Sciences Library, the PDA program presented the opportunity to observe patterns of e-book use versus use patterns of print titles that might have come in on an approval plan. The higher percentage of titles used just once and the savings afforded by paying a percentage of the list price for that minimal usage proved successful for the Medical Sciences Library. The approval plan profile applied adequate parameters and all the titles, whether loaned or purchased, were within the scope of the collection. Particularly in subject areas where many titles are regularly released, there was certainly increased reliability in having patrons select the most useful e-books.

RESULTS

From April 12, 2012, through March 20, 2013, there have been 17,352 PDA records loaded into the TAMU Libraries OPAC. Of these titles, 927 titles have been triggered and purchased, totaling $105,758.45. Figure 9.3 illustrates the call number ranges of the titles purchased for the TAMU Libraries collection during the eleven-month period. For the same time period, 3,084 PDA records were loaded into the Medical Sciences Library catalog for a total of $6,522.68; of these, 98 incurred 155 STL charges for a total of $2,260.97 and 47 were purchased for a total of $4,261.71. The call number ranges for the Medical Sciences Library purchases and loans are illustrated in figure 9.4.

Library of Congress Classifications	Purchased title counts	Net expenditure
A - GENERAL WORKS	3	$334.86
B - PHILOSOPHY Total	75	$6,705.60
C - HISTORY, AUXILIARY SCIENCES	3	$524.93
D - HISTORY, EASTERN HEMISPHERE	38	$5,655.26
E - HISTORY, NORTH AMERICA	24	$2,451.94
F - HISTORY, WESTERN HEMISPHERE	9	$1,066.17
G - GEOGRAPHY	42	$3,963.60
H - SOCIAL SCIENCES (GENERAL)	227	$21,541.45
J - POLITICAL SCIENCE (DOCS)	51	$7,223.34
K - LAW (GENERAL)	31	$3,156.16
L - EDUCATION (GENERAL)	38	$3,972.77
M - MUSIC	15	$1,352.09
N - VISUAL ARTS (GENERAL)	8	$624.58
P - PHILOLOGY & LINGUISTICS	97	$9,929.81
Q - SCIENCE (GENERAL)	119	$16,786.71
R - MEDICINE (GENERAL)	8	$920.62
S - AGRICULTURE (GENERAL)	14	$1,882.64
T - TECHNOLOGY (GENERAL)	104	$15,635.63
U - MILITARY SCIENCE (GENERAL)	5	$476.00
V - NAVAL SCIENCE (GENERAL)	5	$640.00
Z - LIBRARY SCIENCE. BIBLIOGRAPHY	11	$914.29
Grand total	927	$105,758.45
Average cost		$114.09

FIGURE 9.3
TAMU Libraries PDA purchases.

Library of Congress Subclassifications	Purchases		Short-term loans		
	Title counts	Net expenditures	STL title counts	STL loan counts	STL charges
KF - LAW - UNITED STATES (GENERAL)			1	1	$11.99
QD - CHEMISTRY			1	1	$27.15
QH - NATURAL HISTORY			1	1	$22.32
QM HUMAN ANATOMY	3	$179.85	2	3	$56.69
QP - PHYSIOLOGY	1	$40.95	10	14	$313.46
QR - MICROBIOLOGY	3	$258.45	4	8	$88.94
R - MEDICINE (GENERAL)	3	$115.88	10	13	$235.95
RA - PUBLIC ASPECTS OF MEDICINE	7	$518.45	23	43	$533.54
RB - PATHOLOGY	4	$222.80	4	4	$87.80
RC - INTERNAL MEDICINE	14	$2,049.24	17	34	$307.61
RD - SURGERY	6	$495.80	4	4	$130.80
RE - OPHTHALMOLOGY	1	$64.95	1	1	$44.99
RG - GYNECOLOGY AND OBSTETRICS			3	3	$38.04
RJ - PEDIATRICS			6	8	$176.69
RL - DERMATOLOGY	1	$57.95			
RM - THERAPEUTICS, PHARMACOLOGY	2	$131.90			
RT - NURSING	2	$125.49	11	17	$185.00
Totals	47	$4,261.71	98	155	$2,260.97
Average cost		$90.67			$14.59

FIGURE 9.4
Medical Sciences Library PDA activity.

CONCLUSION

As libraries of all types struggle with the ability to meet the needs of their customers while managing with lower budgets and space constraints, patron-driven acquisitions can be used to supplement a balanced collection. Utilization of an existing approval plan can ensure that titles in the PDA will be within the scope of the collection development policy and will facilitate efficiencies and duplication control. Careful planning and prior workflow mapping are critical to a successful PDA implementation. Other critical tasks are to identify funding and stakeholders and to define objectives. The decision to select purchase or short-term loan options will vary from library to library based on individual needs and budgets of each organization. While a PDA program should not be used to fulfill all the collection needs of academic libraries, it can be used effectively to enrich the collection with titles that are needed by customers when they need them without the delays of acquiring and processing titles that may never be used.

REFERENCES

Ammerman, Sarah. 2010. "Loftin Announces Cuts." *The Battalion*. July.

Anderson, Kristine J., Robert S. Freeman, Jean-Pierre V. M. Herubel, Lawrence J. Mykytiuk, Judith M. Nixon, and Suzanne M. Ward. 2010. "Liberal Arts Books on Demand: A Decade of Patron-Driven Collection Development, Part 1." *Collection Management* 35 (3, July): 125–41.

Carrico, Steven, and Michelle Leonard. 2011. "Patron-Driven Acquisitions and Collection Building Initiatives at UF." *Florida Libraries* 54 (1, Spring): 14–27.

Cook, Colleen, and Michael Maciel. 2010. "A Decade of Assessment at a Research-Extensive University Library Using LibQUAL+." *Research Library Issues* 271 (August): 4–12.

Fischer, Karen S., Michael Wright, Kathleen Clatanoff, Hope Barton, and Edward Shreeves. 2012. "Give 'Em What They Want: A One-Year Study of Unmediated Patron-Driven Acquisition of E-Books." *College & Research Libraries* 73 (5, September): 469–92.

Herrera, Gail, and Judy Greenwood. 2011. "Patron-Initiated Purchasing: Evaluating Criteria and Workflows." *Journal of Interlibrary Loan, Document Delivery & Electronic Reserves* 21 (1, January): 9–24.

Hodges, Dracine, Preston Cyndi, and Marsha J. Hamilton. 2010a. "Patron-Initiated Collection Development: Progress of a Paradigm Shift." *Collection Management* 35 (3, July): 208–21.

———. 2010b. "Resolving the Challenge of E-Books." *Collection Management* 35 (3, July): 196–200.

Lenares, Deborah, and Emilie Delquie. 2011. "Give the People What They Want: Patron Driven Acquisition." Available online at www.stm-assoc.org/2010_04 _27_Spring_Conference_Lenares_Patron_Driven_Acquisition.pdf.

Library of Congress. 2010. *Library of Congress Rule Interpretations 1.11A*. Washington, DC: Library of Congress. Available online at www.loc.gov/cds/PDFdownloads/ lcri/LCRI_2010–03.pdf.

————. 2001–2012. *MARC 21 Format for Bibliographic Data*. Washington, DC: Library of Congress, 1999, Update no. 1, 2001, through Update no. 15, 2012. Available online at www.loc.gov/marc/bibliographic.

Macicak, Susan, and Lindsey E. Schell. 2009. "Patron-Driven, Librarian-Approved: A Pay-per-View Model for E-Books." *Serials* 22, supplement (November): S31–38.

Martin, Kristin E. 2007. "ATG Special Report—Cataloging eBooks: An Overview of Issues and Challenges." *Against the Grain* 19 (1, February): 45–47.

Nabe, Jonathan, Andrea Imre, and Sanjeet Mann. 2011. "Let the Patron Drive: Purchase on Demand of E-Books." *Serials Librarian* 60 (1–4): 193–97.

Perdue, Jennifer, and James A. Van Fleet. 1999. "Borrow or Buy? Cost-Effective Delivery of Monographs." *Journal of Interlibrary Loan, Document Delivery & Information Supply* 9 (4): 19–28.

Pickett, Carmelita, Simona Tabacaru, and Jeanne Harrell. 2012. "E-Approval Plans in Research Libraries." *College & Research Libraries*. Available in preprint at http://crl.acrl.org/content/early/2012/12/19/cr112-410.full.pdf | html.

Program for Cooperative Cataloging. 2009. *MARC Record Guide for Monograph Aggregator Vendors*. Washington, DC: Library of Congress. Available online at www.loc.gov/aba/pcc/sca/documents/FinalVendorGuide.pdf.

————. 2009. *Provider-Neutral E-Monograph MARC Record Guide*. Washington DC: Library of Congress. Available online at www.loc.gov/aba/pcc/bibco/documents/PN-Guide.pdf.

Reynolds, Leslie J., Carmelita Pickett, Wyoma vanDuinkerken, Jane Smith, Jeanne Harrell, and Sandra Tucker. 2010. "User-Driven Acquisitions: Allowing Patron Requests to Drive Collection Development in an Academic Library." *Collection Management* 35 (3, July): 244–54.

Sharp, Steve, and Sarah Thompson. 2010. "'Just in Case' vs. 'Just in Time': E-Book Purchasing Models." *Serials* 23 (3, November): 201–6.

Tyler, David C., Yang Xu, Joyce C. Melvin, Marylou Epp, and Anita M. Kreps. 2010. "Just How Right Are the Customers? An Analysis of the Relative Performance of Patron-Initiated Interlibrary Loan Monograph Purchases." *Collection Management* 35 (3, July): 162–79.

VanDuinkerken, Wyoma, Jane Smith, Jeanne Harrell, Leslie J. Reynolds, Sandra Tucker, and Esther Carrigan. 2008. "Creating a Flexible Fund Structure to Meet the Needs and Goals of the Library and Its Users." *Library Collections, Acquisitions, & Technical Services* 32 (3): 142–49.

Walker, Kizer. 2012. "Patron-Driven Acquisition in U.S. Academic Research Libraries: At the Tipping Point in 2011?" *Bibliothek* 36 (1): 126–30.

Wu, Annie, and Anne M. Mitchell. 2010. "Mass Management of E-Book Catalog Records: Approaches, Challenges, and Solutions." *Library Resources & Technical Services* 54 (3, July): 164–74.

APPENDIX 9

Questions for the Patron-Driven Acquisitions Presentation

September 20–28, 2011

1. What is involved in setting up your PDA and how long does this setup generally take?

2. Knowing our library's goals and budget, what kind and size of program would you recommend?

3. How does your browsing period work? How is it tracked across sessions and users?

4. When the browsing period results in a purchase, what is the process for notifying the library that the title has been purchased?

5. What type/number of uses triggers a purchase?

6. What profiling options are available?

7. What publishers and content are included in your PDA titles? How many total titles are available?

8. What procedures are in place to avoid duplication of titles with titles already in the library's collection?

9. How and how often can I change the settings for my profile?

10. Can multiple users access a nonowned title simultaneously?

11. What cataloging and discovery service options do you provide?

12. What tools are available for tracking expenditures and how often are they updated?

13. What options are available for putting my program on hold?

14. How do I identify the MARC records that need to be deleted/suppressed?

15. How long are your customers leaving MARC records in the catalog before pulling the unpurchased titles?

16. What usage data is available? How often is it updated? How do I access it?

17. How many Voyager sites do you work with? What are the largest ones?

JOHN BUSCHMAN

10

Seven Reasons to Be Skeptical about Patron-Driven Acquisitions

A Summary

What a piece of work is a man, how noble in reason, how infinite in faculties, in form and moving how express and admirable, in action how like an angel, in apprehension how like a god!

Shakespeare, Hamlet

If there be nothing new, but that which is
Hath been before, how are our brains beguiled,
Which, labouring for invention, bear amiss
The second burden of a former child.

Shakespeare, Sonnet 59

LOTS OF SMART THINGS HAVE BEEN WRITTEN AND SAID ABOUT patron-driven acquisitions (PDA) (in fact, some of those smart things are too smart by half—but more on this later). This chapter will be neither a comprehensive literature review nor an original dig-down-deep skeptical analysis of the claims made for PDA (though maybe a bit of an eye-rolling exercise at trendiness). The task here is to produce a useful summary of the questions and issues that have already surfaced, albeit in a broad and scattered way among a wide variety of forums like formal studies, blogs, surveys, literature reviews, commentary, and conference presentations. This summary will focus on the reasons for a certain amount of skepticism in adopting, implementing, or exploring PDA for decision makers at all levels in libraries. In other words, this chapter is meant to gather and organize much of the widely scattered evidence and analysis that casts doubt on the PDA trend. Since many of these issues have been raised multiple times and in multiple ways, the approach here will be to document some (not all) of the instances where the evidence was gathered or the analysis put forth to make the point (sometimes moments of doubt appear like a cloud in any otherwise sunny report, and therefore tend to be buried a bit). It will proceed somewhat arbitrarily through a series of enumerated points marshaling analysis and evidence and end with a short conclusion. Throughout, I will freely mix general studies and surveys of library users with those focusing on specific groups (public library users, students, etc.).[1] We should probably begin by acknowledging the prima facie arguments *for* PDA: libraries can offer their users "access to the broadest range of high-quality content [by] taking advantage of the increasing availability of . . . content in digital form . . . [which] permit libraries to purchase e-books only when library users have requested them with a given frequency [and still] give the institutions some control over their costs" (DeGruyter 2012). PDA is identified "as an inevitable trend for libraries" and is "poised to become the norm" (ACRL Research Planning and Review Committee 2012, 314). Cutting through the hype larded into those last statements, the bottom line is that PDA "data tells a compelling story that confirms patrons can positively contribute to collection development" (Hoesly 2012, 524). Thus, PDA is part of a broader set of trends taking place in libraries that seek to more sensitively shape library spaces and environments around use and user patterns (Buschman 2012, 4–5) to take advantage of the affordances of e-distribution of reading and research resources. If these are good reasons to take PDA seriously (and they are), the obverse also holds: as professionals charged with guiding our institutions we have a responsibility to take seriously the evidence and analyses that raise penetrating questions about this "inevitable" new "norm." It is to this task that we now turn.

REASON ONE

Librarians Have Been Doing This (PDA) All Along (or at Least for a Long While)

Even the most enthusiastic proponents of PDA admit that it is "nothing new . . . , especially for the print format. Libraries have been using patron requests to help drive collection building for years, through interlibrary loan (ILL) suggestions . . . librarians concluded that they could buy books for about the same cost as obtaining them through ILL and the books tended to circulate more than regularly acquired books" and we have known this for much more than a decade (Dinkins 2012, 249; Howard 2010; Hoesly 2012). It in fact goes back to the use studies of the 1970s and a culture of poor or prescriptive or librarian-centered selections by librarians—pejoratively cast as "traditional" collection development by PDA proponents (Nixon, Freeman, and Ward 2010; Howard 2010; Wiegand 2011). After all, we are awash in information: "There's a lot of bad books, and if readers are more involved in the selection, some of those bad books are going to have to go away" (Dillon in Howard 2010). We will return to the virtues of such a collection so built in light of a more considered role of a library near the end of this chapter, but the point here is that PDA is in no way a new and revolutionary idea for librarians and librarianship. Wayne Wiegand (2011) has long shown us that local preferences and usage have effectively shaped libraries over and against prescriptive and traditional models. In other words, libraries have been shaped for many decades by their users' habits and preferences, and it is a fair assumption that they could not have done so without the tacit cooperation and support of librarians (even if only minimal at times). Those professionals were shaping their collections around patron demand. It is the affordances of Internet sales of books *and* the advent of aggregations of and access to electronic books by vendors that has surmounted some of the difficulties of earlier attempts (Nixon, Freeman, and Ward 2010). The idea, however hyped (and this is what we're skeptical about here), is not new; it is simply now more efficiently realized.

REASON TWO

Many Readers Still Don't Much Care for the E-Books That PDA Best Provides

I can hear the howls of protest: the devices have gotten so much better; you can use them in ways that mimic print books now; the (insert fake marketing/demographic moniker for young people that denotes their affinities to technology here) generation is "more comfortable" with e-text; screens don't cause so much eyestrain; and on and on. Recall that F. W. Lancaster predicted we would be "paperless" in the late 1970s, and a cursory familiarity with the history of technology shows that—even in libraries—they tend to accrete, rather than purely displace older technologies (Harris, Hannah, and Harris 1998; O'Donnell 1998).[2] That aside, readers across the spectrum still expect and mostly prefer the affordances of print: 63 percent in a recent *American Libraries* survey expected print books to "never" disappear[3] (Helgren 2011). While the recent Pew study fell into the "young are more adaptable" style of preset analysis in reporting the data, they found that the young were "especially likely to have read a book or used the library in the past 12 months" and that "75% read a print book, 19% read an e-book, and 11% listened to an audiobook" (Zickuhr et. al 2012); most tellingly, college students over the course of a half decade or more persistently tell us through the research that for their academic work they dislike the opportunity costs of e-books and their readers (they *do* tend to like the convenience and access) and prefer the study "environment" or "space" of print as most conducive to learning (Levine-Clark 2006; Li et al. 2011; Staiger 2012; Internet2 e-Textbook Pilot 2012).[4] Two studies a decade apart bookend each other and summarize the issue: two-thirds of the people surveyed in 2002 reported using a library and almost that amount had a library card, and of those who had used a library two-thirds had checked out a book (Davis 2006); in 2012 there are *still* "few differences between readers under age 30 and older adults when it comes to reading books in print" and "some 56% of all Americans ages 16 and older have used the library in the past year, including 60% of those under age 30" in the recent Pew study (Zickuhr et al. 2012). The reason for this continuity of preference for print is fairly simple: "Most . . . read only small portions of e-books, suggesting perhaps that print volumes are a better alternative for immersion in the text" (Levine-Clark 2006; Staiger 2012). In other words, if we really *are* building our collections around patron-driven preferences, these strong preferences *should* actually show up in our analysis: the young have not flocked en masse to e-books, and they are *not* the only users of library materials (so let's focus on all our users, not our preferred false marketing demographic). The buzz—essentially that the combination of e-books and PDA is "inevitable" and transformative for libraries—is an excellent example of the classic "congealing oil" thesis of Starbuck (1982): we're "inventing ideologies to justify acting ideologies out."[5] E-books and PDA methods are not an inexorable force, but rather will take their place *alongside* the other means that libraries deploy to continue to provide access to information.

REASON THREE

PDA Selects E-Books, Which Are Very Expensive in a Couple of Ways

First, as we have said, PDA has come to focus on the synergy between patron demand and the ability to quickly provide e-books. The problem is e-books are expensive. I am not speaking of the 99 cents for a Kindle book rental for an individual customer, but the premium libraries pay for e-books and the ability to lend them. Leasing them in the aggregate is fairly affordable right now, but PDA-selected academic books most often cost more than $100, and frequently limits (below $150, for instance) on cost and content must be set (Howard 2010). For public library general reading/readers, publishers have significantly jacked up prices for libraries, or limited use, or both (*State of America's Libraries* 2012). PDA costs more. Period.[6] A PDA advocate states that, in the face of "significant budget cuts, and when the money gets tighter, it gets harder and harder to justify spending money on materials nobody wants" (Anderson in Howard 2010). But the notion that PDA provides much more bang for the buck had better demonstrate *proportionately* more to justify what is most of the time a doubling or tripling of acquisition costs: the so-called data-driven, hard-nosed approach can't fall back on the soft talk of *possible* uses or the convenience of access without data to back up those investments. And better use data on print collections beyond circulation should *also* be part of that mix if we are making legitimate comparisons. Second (and briefly), preservation/curation of e-books is—and has remained for some time now—dreadfully expensive and elusive: Warner (2002, 53) cites a study from the 1990s that stated flatly that "a great deal of money can be wasted . . . without due regard to long-term preservation. It is now relatively easy to [acquire] digital . . . texts or images. However, if there is no plan in place for archiving . . . preservation will be expensive or may even result in the work having to be repeated." In 2012 it is *still* reported that the "ALA identified sustainability as a core principle for e-book collections [and] sustainability requires secure and ongoing funding, technology solutions that are appropriate to the longevity of the cultural record and long-term management capabilities" (ACRL Research Planning and Review Committee 2012, 314). Little in terms of the structural costs and challenges of preservation has changed in fifteen years—e-preservation is very expensive for libraries—or it is simply obviated altogether in PDA's leasing/licensing environment (Coffman 2012).[7]

REASON FOUR

We Have Good Reason to Doubt Some of the Usage Claims and Impacts of PDA

There is much chest-beating about PDA's efficacy: "I've got limited resources, the purchase doesn't happen until the need is demonstrated" (Anderson in Howard 2010). But this is merely an exercise in the obvious: like interlibrary loan requests, PDA captures users when "they're pretty far along the road of knowing what they want" (Nixon in Howard 2010). In other words, PDA is a form of preaching to the choir. These are already library users relatively deep into the discovery or access tools libraries provide and they are requesting materials. Of course those materials are going to be used; they're being requested *for* use. It is the *follow-up* that gets a little vague, with little data systematically collected. There, *assumptions* tend to take over. When ILL books were purchased in an early version of PDA, "*if* the book is read twice, *we feel* the book is well worth the purchase price"—but there is no systematic follow-up data (italics added, Nixon in Howard 2010). The same applies to PDA purchased e-books: "Not only are the requesting patrons' needs satisfied, but also it is *highly likely* that those books will interest other patrons in the future" (italics added, Nixon, Freeman, and Ward 2010, 120; Arch et al. 2011); "*I am convinced* it will be either cheaper or deliver more use or both" once the PDA model is more worked out[8] (italics added, Lewis in Schwartz 2012). But those are assumptions and hopes, not data-driven decisions. In fact, we have excellent usage data for our e-book aggregations and of the data points that trigger purchase, but like the ILL-generated purchases, little to no follow-up data on second, third, and more uses of PDA-generated purchases. A study identified the top fifty used PDA titles (out of 12,000 catalog records available to search) at a very large state university research library, and found around 70 uses per title or less for the bottom quintile—in other words, those 50 titles represented .0416 percent of the universe of items which *could* have been found and used with some frequency, and the bottom quintile showed relatively modest use given the very large population served and the academic- and research-intensive nature of the environment (Fischer et al. 2012). As a brief corollary, e-book purchases (whether PDA-generated or not) still represent a low percentage and low raw numbers among library purchases (this is sensible given the added costs) and circulation, the vast majority of libraries do not loan the reading devices (ditto), and patrons still widely find the interfaces difficult (*State of America's Libraries* 2012; Howard 2010; Doyle and Tucker 2011; Dinkins 2012; Esposito March 27, 2012; May 8, 2012; Duncan and Carroll 2011). This is an awful lot of sound and fury over a small market and hesitant use and adoption.

REASON FIVE

PDA Isn't about Us

. . . or most of us at the very least. An earlier analysis showed the number of "page views you need to drive to get to only $50 million in revenue—the size of a mid-sized publisher. Short answer: way more than most people ever imagine"—a 200-page book selling 20,000 copies would generate 4 million page views and only a few thousand dollars of ad revenue—so "publishers and authors have to get a LOT more readers to bring you up to the level of revenue you get today from a printed book" (O'Reilly 2007) In PDA Big Thinker-World, this paradoxically means that collections *will inevitably* be PDA-driven, electronic, smaller, and specialized, relying on the yet-to-be-invented-or-funded "national infrastructure [and] Web scale enterprises tak[ing] on an increasing role in preserving and providing the content that is not unique to a particular" library (Schwarz 2012). If this kind of Library Magical Realism confuses you, that is because your/our frame of reference is off. Most of the Big Thinkers are looking at the *overall* market for e-books and the role of PDA in helping to develop that emerging market, and it has more to do with Amazon and Google and Apple than it does, for example, with Appalachian State University Library or the Monticello (Indiana) Public Library: "The purpose of this meditation is not to deliver yet another angst-filled blog post about the horrors of capitalism. . . . Rather the point is to come up with scenarios against which strategic plans can be made. Publishers now have a glimpse of . . . consumer book markets and now should be thinking about a significantly restructured library market" (which is, by the way, a grave threat to university presses) (Esposito March 27, 2012; May 8, 2012; January 3, 2012; Brantley 2011). Thus in another wing of PDA Big Thinker World, "open access will be the dominant model, . . . many university presses will have gone under, and the rest will have been reorganized into broader units" (Schwartz 2012). The real market and money is in the STEM (science, technology, engineering, and medicine) literature which *is* much more highly and easily monetized, and endlessly discussed (by the Big Thinkers): open access (OA), versions of OA, the economic models and their (de)merits in the possible/desirable transition to OA, and on and on in blogs like *The Scholarly Kitchen*[9] and Yale's LibLicense e-mail list. It is clear that *here* the economic stakes are quite high, and it is here that the much earlier visions of reshaping and monetizing library collections and services[10] have been most thoroughly realized. In other words, the trunk from which current PDA discussions emanated *never really concerned patrons* in the broadest sense, but rather the "saving" of libraries by monetizing their services and assets, transforming them, the big-market shift to e-content, and how to manage the billions in assets of the economically important STEM literature for STEM researchers. Main Street Public Library, the garden variety non-research academic library, and your local school library are *not* the point, and never were.

REASON SIX

PDA Strongly Smacks of Just Plain Old Marketing

To be very clear at the outset: librarians' motives are not in question concerning PDA. The publishers and the vendors are, well, out to create and massage a market—the publisher and vendor white papers frankly say so. PDA is just another way to market their products. There is nothing nefarious in that. But as was characterized a while ago, it is those within librarianship "oriented toward national and international networking trends, and frequently remote from professional concerns and routine organizational problems [who are] often openly allied with . . . administrative networks [and] the elite corporate culture that controls [network] technology" who tend to skew the issues (Winter 1993, 184)—PDA now included. Some characteristic prior bold predictions and "visionary" directions for libraries have been quoted here. The point isn't that they are venal in the "innovations" heavily promoted, but rather the point is the climate in which few professionally prosper by taking the sensible position that most people still like to read print books and that to actually learn something requires lots of hard work and study in a rationally constructed collection. That is, the path to professional publication, notoriety, publicity and promotion is simply often easier trod by exploring and researching and explaining the affordances of the latest publisher/vendor-sponsored information tool or package. The *result* is that much research and professional discussion appear as mere adjuncts to vendor/publisher marketing efforts. A previously cited study is a good example. Despite a heavy preponderance of negative comments from the *actual* users, the study skewed presentation of the results to highlight first and foremost that "only a minority of users elected to purchase a paper copy (12%)" vs. an eText, that "lower cost . . . was considered the most important factor[11] [with] the portability of eTexts also ranked very high as a factor leading to future purchase." The study therefore concluded that "each institution [should] proceed in developing a plan for . . . optimal procurement, distribution, funding, and management [of eTexts and] focus on the impact . . . on [the users] as one of the most important considerations." Where there *were* problems others were to blame: "the enhanced eText features [were not used, thus] little benefit from the . . . platform's capability" was realized (Internet2 e-Textbook Pilot 2012). In other words, the *core* constituencies that *used* these e-books didn't use their features and/or didn't particularly like them, but the answer was to double down and figure out how to finance, distribute, and promote them. As should be clear from many of my earlier comments, these investigations too often and too easily slide over into marketing itself (or pretty close) or at best, why-we-should-try-and-promote-the-resource/tool-of-the-moment.[12]

Outside of moralizing or inveighing against this slippage and these practices in the name of a measure of professional authenticity and autonomy[13] there are real costs. First and foremost, the long-advocated move to business-style marketing of the library, its "products" and services, makes the overt claim that libraries operated "without regard to . . . needs or demand" (Koontz, Gupta, and Webber 2006, 224; Weingand 2002; 1995). PDA is clearly cast as rectifying that. Within the marketing ethos, privacy is simply less of a value: patron records represent a "competitive opportunity" (Estabrook 1996). With the synergies of PDA and e-books, privacy is out the window: reading devices either owned by the individual (using a library e-book) or loaned out by the library itself capture and convey information about who is reading what and use it for marketing purposes (Caldwell-Stone 2012; Electronic Frontier Foundation 2012). PDA is just another step in this broader marketing process and the obviation of private inquiry in the (library) name of "efficiency, predictability, calculability, and control" (Quinn 2000, 259). The fact is that practices like PDA that emanate more from concerns for monetization, marketing, and the economically important STEM literature *do* have an impact not just on the practices of librarianship, but on its purpose and ethos as well:

> Supplying books that patrons (or should I say "customers"?) order from a catalog of possibilities alters the fundamental nature of libraries. The library is not a mall where individuals select the goods they plan to consume, like groceries or shoes. It's a commons, a resource for the entire community furnished with books that can be shared amongst ourselves and beyond local boundaries so that, by pooling our library holdings, we all can accommodate the unanticipated and occasional need. Sharing among libraries is something that most ebooks don't allow. And building a collection for the future seems to be a thing of the past. (Fister 2010)

Coffman (2012) confirms this with his usual blatant advocacy and lack of tact: "The fact is that well over half the ebooks currently available can be read at no cost whatsoever and most of the rest are available at prices so low as to unlikely challenge any but the most destitute among us. And this raises some very real questions about the continued value of the 'free' lending library in the age of the ebook"—and PDA, I would add.[14] *Any* notions of social solidarity or sharing (core to common support of a common resource like a library) are just blown away by practices like PDA when they are not introduced and contextualized intelligently and professionally—marketed and hyped, in other words (Buschman 2012; Jaeger et al., 2011).

REASON SEVEN

PDA Doesn't Necessarily Support the Broader Aims of a Library

Fister (2010) again sums up a central point:

> [A] library is more than a shopping site built to satisfy immediate patron needs. A well-chosen collection is a cartography of knowledge that helps guide the novice researcher toward books that they would never think to ask for. Patron-driven acquisition puts an enormous amount of faith in catalogs. With all due respect, they work pretty well when you know what you're looking for, but I have yet to meet the metadata that is better than what cataloging and classification can provide in combination. Umberto Eco . . . said . . . that "the whole idea of a library is based on a misunderstanding: that the reader goes into the library to find a book whose title he knows." Its real purpose, he said, "is to discover books of whose existence the reader has no idea." For him, open stacks were a triumph. When libraries turn to ebooks, browsing will be circumscribed by the cleverness of your interface and the dimensions of your computer screen.

And behind PDA are some other highly questionable assumptions. The first is that libraries (through tactics like PDA) can be a part of the royal road to learning-made-easy by crowd-built collections which are inherently better/ more useful. Remember gaming and the theory/wish that it would dramatically enhance learning and literacy through the enthusiasm of gamers and the concomitant enthusiasms of librarians (Gee 2003; Lipschultz 2009)? That trend seems not to have worked out if national test scores are to be believed after decades of gaming from Pac-Man to current sophisticated shooter games. Leckie (1996) aptly summarizes the reasons why: researching something to learn requires mastering at a minimum a measure of the broader context in which the subject resides, and then being able to ask a sensible (and answerable) question about the subject, and *then* being able to systematically query the organized literature about it to read/learn.[15] An expert, Leckie argues, knows that one doesn't simply "research" a topic like climate change as a beginner; one reads to get an introduction to *how climate change is thought about and researched* (the polar ice cap, ocean temperatures, rising land temperatures, the increasing occurrences and severity of separate—and specific— forms of weather like hurricanes and tornadoes, and so on). Then one picks an area of interest and queries that through its organized literature (that is, what a library provides access to in a multiplicity of ways, including a classified print collection). PDA, as noted, obviates this kind of learning and learning by those things "accidentally found on purpose" (Duff and Johnson 2002; Mann 2007) that a library enables. After all, things have to be *there* and structured to be queried in the first place. In fact, PDA advocates *celebrate* the hopscotch and out-of-nowhere selections made for their libraries (Howard 2010), but that clearly only works *within* a reasonably constructed context—a library already extant. PDA-built collections obviate the central point of discovery: what one *doesn't* know. Second (and closely related), PDA represents (illustrated by the Fister quotes) a furthering of the library-as-hardware-store model to provide "instant information gratification" (Isaacson 2002; Budd 1997). Libraries are built to enable a community of inquiry, not the exchange value of I-want-it-so-you-buy-it-for-my-specific-needs. Third, the all-too-quick response is that PDA simply enables people to get their hands on what they find with broader/bigger/faster "research" tools (think Google). Mann (2007) explodes this myth: a hyper-abundance of "results" simply makes the inquiry incoherent and disenables systematic ("accidentally found on purpose") inquiry. Either that or demand is often/largely driven by simple marketing: the PDA-generated product is in demand because it is out there in the zeitgeist in the form of marketing and advertising. Fourth and last, like the *Citizens United* decision in politics (Buschman 2012), PDA privileges a set of library "speakers"—those who can and do engage this particular choice process and "speak" through PDA. But a library is supported by its *community* (town, county, university, school) to serve more than just a vocal or savvy clientele:

> It is tautological that a perfectly functioning market [which is what PDA aspires to] responds properly to *market-expressed* preferences. However, people identify and reveal preferences [and needs, I would argue] in many different ways and at many different times and in many different contexts. . . . Why should the . . . expression that tends to be the most impulsive or the most self-centered be privileged over . . . other[s]? (Baker 1997, 398–400)

PDA—if overrelied upon and oversold—will skew collections as badly or worse than the practices it represents as outmoded. And again, PDA simply serves those particular library users already deep into the discovery or access tools libraries provide.

CONCLUSION

At the outset I noted that the order of the reasons given would be a bit arbitrary, and they also do not entirely cohere as a group: we've-been-doing-a-version-of-this-for-a-while (Reason One) doesn't sit comfortably with the inherent argument that PDA essentially moves us further toward a consumer/

customer model that doesn't serve us well (Reason Seven). Likewise, the notion that we're not that important as a market (Reason Five) is belied some by the idea that vendors/publishers are eager to cooperate with us to market (Reason Six). That's okay. In fact, the reasons and arguments *for* PDA are all over the map (since they come from many corners and perspectives), and the purpose of this chapter was to organize the scattered reasons for skepticism about the varieties of those arguments, claims, evidence, approaches, and assumptions. In other words, the case for PDA doesn't necessarily cohere without its internal contradictions either, but that doesn't mean we can simply ignore the case. Nor is this a purely intellectual exercise: it is a contribution to a practical discussion about an ongoing and developing practice in the field which no one is going to "win" on debating points. Finally, this isn't about stopping PDA dead in its tracks. Rather, it is about developing a *taurus cacas olefacto* concerning the subject: the vague and the qualitative nature of PDA assertions/evidence can have a number of interpretations; if there's a chain of argument with PDA (and there is), each step must work (including the premise)—not just most of them; it is worth remembering Occam's Razor (when there are multiple interpretations of PDA, the simplest one is likely the most accurate); and last, can the evidence for PDA be falsified? (Sagan 2011). If, as a result, PDA takes its place as a sensible tool in librarianship's toolkit—and not as an overhyped savior to libraries/librarianship, then it will have an honorable role. This chapter was a contribution toward this tactic of librarianship assuming that honorable role.

NOTES

1. I leave it to any critics to convincingly point out real differences among them more significant than those fleeting distinctions in marketing categories that are themselves products conjured up whose purpose is to market and sell or set the stage for same (Buschman 2007).

2. For that matter, how many of us still have our teeth set on edge that we are, for the foreseeable future, still dependent on microform machines and their bulky/balky reading/copying mechanisms for access to valuable bought-and-paid-for collections?

3. In the typical fashion of hype around this subject the prediction that e-books would circulate from libraries at about the same rate or more as print books made the splash.

4. This last study is a particularly egregious example of trying to tease out "support" for e-textbooks from manifestly mixed or negative results. The treatment of the literature review is especially revealing.

5. As Fister (2010) put it, this is "a prediction combined with an assumption: this is what people will want as soon as they wake up to the new

reality"—confirmed by one publishing industry study: "The users must be gradually brought to accept them. . . . They won't go away this time; this time they're here to stay" (Renner 2009).

6. Tim O'Reilly (2007) laid out the basic math of why this is so a while back (more on this in a bit). His analysis stands in direct contrast to the PDA-slanted coverage. For example: "Contrast those approximately 350 e-book purchases per year, all bought based on usage, with the 10,000 physical books . . . acquire[d] on speculation. Of those 10,000 titles, only about half will be checked out." In other words, the $69,000 spent on those 350 e-books were somehow of less value than the $600,000 spent on the 5,000/10,000 books of the print books acquired that circulated (Kolowich 2011). By PDA's hard-nosed cost calculations, it fails: PDA e-books cost just under $200 per used copy but the print books cost $120 per used copy—or 40 percent less with a potential future use on hand double that.

7. Coffman doesn't lament this and in fact celebrates it. He has been beating the drum for over 30 years to monetize and privatize library services and collections, as will be seen from other citations to his writings.

8. This from a PDA Big Thinker who has *not yet* implemented PDA in his library.

9. See for one example the article and discussion at http://scholarlykitchen .sspnet.org/2012/07/16/predictable-problems-the-uks-move-to-open-access.

10. "Commercialization will change the strategic directions for library customer services. . . . Fee-based access and retrieval services could provide the necessary capital to continue funding high-cost technology. Ultimately [it] may be what makes libraries more expensive, more lucrative, and, ironically, more customer-service oriented because it will be the marketplace that will determine which services are essential" (Hirshon 1996, 19–20; Coffman and Josephine 1991; Coffman 1998; Esposito 2006). This is a particularly good example of what Day (2002; 1998) has called a "transformational discourse" or a "discourse fashion."

11. They were given away.

12. Hence the aptness of the Starbuck (1982) thesis noted earlier: inventing an ideology to justify acting an ideology out.

13. I do not use the term pejoratively here. Budd (1997; Higgs and Budd 2007) is particularly incisive about the problems and values larded into unmindful adaptation of practices and vocabularies not informed by conscious reflection on professional and social values.

14. It is breathtaking how Big Thinkers (like Coffman) pass over the needs of the poor—or even those in some straits during our recent and ongoing economic struggles when library use picked up dramatically (www.cbsnews.com/8301 –18563_162–4770599.html).

15. To say nothing of the hard work of literacy and all that it enables as Postman (1979; 1985) has long demonstrated.

REFERENCES

ACRL Research Planning and Review Committee. 2012. "2012 Top Ten Trends in Academic Libraries." *College & Research Libraries News* 73 (6): 311–20.

Arch, Xan, Robin Champieux, Susan Hinken, and Emily McElroy. 2011. "By Popular Demand: Building a Consortial Demand-Driven Program." In *Proceedings of the Charleston Library Conference*. http://dx.doi.org/10.5703/1288284314974.

Baker, C. Edwin. 1997. "Giving the Audience What It Wants." *Ohio State Law Journal* 58:311–417.

Brantley, Peter. 2011. "Renting Out the Library." *Publishers Weekly* blog (December 9). http://blogs.publishersweekly.com/blogs/PWxyz/2011/12/09/renting-out-the -library.

Budd, John M. 1997. "A Critique of Customer and Commodity." *College & Research Libraries* 58 (4): 310–21.

Buschman, John. 2007. "Talkin' 'Bout My (Neoliberal) Generation: Three Theses." *Progressive Librarian* no. 29:28–40.

———. 2012. *Libraries, Classrooms, and the Interests of Democracy: Marking the Limits of Neoliberalism*. Lanham, MD: Rowman & Littlefield/Scarecrow.

Caldwell-Stone, Deborah. 2012. "A Digital Dilemma: Ebooks and Users' Rights." *American Libraries* online (May 29). http://americanlibrariesmagazine.org/ features/05292012/digital-dilemma-ebooks-and-users-rights.

Coffman, Steve. 1998. "What If You Ran Your Library Like a Bookstore?" *American Libraries* 29 (3, March): 40–46.

———. 2012. "The Decline and Fall of the Library Empire." *Searcher* 20 (3, April). www.infotoday.com/searcher/apr12/Coffman—The-Decline-and-Fall-of-the -Library-Empire.shtml.

Coffman, Steve, and Helen Josephine. 1991. "Doing It for Money . . . a Growing Number of Libraries Are Developing Fee-Based Services." *Library Journal* 116 (17): 32–36.

Davis, Denise M. 2006. "What We Know about Libraries." In *The Whole Library Handbook 4,* edited by George M. Eberhart, 2–9. Chicago: American Library Association.

Day, Mark Tyler. 1998. "Transformational Discourse: Ideologies of Organizational Change in the Academic Library." *Library Trends* 46 (4): 635–67.

———. 2002. "Discourse Fashions in Library Administration and Information Management: A Critical History and Bibliometric Analysis." *Advances in Librarianship* 26:231–98.

De Gruyter. 2012. *Patron Driven Acquisition: A Model for Providing Complete Access to Electronic Content while Limiting Costs for Libraries—a White Paper*. Berlin: De Gruyter. www.libraries.wright.edu/noshelfrequired/2012/10/04/degruyter -white-paper-on-patron-driven-acquisition.

Dinkins, Debbi. 2012. "Individual Title Requests in PDA Collections." *College & Research Libraries News* 73 (5): 249–55.

Doyle, Greg, and Cory Tucker. 2011. "Patron-Driven Acquisition—Working Collaboratively in a Consortial Environment: An Interview with Greg Doyle." *Collaborative Librarianship* 3 (4): 212–16.

Duff, Wendy M., and Catherine A. Johnson. 2002. "Accidentally Found on Purpose: Information-Seeking Behavior of Historians in Archives." *Library Quarterly* 72 (4): 472–96.

Duncan, Jennifer, and Jeff Carroll. 2011. "Patron-Driven Acquisition Practices of US Research Libraries: East vs. West." In *Proceedings of the Charleston Library Conference.* http://dx.doi.org/10.5703/1288284314955.

Electronic Frontier Foundation. 2012. *E-Reader Privacy Chart, 2012 Edition.* www.eff .org/pages/reader-privacy-chart-2012.

Esposito, Joseph J. 2006. "What If Wal-Mart Ran a Library?" *Logos* 17 (1): 5–11.

———. 2012a. "A Dialogue on Patron-Driven Acquisitions." *The Scholarly Kitchen Blog.* (January 3). http://scholarlykitchen.sspnet.org/2012/01/03/a-dialogue -on-patron-driven-acquisitions.

———. 2012b. "Amazon, PDA, and Library Sales for Books." *The Scholarly Kitchen Blog.* (March 27). http://scholarlykitchen.sspnet.org/2012/03/27/amazon-pda -and-library-sales-for-books.

———. 2012c. "Sizing the Market for Patron-Driven Acquisitions (PDA)." *The Scholarly Kitchen Blog.* (May 8). http://scholarlykitchen.sspnet.org/2012/05/08/ sizing-the-market-for-patron-driven-acquisitions-pda.

Estabrook, Leigh S. 1996. "Sacred Trust or Competitive Opportunity: Using Patron Records." *Library Journal* 121 (2, February 1): 48–49.

Fischer, Karen S., Michael Wright, Kathleen Clatanoff, Hope Barton, and Edward Shreeves. 2012. "Give 'Em What They Want: A One-Year Study of Unmediated Patron-Driven Acquisition of E-Books." *College & Research Libraries* 73 (5): 469–92.

Fister, Barbara. 2010. "Problematizing Patron-Driven Acquisitions." Peer-to-peer review column (November 11). www.libraryjournal.com/lj/communityacademic libraries/887739-419/problematizing_patron-driven_acquisitions_ peer.html .csp.

Gee, James Paul. 2003. "What Video Games Have to Teach Us about Learning and Literacy." *ACM Computers in Entertainment* 1 (1, October): 1–4.

Harris, Michael H., Stan A. Hannah, and Pamela C. Harris. 1998. *Into the Future: The Foundations of Library and Information Services in the Post-Industrial Era.* 2nd ed. Greenwich, CT: Ablex.

Helgren, Jamie E. 2011. "Booking to the Future." *American Libraries* 42 (1–2): 40–43.

Higgs, Graham E., and John Budd. 2007. "Toward an Authentic Ethos for Online Higher Education." *Policy Futures in Education* 5 (4): 507–15.

Hirshon, Arnold. 1996. "Running with the Red Queen." *Advances in Librarianship* 20:1–26.

Hoesly, Jody. 2012. "Review of *Patron-Driven Acquisitions: Current Successes and Future Directions,*" ed. Judith Nixon, Robert Freeman, and Suzanne Ward. *Library Quarterly* 82 (4): 522–25.

Howard, Jennifer. 2010. "Reader Choice, Not Vendor Influence, Reshapes Library Collections." *Chronicle of Higher Education* 57 (12): A11–A12.

Internet2 e-Textbook Pilot. 2012. www.internet2.edu/netplus/econtent/docs/eText -Spring-2012-Pilot-Report.pdf.

Isaacson, David. 2002. "Instant Information Gratification." *American Libraries* 33 (2, February): 39.

Jaeger, Paul T., John Carlo Bertot, Christie M. Kodama, Sarah M. Katz, and Elizabeth J. DeCoster. 2011. "Describing and Measuring the Value of Public Libraries: The Growth of the Internet and the Evolution of Library Value." *First Monday* (online) 16 (11): 1–14.

Kolowich, Steve. 2011. "P.D.A. in the Library." *Inside Higher Ed* (October 28). www.insidehighered.com/news/2011/10/28/e-book-acquisition-based-use -and-demand-could-save-libraries-thousands.

Koontz, Christie M., Dinesh K. Gupta, and Sheila Webber. 2006. "Key Publications in Library Marketing: A Review." *IFLA Journal* 32 (3): 224–31.

Leckie, Gloria J. 1996. "Desperately Seeking Citations: Uncovering Faculty Assumptions about the Undergraduate Research." *Journal of Academic Librarianship* 22 (3): 201–8.

Levine-Clark, Michael. 2006. "Electronic Book Usage: A Survey at the University of Denver." *Portal: Libraries & the Academy* 6 (3): 285–99.

Li, Chan, Felicia Poe, Michele Potter, Brian Quigley, and Jacqueline Wilson. 2011. "UC Libraries Academic E-Book Usage Survey." www.cdlib.org/services/uxdesign/ docs/2011/academic_ebook_usage_survey.pdf.

Lipschultz, Dale. 2009. "Gaming@ Your Library." *American Libraries* 40 (1–2): 40–43.

Mann, Thomas. 2007. "The Research Library as Place: On the Essential Importance of Collections of Books Shelved in Subject-Classified Arrangements." In *The Library as Place: History, Community, and Culture,* ed. John Buschman and Gloria J. Leckie, 191–206. Westport, CT: Libraries Unlimited/Greenwood.

Nixon, Judith M., Robert S. Freeman, and Suzanne M. Ward. 2010. "Patron-Driven Acquisitions: An Introduction and Literature Review." *Collection Management* 35 (3–4): 119–24.

O'Donnell, James J. 1998. *Avatars of the Word: From Papyrus to Cyberspace.* Cambridge, MA: Harvard University Press.

O'Reilly, Tim. 2007. "Bad Math among Ebook Enthusiasts." *Tools of Change for Publishing Newsletter* (December 5). http://toc.oreilly.com/2007/12/bad-math -among-ebook-enthusias.html.

Postman, Neil. 1979. *Teaching as a Conserving Activity.* New York: Dell.

———. 1985. *Amusing Ourselves to Death: Public Discourse in the Age of Show Business.* New York: Penguin Books.

Quinn, Brian. 2000. "The McDonaldization of Academic Libraries?" *College & Research Libraries* 61 (3): 248–61.

Renner, Rita A. 2009. "Ebooks—Costs and Benefits to Academic and Research Libraries." Springer.com. Available at www.springer.com/librarians/ e-content?SGWID=0-113-2-773809-0.

Sagan, Carl. 2011. "Carl Sagan's 'Skeptical Thinker's Toolbox.'" *Activate the Mechanism Blog* (May 19). http://abaldwin360.tumblr.com/post/5639195814/carl-sagans -skeptical-thinkers-toolbox.

Schwartz, Meredith. 2012. "Academic Libraries Should Give Up Book-by-Book Collecting." (February 22). http://lj.libraryjournal.com/2012/02/academic -libraries/article-argues-academic-libraries-should-give-up-book-by-book -collecting.

Staiger, Jeff. 2012. "How E-Books Are Used: A Literature Review of the E-Book Studies Conducted from 2006 to 2011." *Reference & User Services Quarterly* 51 (4): 355–65.

Starbuck, William. 1982. "Congealing Oil: Inventing Ideologies to Justify Acting Ideologies Out." *Journal of Management Studies* 19 (1): 3–27.

The State of America's Libraries: A Report from the American Library Association. 2012. www.ala.org/news/sites/ala.org.news/files/content/StateofAmericas LibrariesReport2012Finalwithcover.pdf.

Warner, Dorothy. 2002. "'Why Do We Need to Keep This in Print? It's on the Web . . .': A Review of Electronic Archiving Issues and Problems." *Progressive Librarian* no. 19–20:47–64.

Weingand, Darlene. 1995. "Preparing for the New Millennium: The Case for Using Marketing Strategies." *Library Trends* 43 (3): 295–317.

———. 2002. "Managing Outside the Box: Marketing and Quality Management as Key to Library Effectiveness." In *Education and Research from Marketing and Quality Management in Libraries,* ed. Réjean Savard, 9–17. Munich: K.G. Saur.

Wiegand, Wayne A. 2011. "Tourist Attraction: The Moore Library of Lexington, Michigan, 1903–1953." *Library Quarterly* 81 (3): 251–76.

Winter, Michael F. 1993. "Librarianship, Technology, and the Labor Process: Theoretical Perspectives." In *Critical approaches to information technology in librarianship: Foundations and applications,* ed. John Buschman, 173–95. Westport, CT: Greenwood Press.

Zickuhr, Kathryn, Lee Rainie, Kristen Purcell, Mary Madden, and Joanna Brenner. 2012. "Younger Americans' Reading and Library Habits." Pew Internet & American Life Project. http://libraries.pewinternet.org/2012/10/23/younger -americans-reading-and-library-habits.

11

Patron-Driven vs. Librarian-Selected

Three Years of Comparative E-Book Usage

L IBRARY PHILOSOPHIES FOR COLLECTION BUILDING ARE RAP-
idly morphing. Libraries are in a period where traditional methods of collection development must be maintained, while concurrently moving toward
a future with increasing focus on patron-driven collection development
(PDCD). This paradigm shift has received much fanfare in the profession,
but there is a healthy amount of critical hesitancy to embrace models of this
type.[1] Many argue against the idea of patron-driven collection development
as the magic bullet for the shortcomings of traditional collection development
practices.

PDCD practices are evolutionary, not revolutionary, in that they complement but do not completely supplant existing selection by trained library professionals. Philosophical discussions abound with PDCD. Having nonlibrary
selectors acquire titles of interest or for immediate use fulfills one function,
namely access, but by removing the librarian selector it also affects overall collection-building strategies and allows purchase of titles that might not have
been considered appropriate for a specific academic collection. On the other
hand, PDCD allows patrons to acquire titles that fall in the interdisciplinary

gaps, which are often a blind spot for collection managers who have specific subject areas for which they are responsible.

In the face of the oft-quoted 80/20 rule for expected circulation of library materials, it is hard to argue against content that generates at least one use for every purchased title. In many instances PDCD content has proven to circulate at greater rates than librarian-selected content.[3] The question then remains whether PDCD-acquired titles continue to show relevancy over time by demonstrating comparable or higher levels of sustained patron usage compared to librarian-selected e-books.

This chapter will briefly summarize the Ohio State University Libraries' (OSUL) 2009–2010 patron-driven acquisitions (PDA) e-book pilot project. It will provide analysis of three years of comparative e-book usage data for titles purchased during the pilot versus librarian-selected e-books purchased during the same fiscal year. These two groups are deemed similar enough for valid usage data comparison. The chapter will conclude with a discussion of major barriers to PDCD e-book use and availability including lack of standardization in the publishing world for simultaneous publication across formats, restrictive digital rights management, and cost inflation, as well as discovery and platform challenges.

DEFINING USE

Usage data is not a new phenomenon for libraries. Door counts, reference transactions, interlibrary loan lending and borrowing requests are just a few of the ways in which data is captured to help professionals comprehend trends and develop best practices.

The management of library collections, both print and electronic, has made measuring usage a particularly important decision-making tool. Data provides insight into what resources are meeting the needs of users, especially when confronted by cost increases and budget limitations. This information is valuable for librarians in their stewardship of collections and users who remain skeptical of e-books and the bombarding hype that surrounds them. Usage data for e-books provides evidence of what and how content is used. It demonstrates value and frequently makes the most reticent of collection development librarians more open to buying them.

Conversely, it is also important to check expectations when thinking and talking about e-book use in comparison to print. Many discussions around e-books often perpetuate the idea that e-books are used more often than print. This isn't necessarily true because the measures of use are different for each format. Table 11.1 shows the very distinctive aspects of measurement used for OSUL print circulation vs. the units of measurement for e-book

TABLE 11.1

Use Metrics by Format.

Print Book Use Data Points		E-Book Use Data Points	
Patron Type	*Loan Period*	*Activity*	*DRM**
Undergraduates	3 weeks	Views	Unlimited
Graduates	10 weeks	Printing	Variable (60 max*)
Faculty, Staff	10 weeks	Copying	Variable (60 max*)
Guests	3 weeks	Downloads (page range, chapter, full)	Variable (60 max*)
All have unlimited renewals			

*Digital Rights Management restrictions set by publisher for max amount of activity per book, per user session. Some publishers impose more restrictive limits than the max set by ebrary.

usage. A single OSUL print book checked out for ten weeks could be used every day for the seventy-day circulation period. However, it is only counted as one circulation. The electronic version of that same book could be used every day for the same 70-day period resulting in a usage tally of 70. Many libraries do not formally track in-house use of print materials, but print materials are frequently and often intentionally used inside the library without thought or need of checkout. Additionally, e-book usage data is subject to the permissions allowed under license agreements as well as the robustness of supporting data-gathering tools. For that reason, comparing print to e-book circulation is often an apples to oranges comparison. Of more value is a look at the comparative circulation of e-books acquired through different selection methods.

To determine how PDCD e-book usage compares to usage of librarian-selected e-books, it is necessary to employ a standard measurement. Usage statistics are an accepted determinant of value for most electronic resources. Project COUNTER, a nonprofit organization, has led the charge to standardize how electronic resource use is counted and reported. This group has also created several report models to define specific measurements for journals, books, and databases.

Under the *Code of Practice for Books and Reference Works,* Project COUNTER outlines six styles of Book Reports to track and format usage data. This study uses Book Report 2, which targets e-books accessed at the section level instead of the title level. It captures the number of successful section requests by month and title. Sections are defined as a subdivision of a book or reference work.[4] Ebrary, the commercial e-book aggregator from which usage data was retrieved for the OSUL pilot, provides access to e-book content at the section or chapter level. In compliance with Book Report 2, ebrary further defines successful session requests as the sum of all views, prints, and copies for an individual title over a requested time frame.[5] Another facet of Report 2 is that if a title is opened, but no action such as view, copy, print, or download is taken then it falls into the "no usage" category. These titles are not included in the usage report. It should also be noted that as patron-driven e-book models have evolved, many aggregators make allowances for user browsing habits by not using views of front or back matter to trigger purchases (i.e., table of contents, index, etc.). It is not clear if uses of these portions of an e-book are also excluded from usage data tallies.

METHODOLOGY

For the purposes of this study, several years of usage data were obtained for comparison of titles purchased during the 2009–2010 OSUL PDA e-book pilot as well as librarian-selected e-books purchased during the 2009–2010 fiscal year. The retrieved data reflects three years of usage, covering October 2009 through October 2012.

1. *Patron-Driven Acquisition E-Book Data*

   Usage data for PDA e-books was collected from the ebrary partner site. Because ebrary e-books are accessible at the section or chapter level, the data was formatted in accordance with the Project COUNTER Book Report 2 style. The report covers three years of usage data for *all* ebrary titles purchased by OSUL. The ebrary trigger report received at the conclusion of part 1 of the OSUL PDA pilot was used to identify and isolate 393 titles. Patron-initiated activity triggered the purchase of these titles during part 1 of the pilot, which ran from October to November 2009. The PDA pilot usage data is restricted to part 1 because records and access for ebrary's Academic Complete collection used during part 2 were subsequently removed.

2. *Librarian-Selected E-Book Data*

   Usage data for librarian-selected e-books was initially gathered by running a Boolean search in the Millennium integrated library system order record file. In order to capture librarian-selected e-book firm orders, a search was run on order records with location = wwb, vendor = ebrary, and receipt dates falling within the 2009–2010 fiscal year (July 2009–June 2010). Location "wwb" is the tag for e-books on the library system. The decision to use librarian-selected e-book data for the entire fiscal year was made so that there were enough titles for comparison. The search successfully identified 1,260 titles that met the expressed parameters. PDA e-book titles were excluded because they lack attached order records. This list was used to identify and isolate titles in the ebrary Book Report 2.

After both data sets were retrieved, usage information was aggregated and assessed to compare relevant usage pattern commonalities and differences in the overall use as well as comparative use among the top five publishers.

BACKGROUND ON OSUL PDA PILOT PROJECT

The Ohio State University Libraries participated in a patron-driven acquisitions e-book pilot with ebrary during the 2009–2010 academic year. Ebrary provided an initial spreadsheet of close to 100,000 e-book titles from their catalog as a potential PDA pool. Due to other e-book purchasing activities via local and consortia acquisitions, significant de-duplication was required prior to making the pool available to users. In addition, the OSUL Collections Advisory Council (CAC), a committee primarily made up of subject librarian representatives from the humanities, science, and social science disciplines, put a set of criteria forward. The criteria assisted in aligning the PDA discovery pool with collection development principles while avoiding duplication and acquisition of content deemed inappropriate. The pilot excluded the short-term loan patron-driven acquisition option. The criteria excluded the following:

- Pre-2007 imprints
- List price over $299.99
- Forty publishers (not wanted or already acquired via standing orders or OhioLINK)
- Twenty subject headings (e.g., Juvenile Fiction, Self-Help)
- Computer manuals
- Technical areas in law
- Foreign-language texts with no English-language content
- Fiction (literary fiction and short stories were included)

This resulted in a PDA discovery pool of almost 16,000 PDA titles that were loaded into the local OPAC. A full accounting of the OSUL PDA pilot and its initial results can be found in the previously published article.[6]

USE OBSERVATIONS

A cursory glance at the data in table 11.2, a snapshot of e-books analyzed in this chapter, shows librarian-selected e-books having the highest number of uses overall because of the larger sample size. However, the average use per title for patron-driven e-books is nearly three times the rate of average

TABLE 11.2

E-Book Snapshot.

E-book type	# of titles	Total uses	Avg UPT*	Avg CPT*	Avg CPU*
PDA	393	220,725	187	$90.60	$0.49
Librarian	1,260	270,045	64	$84.75	$1.32
All Titles	1,653	490,770	99	$86.15	$0.87

*Average use per title, cost per title, cost per use.

use for librarian-selected titles. In terms of cost per title and per usage, the average cost per patron-driven title at $90.60 is slightly more expensive than the average cost of librarian-selected e-books at $84.75. This may stem from librarians being aware of the price at the point of selection and using it to determine value as it relates to building a collection to support specific learning and research agendas. Despite being more expensive than OSUL librarian-selected e-books, the OSUL patron-driven e-book average cost is still less than the $98.24 average list cost for all ebrary titles profiled in 2012.[7]

As for cost-per-use, the higher rate of use per patron-driven title means a very economical $0.49 cost-per-use. This is over two and a half times cheaper than the cost-per-use of librarian-selected titles at $1.32. This could be a result of the currency of the materials as well as the availability of content that subject librarians might not choose due to interdisciplinary content overlap or publisher preference. The cost-per-use for librarian-selected titles is not exorbitant, but it does add up over time because many of the benefits or cost-savings libraries have leveraged in print acquisition models have been lost in the transition to electronic content. One example of this can be seen in the comparative list price of $98.24 for the average ebrary e-book profiled vs. the average list price of U.S. print titles at $83.59. This does not take into account annual platform fees and subsequent inflation generally associated with publisher- or vendor-hosted electronic content.

Long-term use for e-books is a discussion still in the making, as this format becomes a systematic and seasoned part of library collections. As time passes, library professionals will be better able to understand the obsolescence, or the variation in demand for a title through time of PDA vs. librarian-selected e-books.[8] This issue is particularly important as previous studies indicate a significant impact on use in relation to the currency of e-book collections.[9]

Obsolescence has long been a measure of assessment for print materials, and eventually as libraries begin to confront collection management issues like de-selection it will be paramount for e-books as well. In comparing the Ohio State University Libraries' e-book use data as shown in figure 11.1, it is immediately apparent that PDA titles were used on average almost twenty times more often within the first month of availability than librarian-selected

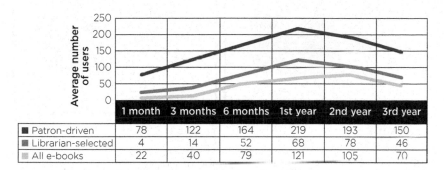

	1 month	3 months	6 months	1st year	2nd year	3rd year
■ Patron-driven	78	122	164	219	193	150
■ Librarian-selected	4	14	52	68	78	46
▨ All e-books	22	40	79	121	105	70

FIGURE 11.1
Average use per title.

titles. This is particularly significant because the PDA sample was so much smaller than the sample of librarian-selected titles. PDA titles also showed a gradual increase in usage over the course of the first year. The same use pattern can be observed in the librarian-selected e-books during the first year. It is reassuring evidence of the viability of PDA e-books beyond the initial trigger. There continues to be remarkable use of PDA e-books in the second year while librarian-selected e-books show a slight climb in use as well. This is clear evidence of e-books being used at regular intervals. However, the third year appears to indicate the beginning of a decline in use or what Buckland describes as "diachronous obsolescence" in the use of a document in successive years or over time.[10] Both e-book categories show a significant drop in use with PDA titles down 22 percent and librarian-selected titles down a worrying 41 percent. Even with the notable decline, patron-driven usage remains significant and continues to exceed usage of librarian-selected titles.

Another surprising finding was the percentage of e-book titles in both categories with over 100 uses. As seen in figure 11.3, nearly half (45 percent) of the librarian-selected e-books generated 100 uses or more. In comparison, figure 11.2 displays the 65 percent of PDA e-book titles with 100 or more uses. These percentages are especially striking considering the sample sizes: 393 total titles for PDA and 1,260 for librarian-selected e-books.

A comparative view of patron-driven vs librarian-selected e-book use of the top five publishers can be seen in figures 11.4 and 11.5, respectively. This group includes the following publishers and respective counts for PDA and librarian-selected categories; Cambridge (41, 100), Elsevier (31, 78), McGraw-Hill (40, 16), Taylor & Francis (68, 267), and Wiley (115, 219).

The initial and perhaps most astonishing observation is that McGraw-Hill, the publisher with the smallest number of titles, has yielded the highest use for patron-driven titles in the first year. By comparison, the patron-driven use for McGraw-Hill titles had eight times the use of librarian-selected titles

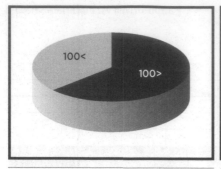

FIGURE 11.2
Patron-driven titles with
100 or > uses.

FIGURE 11.3
Librarian-selected titles with
100 or > uses.

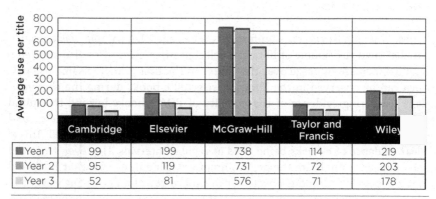

	Cambridge	Elsevier	McGraw-Hill	Taylor and Francis	Wiley
■Year 1	99	199	738	114	219
■Year 2	95	119	731	72	203
■Year 3	52	81	576	71	178

FIGURE 11.4
Average patron-driven use by publisher (top five).

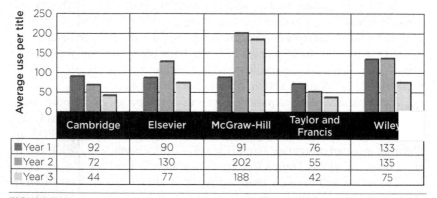

	Cambridge	Elsevier	McGraw-Hill	Taylor and Francis	Wiley
■Year 1	92	90	91	76	133
■Year 2	72	130	202	55	135
■Year 3	44	77	188	42	75

FIGURE 11.5
Average librarian-selected use by publisher (top five).

in the first year. The use of McGraw-Hill titles is also exceptional when compared with use across the other four publishers.

The next highest patron-driven e-book use was for Wiley titles. Here patron-driven titles demonstrate a use of one and a half times the use of librarian-selected Wiley titles. Most of the remaining publishers demonstrate a similar pattern, with the exception of librarian-selected Elsevier titles yielding higher comparative use in the second year.

There is an exceptional use rate for McGraw-Hill titles in both the librarian-selected and patron-driven categories. However, the striking use of patron-driven titles in particular might be attributed to the publisher's portfolio of content. It is particularly known for textbooks, how-to manuals, and handbooks as well as introductory and reference titles. This type of content is thought to be consumed in small bites or piecemeal rather than as a whole and is well suited to the electronic format. In addition, this form of piecemeal interaction is increasingly described as use over reading to distinguish this behavior.[11] Users interacting with content in this manner are known to have specific objectives such as finding facts, retrieving content to support a research paper, and accessing recommended or required course reading.[12]

The overall usage over a three-year-period pattern is not replicated exactly in the top five publishers for the PDA sample. Peak use is yielded in the first year, with slightly less, but consistent use taking place in the second year. The analysis of overall e-book average use showed the reverse. Librarian-selected titles falling in the top five publisher group, charted in figure 11.5, is markedly less than their top five patron-driven counterparts. Also, librarian-selected titles show mixed results across publishers between the first and second years.

Summarily, the results show the top five are split between publishers (Wiley, McGraw-Hill, Elsevier) who see slight or significant use increase, and publishers (Taylor & Francis, Cambridge) with notable decrease in use. However, the decline of use for both categories in the third year is consistent with the decline observed earlier in the overall use. Examination of this select group of five publishers continues the pattern of use declining in the third year and perhaps the notion of the beginnings of obsolescence. These publishers are the top five in the discovery pool. However, some publishers were excluded from the pool because they were being acquired through separate e-book deals or through OSUL consortia. It is possible other publishers' e-books might actually have higher overall system usage than these five.

LIMITATIONS OF RESEARCH

Neither patron-driven nor librarian-selected e-books are free from outside influence. It is necessary to acknowledge that some use may be attributed to technical services processing of both patron-driven and librarian-selected e-books.

More important, many patron-driven acquisitions programs have some form of librarian mediation imposed upon them during the profile setup, which generates the eligible title discovery pool. Librarians provide oversight of these programs to stay within limited budgets and to present content relevant to known curricula, research agendas, and institutional priorities. Libraries with smaller budgets may impose very strict limitations around the cost of a PDA title. Other scenarios might have a technical college excluding advanced humanities texts or an undergraduate-degree-granting university excluding law and medical titles.

Ultimately users trigger the purchase of a PDA e-book, but librarians do impact the process. Similarly, many e-books are selected by collection development librarians using their expertise and subject knowledge to make decisions based on research processes, established courses, publisher pedigree, and context within a library's collections.[13] Faculty and subsequently students set much of the institutional research and curriculum agenda. As a result, some e-book titles that are informally tied to course assignments in either category might result in higher use than expected. In addition, librarian selections are frequently based upon requests from faculty, staff, and students to purchase content that is relevant to their specific teaching, learning, and research pursuits. In this way, both librarian-selected and patron-driven purchases form part of a collaborative process benefiting the library collection and the university community as a whole.

CONCLUSION

When it comes to e-books, librarians and users have different end goals. The selection process is also different for both groups. Users aren't aware of their decision-making role in patron-driven acquisition models, but they do have recognized research "use" versus "reading" behaviors that work well with the e-book format. Users are triggering purchases and using the e-book format at the point of need to retrieve bites of information to support research and learning. Librarians are building a more balanced scholarly collection to enhance teaching, learning, and research now and in the future. Although the two approaches may overlap considerably, there will be unique titles selected by either group that would not necessarily be purchased by the other.

The average use of PDA titles during the three-year time period shows sustained relevance and use of content chosen by users. In comparison, librarian-selected titles, while not used as frequently, show worthwhile use as well. Commonalities are seen in the makeup of the top five publishers for each sample, though there are notable variations in the patterns of use over time for each e-book category. These two approaches to collection development should not be viewed as competitive. Instead, they can be deployed as complementary tools for creating collections that have immediacy in impact on the end-user as well as the potential to enhance more in-depth or advanced study of a topic in the present and as it develops in the future. One size does not fit all, and the more proven options available for supporting scholarly pursuits with meaningful collection development practices, the better for the end-user.

PDA is not perfect, but more important neither is the e-book format. However, patron use over time cannot be ignored when deciding how best to use limited acquisition budgets. It can be expanded and refined as both PDA models and the e-book market evolve. Just as print and e-book formats concurrently occupy space within a library collection, so must patron-driven and librarian-selected models become coexisting best practices. PDA enthusiasts or apologists must move away from arguing the value of patron-driven collection development as a replacement for librarian selection. Instead, energy should be focused on removing barriers to the availability and use of all e-books.

There are several issues that have slowed the cooperative success of multiple approaches to building library e-book collections. Cost is certainly a consideration for many institutions still trying to understand the best available e-book acquisition models. The loss of major pricing discounts for selected, as opposed to packaged or bundled e-books, is noteworthy. Opportunities for individual institutions to buy print titles at a cost less than list price resulted in long-standing discount rates ranging roughly from 5 percent to 20 percent. There are also maintenance costs associated with electronic content, regardless of whether it is hosted by vendor (platform/hosting fees) or locally (server/staffing costs). These particular costs can also be subject to inflation rates beyond institutional control.

E-books also present many limitations to one of the major benefits of developing library collections, which is the lending and borrowing of materials in cooperation with shared resource partners. The excessively restrictive digital rights management (DRM) of e-book publishers is fast becoming a serious threat to one of the crowning achievements of libraries.[14]

There is also a need for innovative format operability standards for all mobile platforms. Many libraries are exploring and implementing mobile discovery layers in order to meet more users where they are and these efforts could only be enhanced by mobile content. Interested e-book users are often deterred by format difficulties with mobile devices and platforms. Clearly, many of today's users want simple access to content more than exhaustive research capability.[15]

Finally, in order to fully enable use of both patron-driven and librarian-selected e-books, simultaneous publication of titles across formats must become a publisher standard. Available academic e-books represent just over

30 percent of new titles profiled annually.[16] This number is growing as more publishers move into the e-book market, but not at an encouraging rate. In addition, some publishers who offer titles in multiple formats frequently impose embargoes on digital content to provide a period of advantage to the print format. This further slows the availability and use of e-book content when e-book PDA programs are not able to include discovery for new content because it isn't available electronically. It also forces librarians to select content in print to keep collections current in a timely manner.

Use of content is the primary goal of patron-driven and librarian-selected collection development models. Utilizing both approaches in a kind of complementary hybrid model creates more opportunities to match users with content that meets their educational needs. Both libraries and publishers as the principle stakeholders must find ways to make the e-book format a more tenable market by removing barriers to availability and use. Nevertheless, it is libraries in particular who must remain sensitive to the needs of users as progress is made in order to keep collection development activity, patron-driven or not, a flexible practice.

ACKNOWLEDGMENT

The author would like to give particular thanks to Nichole Collier for invaluable assistance in the retrieval and organization of usage data for this research.

NOTES

1. Judith M. Nixon, Robert S. Freeman and Suzanne M. Ward, eds., "Patron-Driven Acquisitions: Current Successes and Future Directions," *Collection Management,* special issue 35, no. 3–4 (2010): 119–259.
2. Meredith Farkas, "Ebooks and Libraries: A Stream of Concerns," *Information Wants to Be Free.* January 18, 2011, http://meredith.wolfwater.com/wordpress/2011/01/18/ebooks-and-libraries-a-stream-of-concerns.
3. Rebecca Schroeder, "When Patrons Call the Shots: Patron-Driven Acquisition at Brigham Young University," *Collection Building* 31, no. 1 (2012): 14.
4. Project COUNTER, "Release 4 of the COUNTER Code of Practice for e-Resources," *Codes of Practice,* www.projectcounter.org/code_practice.html.
5. Ebrary Support Center, "New Release 4 COUNTER Report," For Admins, http://support.ebrary.com/kb/counter-reports-new.
6. Dracine Hodges, Cyndi Preston, and Marsha J. Hamilton, "Patron-Initiated Collection Development: Progress of a Paradigm Shift," *Collection Management* 35, no. 3–4 (2010): 208–21.

7. Nat Bruning, "Annual Book Price Update" (Contoocook, NH: YBP Library Services, 2012), www.ybp.com/book_price_update.html.

8. Michael K. Buckland, *Book Availability and the Library User* (New York: Pergamon, 1975), 12.

9. Catherine S. Herlihy and Hua Yi, "E-Books in Academic Libraries: How Does Currency Affect Usage?" *New Library World* 111, no. 9–10 (2010): 378–79.

10. Buckland, *Book Availability and the Library User,* 12.

11. Leo Appleton, "The Use of Electronic Books in Midwifery Education: The Student Perspective," *Health Information and Libraries Journal* 21, no. 4 (2004): 250.

12. Abdullah Noorhidwaati and Forbes Gibb, "How Students Use E-Books— Reading or Referring?" *Malaysian Journal of Library and Information Science* 13, no. 2 (2008): 5.

13. William H. Walters, "Patron-Driven Acquisition and the Educational Mission of the Academic Library," *Library Resources & Technical Services* 56, no. 3 (2012): 205.

14. Charles Hamaker, "Ebooks on Fire: Controversies Surrounding Ebooks in Libraries," *Searcher* 19, no. 10 (December 2011): 25.

15. Rachael Hu and Alison Meier, "Planning for a Mobile Future: A User Research Case Study from the California Digital Library," *Serials* 24, no. 3 (2011): S23.

16. Walters, "Patron-Driven Acquisition," 207.

Contributors

NANCY BURFORD is the veterinary collections curator at the Medical Sciences Library at Texas A&M University. She has a degree in history from Louisiana State University–Shreveport and a master's in information science from the University of North Texas. She has been involved in collection development, acquisitions, and cataloging for many years.

JOHN BUSCHMANN is dean of University Libraries at Seton Hall University in South Orange, New Jersey. He is the author of *Libraries, Classrooms, and the Interests of Democracy: Marking the Limits of Neoliberalism* (2012).

CRISTINA CAMINITA is the agriculture and information literacy librarian at LSU Libraries. She is involved in the Association of College and Research Libraries' Science and Technology Section and the United States Agriculture Information Network. Her research interests include digital libraries, gray literature, historical agricultural documents, and information literacy across the curriculum.

NAOMI IKEDA CHOW is the librarian for the Hamilton Library's Interlibrary Loan/External Services Program Unit at the University of Hawai'i at Mānoa. She has previously served as a reference librarian and in collection development and management at the Cushing/Whitney Medical Library at Yale University. Chow's MILS is from the University of Michigan at Ann Arbor, and she has a BA from Carleton College.

JAMIE CONKLIN is the science and health sciences librarian and instruction coordinator at Lovejoy Library at Southern Illinois University–Edwardsville. Prior to that, she held positions at the University of Central Florida and the Orange County Library System in Orlando, Florida, and received her MLIS from Florida State University. Conklin focuses on meeting users' needs through innovative approaches to her collection management, instruction, and reference responsibilities.

KAY DOWNEY is an assistant professor and collection management librarian at Kent State University Libraries. She also represents Kent State University Libraries on the OhioLINK Cooperative Information Resources Management Committee. Prior to coming to Kent State, she worked at the Ingalls Library, Cleveland Museum of Art, as serials and electronic resources librarian and the Martha Stecher Reed Library at the Akron Art Museum. She is a member of a number of professional organizations and is currently serving on the ALA's CRS Acquisitions Committee. She has a BFA in painting and drawing, and an MLS. in library science.

ERIK SEAN ESTEP has been an academic librarian for over a decade and currently resides in Edwardsville, Illinois. He has worked as a social sciences librarian at Illinois State University, Swarthmore College, East Carolina University, and Southern Illinois University Edwardsville. He is the coeditor, along with Martin Wallace and Rebecca Tolley-Stokes, of *The Generation X Librarian* (2011, McFarland), and is the coeditor, along with Nathaniel Enright, of *Class and Librarianship*, forthcoming from Library Juice Press.

ROBERT S. FREEMAN has worked at Purdue University since 1997, where he is a reference librarian and liaison to the School of Languages and Cultures and the Department of English. He has an MA in German from the University of North Carolina–Chapel Hill and an MS in library and information science from the University of Illinois at Urbana-Champaign. Interested in the history of libraries and publishing, he coedited and contributed to *Libraries to the People: Histories of Outreach* (2003). He recently coedited a special issue of *Collection Management* (July–December 2010) on PDA with Judith M. Nixon and Suzanne M. Ward.

JEANNE HARRELL is the coordinator of monograph and automated acquisitions at Texas A&M University Libraries. She received her MLS from the University of Oklahoma, and has a research focus in acquisitions management, library material budgets, and e-books.

SARAH HARTMAN-CAVERLY, MS (LIS), MSIS, is an assistant professor and reference librarian and the liaison to Allied Health, Emergency Services and Nursing at Delaware County Community College. Prior to this appointment, she managed electronic resources for academic libraries for more than five years, and was the technical lead for implementation of patron-driven acquisition programs for e-books at Delaware County Community College and the Tri-College Library Consortium of Bryn Mawr, Haverford, and Swarthmore colleges.

JEANNETTE HO is the director of cataloging at Texas A&M University Libraries. She received a master of science degree in library science from the University of Illinois at Urbana-Champaign, and has a research focus in the cataloging of nonbook formats.

DRACINE HODGES is head of the Acquisitions Department at Ohio State University.

JARED L. HOWLAND is the collection assessment librarian and head of catalog services at Brigham Young University. He has a degree in economics from Brigham Young University and a master's in library science from the University of North Texas. His research interests include collection assessment and development.

RYAN JAMES works for the University of Hawai'i at Mānoa Library in the Access Services Department of Hamilton Library as manager of the Interlibrary Loan/External Services Program Unit, where he has spearheaded the implementation, and currently oversees, the ILL purchase-on-demand program. He earned his MLIS from the University of Hawai'i at Mānoa, and his BA in English from Ohio State University. He is currently a PhD candidate in the Communications and Information Science Program at the University of Hawai'i at Mānoa.

AMY M. MCCOLL is the assistant director for collections at the Swarthmore College Libraries, and the TriCollege licensing librarian for the TriCollege Consortium (Bryn Mawr, Haverford, and Swarthmore college libraries). Prior to coming to Swarthmore College in 1998, she was employed at the Free Library of Philadelphia, the Philadelphia Area Consortium of Special Collections

Libraries, and the Biddle Law Library at the University of Pennsylvania. She was the original compiler of the first edition of the *NACO Participants' Manual* published by the Library of Congress in 1994.

NORM MEDEIROS is associate librarian for collection management and metadata services at Haverford College in Pennsylvania. He serves as a director-at-large of the Association for Library Collections and Technical Services (ALCTS), a division of the American Library Association, and as book review editor for *Library Resources & Technical Services*, the official journal of ALCTS.

JUDITH M. NIXON received her BS degree in education from Valparaiso University (Indiana) in 1967 and her MS in library science from the University of Iowa in 1974. She has held appointments as head of three libraries at Purdue University: Consumer & Family Sciences, Management & Economics, and the Humanities, Social Science & Education Library. Currently she is the bibliographer and liaison to the College of Education. She has published more than twenty-three articles and seven books. Most recently her research has focused on evaluation of library science journals and patron-driven acquisitions.

MIKE PERSICK is head of acquisitions and serials at Haverford College Libraries. Along with his coauthors, he created and manages the DDA program for the Tri-College Library Consortium as well as the Tri-Colleges' shared approval plan.

CARMELITA PICKETT is the director of collection development operations and acquisitions services at Texas A&M University Libraries. Her research publication focus includes citation analysis, e-resource business models, collection development, and black studies. She has held previous professional positions at Emory University and the University of California–Santa Barbara.

REBECCA SCHROEDER is the acquisitions librarian at Brigham Young University. She graduated with an MLS from the University of North Texas and is interested in acquisitions and collection development research.

SIMONA TABACARU is the collection development librarian at the Texas A&M University Libraries. She graduated with an MLS from the University of North Texas. Her research interests include collection development and assessment.

ANA UGAZ is the collection development and strategic initiatives coordinator at Texas A&M University Medical Sciences Library. She received her MLIS from Dominican University, and her research interests include electronic resource management, assessment, and collection development.

MAURA VALENTINO began her career as a Microsoft Certified Trainer, teaching programming and database administration. She then returned to school and received a BA in art history from the University of South Florida and an MSLIS from Syracuse University. Beginning in 2009, she served as the coordinator of digital initiatives at the University of Oklahoma and currently is the metadata librarian at Oregon State University. Her research interests focus on digital libraries, metadata, and data management.

SUZANNE WARD holds degrees from UCLA, the University of Michigan, and Memphis State University. She has worked at the Purdue University Libraries since 1987 and is currently head of collection management. Her professional interests include patron-driven acquisitions and print retention issues. She has published two books and over twenty-five articles on various aspects of librarianship. Her book *Guide to Implementing and Managing Patron-Driven Acquisitions* was published in 2012.

TOM WRIGHT is the collection development coordinator and material acquisitions chair at Brigham Young University. He received his MLS from Brigham Young University, and his research interests revolve around collection development.

Index

Locators in *italic* refer to figures/tables/diagrams

CPSIA information can be obtained
at www.ICGtesting.com
Printed in the USA
LVOW01s2254090317

526743LV00006B/200/P